Rachel

Rachel

SAMUEL H. DRESNER

FORTRESS PRESS   MINNEAPOLIS

RACHEL

Scripture quotations are from translations by the author after consulting various published translations.

Excerpt from "A Woman for All Seasons" by Leon Kass in *Commentary* (September 1991). Reprinted by permission.

Poems "Rachel" and "Leah" from *Judaism,* Vol. 36, Number 2, Spring 1987, copyright © 1987 American Jewish Congress. Reprinted by permission.

Poem "Rachel and Leah" by Itsek Manger from *Khumesh Lider,* translated by Kathryn Hellerstein, copyright © 1994 Kathryn Hellerstein. All rights reserved. Reprinted by permission.

Poem "For poor brides who were servant girls" by Kadya Moladowsky from *Kadya Moladowsky's Froyen-Lider,* translated by Kathryn Hellerstein in *Association for Jewish Studies Review* XIII 1 & 2, (1988), copyright © 1988 Kathryn Hellerstein. All rights reserved. Used by permission.

Diary excerpts from *Kever Rachel* by Ely Schiller, copyright © 1977 Ariel Publishing House. Reprinted by permission.

Excerpt from "Midrash and the Dawn of Kabbalah" by Joseph Dan in *Midrash and Literature,* ed. Hartman and Budick, copyright © 1986 Yale University Press. Reprinted by permission.

Cover design: Patricia Boman
Book design: Publishers' WorkGroup
Cover graphic: "Jacob Encounters Rachel at the Well," by William Dyce (1806–64). Photo by Superstock.

Library of Congress Cataloging-in-Publication Data

Dresner, Samuel H.
    Rachel / by Samuel H. Dresner.
      p. cm.
    Includes bibliographical references and indexes.
    ISBN 0-8006-2777-6 :
      1. Bible. O.T. Genesis XXVII–L—Commentaries. 2. Rachel (Biblical matriarch). 3. Midrash. 4. Aggada. I. Title.
    BS1235.3.D7 1994
    222'.11092—dc20   94-2826
                                           CIP

The paper used in this publication meets the minimum requirements of American National Standard for Information Sciences—Permanence of Paper for Printed Library Materials, ANSI Z329.48-1984. ∞™

Manufactured in the U.S.A.   AF 1–2777
98   97   96   95   94   1   2   3   4   5   6   7   8   9   10

Contents

Contents

May your wife be a fruitful vine
within your house.
Your children as olive-shoots
round your table.
May the Lord bless you from Zion
all the days of your life.
May you see the good of Jerusalem
and live to see your children's children.

Peace be upon Israel.

From Psalm 128

Preface

THE NEW FEMALE SELF-AWARENESS MANIFESTED IN the past decades has released a torrent of energy, sweeping away pejorative images as it engages in reexamining the roles and status of women in society. This energy has found wide expression in a literature that ranges from fiction, poetry, and drama to sociological studies of women in our culture. Common to every strand of this literature has been an inquiry into the nature and roles of women, a kind of self-analysis, with women looking inward to their own lives and outward to others who might serve as models.

Because some of those at the forefront of the feminist movement have tended to dismiss the Bible as a document that speaks out of a world of patriarchal autocracy, it has received short shrift as a source of models. One need look no further than the book of Genesis, it is argued, to find ample evidence of a pervading male point of view. For there we are told that while the loss of Eden is assigned to the woman, Eve, the role of pioneering the way that will lead to the ultimate restoration of paradise is given to men, the patriarchs, Abraham, Isaac, and Jacob.

"One cannot deny," writes Leon Kass, "that the text centers mainly on the adventures of the males—though this alone proves nothing—but it is simply wrong to say that the

Bible does not esteem, appreciate, and honor its women. On the contrary, one could argue that the main burden of the Jewish way, beginning with the stories of the patriarchs, is to elevate—in the eyes of male readers especially—the dignity of family life. To this end, it seeks to redirect male attitudes and ambitions away from wealth and glory and toward the proper rearing of the young for the noble work of transmission and sanctification. Indispensable for this transformation of the natural ways of mankind is an elevation in the status and dignity of woman. A careful reading of Genesis shows this to be a major purpose of the text."[1]

In the Bible we find resolute matriarchs as well as pioneering husbands, a courageous queen who delivers the lives of her endangered people, determined midwives who defy a pharaoh's decree, a fearless harlot who saves Israel's leaders, even a general who leads her army to victory. Here too are loyal sisters, compassionate mothers, and faithful daughters. Sarah, Rebecca, Esther, Miriam, Deborah, Ruth, Naomi, and Hannah are names Christians and Jews have bestowed upon one hundred generations of children, names that are commonly given even today. Indeed, it is from the patriarchs and matriarchs, and from the Garden of Eden before them, that the mutuality of the human couple emerges. *Male and female God created them, and called "their" name Adam* (Gen 5:2; cf. 1:27).

As Abraham Heschel has reminded us, "The Bible speaks in every language and in every age. We all draw upon it, and it remains pure, inexhaustible and complete. It is a book that cannot die. Oblivion shuns its pages."[2]

OF THE FOUR BIBLICAL MATRIARCHS, IT IS RACHEL who has inspired the largest creative response in the history of art and literature, a response confirmed a thousandfold by the people Israel, for Rachel is among the most beloved figures in all of Jewish history and in the history of the

Jewish psyche. She wanders—seen and unseen—through almost half the book of Genesis, and her compelling presence there calls forth echoes in Samuel and Jeremiah. Her story is the subject of rich embellishment in the midrash and in the mystical literature. Not unlike Elijah, she early became a folk heroine. The people's imagination was rekindled annually when they heard this most touching of love stories read in the synagogue, when they listened on the New Year to Jeremiah's account of her tears for the exiles, when they gloried in the tales in which the rabbis extolled her, and when they rose at midnight to recite the lamentation, *Tikkun Rachel* in mourning for the exile of the Shechinah, the divine Presence:

> At midnight one laments for Rachel [the Shechinah], for that is the hour she descended into the Exile, by sitting barefoot on the floor next to that doorpost upon which the mezuzah [a reminder of God's presence. Deut 6:9] is fixed, with lowered head, and ashes upon the spot where one places the tefillin . . . shedding tears of grief.[3]

But one way in which Rachel differed from Elijah, who was taken up into heaven by a "fiery chariot" leaving not a worldly trace, was that her people knew of a certainty where her lonely grave was situated on this earth, in Ephrat just outside Bethlehem. There she lies alone, apart from Sarah, Rebecca, and Leah, who rest in sepulchral solemnity in the cave of Machpelah in Hebron. From her solitary, dreary heap of stones, it is said, Rachel rose up to weep for those led captive to Babylonia and to welcome the remnant who later returned. She consoles the never-ending stream of pilgrims who yet continue to make their way to her grave for meditation and heartfelt prayer amidst memories of her tenderness.

Seeking to immerse myself in the study of Rachel, I made

a trip to America's greatest Jewish library and discovered that the index catalogue contained fifteen entries for the celebrated twentieth-century Israeli poet and seven for the famous nineteenth-century French-Jewish actress. Under biblical Rachel, whose name both of them had taken, there was not a single entry! As little interest had been shown in her by scholars as by feminists.

The challenge became even more compelling. There are single chapters about her in other volumes, entries in encyclopedias and commentaries to the books of Genesis and Jeremiah, but there is no book devoted solely to Rachel. Furthermore, most of the studies that have been undertaken are of an ominously technical nature. Some are geographical (was Rachel's grave near Bethlehem or elsewhere?), some archaeological (what did the house-gods of her father, Laban, look like?), some legal (was her husband, Jacob, considered a slave to Laban or part of his family?), and some linguistic or literary. Abraham Heschel once observed that having eyes only for the Bible's literary splendor is much like praising Einstein's theory of relativity for the author's calligraphy. Although modern research has added immeasurably to our understanding of the Bible, detailed studies of this sort cannot serve all our needs. A larger picture must be brought into focus.

Contemporary works of art today rarely have the universal appeal enjoyed by previous works for two reasons: their curious concern with ugliness and their retreat into a world of complex symbols and private concerns, speaking a rarefied language—a hieroglyphic of sorts—that only other artists or critics claim to understand. And when the arts do attempt to speak a more understandable language, they too often lavish their powers upon popular vulgarities. Protected by the prevailing cultural relativism, the once respected word *art* is stamped on anything that claims to be "personal expression," leading to such scandals as the Andres Serrano and Robert Mapplethorpe controversies. It is not surprising to me that the Statue of Liberty replicated by students in Tiannanmen Square in Beijing, the one example in recent years of a work of art so symbolic of the spirit of a people that they were willing to offer their lives for it, raised not an eyebrow in the art journals.

So with the Bible. Contemporary biblical studies are not expected to dwell upon its grand themes. God's search for the righteous person and the righteous people is not a popular topic for research. The Bible has become atomized and desanctified, a curious ancient text lying inert much as a cadaver about to be dismembered—except that once the living God was thought to dwell therein. Consider the only remark of the instructor in a Bible class I once attended on the sublime Isa 40:1—"Comfort, oh comfort my people, says your God"—"One 'comfort' is redundant!" Or the bizarre correction to another noted passage by the author of the latest and largest commentary on Jeremiah: "Thus said the Lord: A cry is heard . . . wailing, bitter weeping—Rachel weeping for her children. She refuses to be comforted, for her children are gone" (Jer 31:15). Because, the writer proposes, the Hebrew word *rahel* means "lamb," we may substitute "a bleating ewe-lamb" for weeping Rachel, giving us in place of "Rachel weeping for her children," "a mother sheep lamenting . . . the loss of her lambs"![4]

In the past, fundamentalist literalists regarded every word of the Bible as divine, leaving little room for human contributions in their rejection of the possibility that the Bible "is not itself revelation, but a humanly mediated record of revelation."[5] At the other extreme, social science reductionists left little room for God in their effort to flatten the scriptural world to a single secular dimension. More recently, literary deconstructionists have attempted to persuade us that no text can have any fully determinable meaning at all. What the first deified, the second trivialized, and the last threatens to dissolve altogether. Over the centuries, however, the Bible has proven that it can survive its interpreters.

Its heaven, though repudiated, continues to shine as brilliantly as ever, and its earth, though spiritualized, continues to throb with life. Both the sacred and the profane remain, and remain joined; we cannot apprehend the one without the other. It is this all-encompassing landscape—time and eternity, spirit and flesh, good and evil—that affords the opportunity to present biblical woman to the modern reader in the fullness of her humanity.

A successful treatment of the Bible should seek to answer three questions: (1) What did the author mean by this or that text? (2) How did the tradition understand it? (3) What is its significance for us today?

Sometimes the answers to these three questions are quite different one from the other. The first refers to the simple meaning of the text, understood within the context of biblical thinking and making use of the tools of modern criticism. The word *tradition* in the second question requires some explanation for the general reader. It refers to the rabbis of the Talmud and the midrash (the postbiblical Jewish expository literature), the philosophers, poets, and mystics, and the collective memory of the people up until our own day. At times tradition deepens and illumines the literal understanding of the text; at other times it takes on a life of its own, spinning tales and meanings not in the biblical text, which the sages felt free to use for their own purposes. Thus, when the midrash says that, in his search for the one God, the young Abraham smashed the idols of his father's shop, it does so knowing full well that there is no biblical source for it: "While the rabbinic creators of the [midrash] looked back into Scriptures to uncover the full latent meaning of the Bible and its wording," Joseph Heinemann observed, "at the same time they looked forward into the present and the future. They sought to give direction to their own generation, to resolve their religious problems, to answer their theological questions, and to guide them out of spiritual perplexities. . . . The [midrashists] do not mean so much to clarify difficult passages in the biblical texts as to take a stand on the burning questions of the day, to guide the people and strengthen their faith."[6]

Our concern is with the story of Rachel. It falls into two sections: the first takes place within her lifetime; the second begins with her death and reaches until our own day. One is no less significant than the other. Most histories of Rachel have dealt only with her life—her meeting with Jacob, her struggle with her sister, Leah, her barrenness, her mothering of Joseph, and her early death in bearing Benjamin. The later references to Rachel in the books of Samuel, Ruth, and Jeremiah and the many legends about her in the midrash, as well as the traditions that grew up around her grave, have been treated in separate studies. But there has been no previous attempt to tie them together, to view the entire landscape from beginning to end, to see a common thread running through the story, from the earliest mention of her in the Bible to the *Kever* (grave of) Rachel near Bethlehem of the present time.

This then is not a book limited to searching for the meaning of the biblical text. Rather we are trying to take the measure of an uncommon woman through a three-thousand-year-old literature. The task has been to gather the references to Rachel through the centuries from all the sources and so to mix them on our palette that there may emerge the portrait of a woman, a matriarch, suggested by Scripture but not bound by it, whose personality infused Scripture and infused too the experience of the people whose lives became a commentary on Scripture. What began as an inquiry into biblical Rachel became the Triumph of Rachel through the ages.

A SYNOPSIS OF THE BIBLICAL STORY, AS WELL AS A genealogy, can be found at the end of the volume. No single translation of Scripture has been used, nor have I always followed standard methods of transliteration. Since the overwhelming number of biblical citations are from the book of Genesis, when citing that book I have used italics and have omitted the name *Genesis*, simply noting chapter and verse.

I am grateful to a number of people who have either read the manuscript or contributed their insights to its creation, or from whose writings I have particularly benefited. They include Professors Nahum Sarna, Edward Greenstein, Leon Kass, and Catherine Chalier, and Rabbi Eliot Gertel. Dr. Saul Rosenberg has improved the style. A special thanks goes to J. Michael West at Fortress Press for his enthusiastic support.

—Samuel H. Dresner

Part I _____

The Covenant

Everything depended upon Rachel.
Therefore are her descendants called by her name.
(Gen. R. 71:2)

Chapter 1————————————————————

The Covenant

IMAGINE AN HOURGLASS, WIDE AT THE TOP AND bottom, narrowing at the center to a slender passage, and you will have an image of the biblical record of the covenant. The metaphor is apt. For the "top" and "bottom," history's beginning and end, its first hope and final fulfillment—each universal in scope and embracing all humanity—are joined by a single man, Abraham.

The story of the Bible is the story of God's search for the righteous person and the righteous people. For nineteen generations only failure is recorded. Adam and Eve might have remained in the Garden of Eden forever had they not transgressed and distorted the divine image in which they were framed. Cain slew his brother Abel. Each generation brought another failure. By the tenth the saturation point for sin had been reached. God's patience was at an end; the heavens overflowed and wiped the slate clean. From the deluge only Noah emerged. Creation, as it were, had begun again with a second Adam. For Noah the rainbow appears, the symbol of God's covenant with nature, and the institution of law begins. But Noah and his clan prove no better than those who preceded him. He too fails God. Another nine generations of sin are recorded. It is not until the tenth, the twentieth after the first beginning, that one is born who at last proves worthy.

The Lord said to Abram, Live in my presence and be blameless. I will establish my covenant between me and you . . . as an everlasting covenant throughout the ages, to be God to you and your offspring to come. . . . I shall bless you . . . and you will be a blessing. . . . And in you will all the families of the earth be blessed (17:1, 6; 12:3). After nineteen generations of disappointment, God found a righteous man and entered into an eternal covenant with him. The covenant with Abraham is a narrowing to a single person of what was meant from the very first for all humankind. From Abraham it was to reach, in succession, one family, one people, one land, and, in the end of days, all lands and all peoples. A solitary person, then, stood between what was intended to embrace every human creature and the beginning of the covenant's realization.

FROM CREATION, TO ABRAHAM, TO THE KINGDOM OF heaven on earth.

"Abraham was the greatest of men," the midrash tells us, "and was worthy of being created before Adam, but the Holy One reasoned thus: If I create Abraham before Adam, 'He [Adam] may sin, and who will set it right? Hence I shall create Adam first, so that if he sins, Abraham will come and set things right.' . . . Just as in the building of a house, one puts the great beam in the center, that it might support the entire structure, so was Abraham placed in the center of the generations that he might sustain all those who came before him and would follow afterwards."[1]

How awesome, then, to consider what might have been lost had the never-silent yet never-fully-heard voice not become audible to Abraham, who, the midrash says, smashed the idols in obedience to the divine command before forsaking his homeland for a new and distant land and a new vision. Nor was this all: might not everything yet end with him with whom it began? Would Abraham—single, fragile, human—find a way to hand down his lonely, newborn bond with God to another generation? That is the problem Scripture implicitly poses: how to prevent what began with Abraham from coming to an end. How might he open the soul of even one of his children to the presence and power of God, how guarantee that another ear would hear the voice and, hearing it, perform its commandments, as he had?

Transmission of the covenant from generation to generation is the crux of the patriarchal story. Indeed, there could be no story, no Bible without it. If the purpose of Israel's destiny is forgotten, then it becomes just another nation in the chronicles of antiquity, no different from the plethora of minor Middle Eastern peoples who arose and disappeared some millennia ago, deserving mention for this or that conquest, this or that potentate, but no more. As a consequence, the transmission of the covenant takes precedence over all else, even to the point of violating hallowed custom. A case in point is the law of primogeniture, which declares that special rights belong to the firstborn male (Deut 21:16-18). But neither Isaac, his son Jacob, Jacob's son Joseph, nor Joseph's son Ephraim is firstborn. The firstborn are, respectively, Ishmael, Esau, Reuben, and Manasseh. Yet the former and not the latter receive the birthright. The law is clear, but it is set aside for the simple reason that these firstborn sons are not deemed worthy of being entrusted with the task of receiving and handing down the covenant—Esau because he *despised* the birthright (25:34); Reuben because he "defiled his father's bed" (1 Chron 5:1). A distinction is clearly made between the biological firstborn and the recipient of the "birthright," usually bestowed through the vehicle of parental blessing. How to supplant the order of birth and strength with the order of merit is the challenge that each of the patriarchal families faces.

The key to understanding the continuity of the covenant is found in these words, *receiving* and *handing down.* As the ancient rabbis put it, "Moses *received* the Torah at

Mount Sinai and *handed it down* to Joshua, and Joshua to the elders, and the elders to the prophets, and the prophets to the men of the Great Synagogue."[2] Receiving and handing down, accepting and giving over, taking and transmitting: these are the poles around which the lives of the patriarchs revolve. What was bestowed upon them they dare not keep for themselves, lest the dream for all humankind die aborning; what they receive, they are obliged to transmit. Lacking one of these two, the venture is destined to fail, for them, for Israel, and for humanity. The sages say that God made many worlds and destroyed them before fashioning our world. Here, similarly, God would have to find another people and another route—and still may.

The fulfillment of creation, which might have been achieved by Adam, rested, after twenty generations of divine search and human failure, with Abraham. Now the hourglass narrows to its thinnest point. It begins a gradual widening only with the story of Joseph and his brothers. Bridging these two events—the divine call to Abraham and the establishment of Jacob's sons as tribal heads—is the collection of colorful, memorable, and precarious tales about the patriarchs and matriarchs—Abraham and Sarah, Isaac and Rebecca, Jacob and the sisters Rachel and Leah—the record of whose lives can be understood only if we remember that they are meant to be the special vehicles for the receiving and transmission of the covenant.

Abraham's receiving, especially significant in that none came before him, is recounted in Scripture and enriched in the midrash. Struggling with Mesopotamian paganism, he is presented as the iconoclast, the spiritual knight who pierces the veils of the ancient cults and hears through the pagan clamor the voice that demands not magic but righteousness, and that requires that he sever all links with his idolatrous past in order to found the new faith in the one God. *And the Lord called to Abram, "Go forth from your native land and your father's house to the land I will show you. . . . And I will bless you . . . and all the families of the earth shall be blessed through you.*" *And Abram went forth as the Lord had commanded him* (12:1-4). His life was presaged in his name, *Abraham the Hebrew* [Heb., *ha-ivri*] (14:13), derived, so the midrash records, from *eyver,* "side," as if to say "The whole world was on one side, while Abraham was on the other."[3]

Sarah, the first of the matriarchs, emerges from the scriptural text as a personality of stature. She joins Abraham in forsaking family and home, surely a more onerous break for a woman. She welcomes the traveler, speaks to the angel, and, while Abraham converts the men, "brings the women under the wings of the divine Presence," a phrase that the sages derive from the verse *the souls "they" made in Haran* (12:5).[4]

As elemental as was Abraham's receiving, that is, his ability to discern the word against the cacophony of pagan voices, so was his handing down. For of what avail is the one without the other? *All the nations are to bless themselves by [Abraham]. For I have singled him out, that he may instruct his children and his posterity to keep the way of the Lord by doing what is just and right* (18:18-19). As the story unfolds, it becomes apparent that the dilemma inherent in handing down was not less than that of receiving, for Abraham and Sarah succeeded only with one of their two sons, Isaac.

As we have said, the backdrop to the family chronicles that constitute so much of Genesis is the precarious process of transmission from one generation to the next. Leon Kass explores the failure of this process in the prepatriarchal story of Noah and his sons, who first witness the rainbow, God's pact with nature, and the beginnings of law.

Noah, an exemplary man, "righteous and simple in his generations," and begetter of three sons, is fit to be a new founder, a saving remnant out of the corrupt age. After the Flood, God establishes the new beginning through a covenant with Noah, and law is instituted for the first time. But transmitting the law involves more than begetting heirs; generation is not yet perpetuation. Genesis shows immediately the impossibility of relying on merely natural means for perpetuating traditions of restraint and reverence. Ham [the father of Canaan], Noah's youngest son, looks upon the uncovered nakedness of his father, and traffics in his discovery. He thereby metaphorically destroys his father as a father, without laying a hand on him, by looking upon him only as source of life and overturning his authority as teacher of a *way* of life. Perpetuation of a way of life requires children who, in order to receive, must have respect and even filial piety, and fathers who, in order to transmit, must remain worthy of the respect of their offspring. Noah's drunkenness reveals that parental authority and respectability are precarious; Ham's shamelessness shows that at least some children rebel against parental authority and tradition. The way of life begun with Noah could not be universally transmitted through natural generation alone, not even for one generation.[5]

That the Canaanites in particular were destined to be characterized by sexual immorality is derived from the story of the drunken Noah, whose *nakedness* was *gazed upon* (9:22) by his son Ham, the father of Canaan. Precisely what Ham had done is unclear in the biblical text, but it is of sufficient magnitude that Ham's son Canaan is cursed and his descendants, the Canaanites, damned with sexual debauchery. One sage suggests that Noah was castrated by his son, another that he was sexually abused. "Both indignities were perpetrated" is the harsh verdict of the Talmud.[6] The sexual immorality and child sacrifice practiced by the Canaanites threatened to debase family life and with it the divine undertaking. The unremitting thousand-year battle against pagan religion is a central theme in both the Bible and the Talmud:

I am the Lord your God. You shall not do as they do in Egypt where you once dwelt, nor shall you do as they do in the land of Canaan to which I am bringing you. . . . You shall not make yourselves unclean in any of these ways; for in these ways the heathen, whom I am driving out before you, made themselves unclean. . . . You, unlike them, shall keep my laws and my rules: none of you, whether natives or aliens settled among you, shall do any of these abominable things. . . . So the land will not spew you out for making it unclean as it spewed them out. . . . I am the Lord your God (Lev 18:1-3, 24, 26).

Pagan immorality provided a stumbling block to the transmission of the covenant. To take a daughter from among such a people would imperil the fragile process of receiving and handing down. Marriage into a pagan family had to be avoided at all costs. That may be why, in a book that wastes not a word and abridges the recitation of even momentous events, the narratives of Abraham and Sarah's search for a wife for their son, Isaac, and, in the next generation, Isaac and Rebecca's search for a wife for their son Jacob are crafted with such care and in such detail, reflecting the considerable importance Scripture imputes to these undertakings. Common to both are long, dangerous journeys to a distant land to avoid liaisons with the local Canaanite women.

How better to assure that Isaac will be loyal to the way of Abraham than by providing a proper wife for him? Then, too, parental influence may reach beyond their child to their child's child, for the proper wife is one who will be a proper mother as well. Where could a wife not tainted by the surrounding corruption be found for Isaac? Where else but in distant Haran, the land of his mother's family? The long trek of the faithful servant Eliezer back to Sarah's family in Haran finds its reward in his encounter with Rebecca. She exemplifies the virtues of kindness, courage, and modesty: kindness in offering to water the animals of others, courage in deciding to leave her family and cross the desert to marry one whom she has never seen, and modesty in covering her face when at the end of the journey she is about to meet Isaac for the first time. Upon her arrival, she proceeds at once to the now deceased Sarah's tent, an act that the rabbis see as a sign of her proper succession. Only then does Isaac marry her and love her and find comfort in the death of his mother (24:66). "So long as Sarah lived, the light she kindled on the Sabbath eve burned until the next Sabbath eve, but at her death the house fell into darkness. When Rebecca came, the light burned again. So long as Sarah lived, a cloud of glory rested upon the entrance to her tent, but at her death it vanished. When Rebecca came, it reappeared. So long as Sarah lived, there was a blessing in the bread she gave to wayfarers, but at her death it vanished. When Rebecca came, it returned."[7]

This midrashic tale reinforces our sense that the covenant is not simply a responsibility passed down the male line of descent, but a merit transmitted from matriarch to matriarch as well. The rabbis see the hand of providence at work. So they comment that "Before the Holy One, blessed be he, permitted Sarah's sun to set, he caused that of Rebecca's to rise," pointing to the order of Scripture where the birth of the latter precedes the death of the former (22:21—23:1), and citing Eccl 1:5, "The sun rises, and the sun sets."[8]

SCRIPTURE TELLS US THAT ABRAHAM'S RECEIVING OF the covenant directly from God, with no human mediation, is especially momentous. But Isaac, the middle and in some ways the least impressive of the patriarchs, is certainly not merely a passive recipient of the faith of his father. Indeed, there is for him a special difficulty, having to deal not so much with the certitude of a divine decree as with the human voice of the parent. According to the biblical account, Abraham was *tested* (22:1) in being commanded to offer up his son at Mount Moriah. But was it not equally a testing of Isaac? He was already at least seventeen years of age at the time. His inquiry into the reason for the journey to Mount Moriah—*Where is the sheep for the burnt offering?*—is not the question of a small child; he did not rebel even when, bound upon the altar, he saw the knife in the hand of his father. Tradition identifies the event less as the testing of Abraham than as the binding of Isaac. Indeed, it is as Isaac's trial that the tale has become a metaphor for Jewish existence, a grim reminder that each Jew must be prepared to face death for the sake of the covenant. Isaac's acceptance of the covenant, then, is as fraught with danger as was Abraham's. The founder of the Hasidic movement, the Baal Shem Tov (1700–1760), is said to have observed that the reason why it is not written "God of Abraham and Isaac" in the daily prayers but "God of Abraham, God of Isaac . . .," repeating the divine name for each patriarch, is to suggest that Isaac was not a silent partner in the transmission from father to son. Like his father, he too struggled to find God. The "God of Abraham" had to *become* the "God of Isaac"; what the father had acquired, the son too must make his own. Only then would Isaac's receiving of the covenant, a delicate thread in the wild fabric of antiquity, hold fast.

The Baal Shem also taught that the opening words of another prayer—"Our God and God of our fathers"—express this same idea in their universal application. The "God of our fathers" is what is handed down to us; "our God" is what we find for ourselves. Alone, each is worthy but insufficient. The "God of our fathers" bears the authority of tradition, but, if not internalized and made our own, may, in time, weaken and be abandoned. "Our God," on the other hand, represents a self-discovered faith that, although admirable in itself, may, without the generational power of family tradition, be forsaken in a moment of confusion. Both are needed. Therefore, concluded the Baal Shem, it is written: "our God" and "the God of our fathers."

As Abraham before him, Isaac too succeeds with only one of his sons. This success is in large measure due to the perspicuity and boldness of his wife, Rebecca. It is

Rebecca, worthy successor to Sarah, who ensures that Isaac's blessing will go not to Esau, the hunter, who though first-born is unfit, but to the younger son, Jacob, whom she, better than the sickly and failing Isaac, discerns to be the proper vehicle for the transmission of the covenant.

The case of Esau points to qualms over the ways of the Canaanites and confirms the importance of succession in the life of the patriarchs. Rebecca's favoring of Jacob over Esau in the matter of the birthright directly relates to Esau's choice of wives. At the close of chapter 26, we are told that Esau took as wives Canaanite (Hittite) women who were a *bitter grief* to Isaac and Rebecca. There immediately follows in chapter 27 Rebecca's decision to deprive Esau of blind Isaac's birthright-blessing and confer it upon Jacob. She, who was herself chosen by Abraham and Sarah as a wife for Isaac in place of the forbidden Canaanite women and who upon her arrival went at once, according to the midrash, to the tent of the deceased Sarah to show honor and pledge loyalty, understood above others the role of the wife in warding off corrupt influences and in handing down the covenant. *And Isaac brought her into his mother Sarah's tent. And he took Rebecca as his wife and loved her. And Isaac found comfort after his mother's death* (24:67).

Nor does Rebecca's part in the transmission of the covenant end here. Once Jacob possessed the blessing and the birthright, her first thoughts are for him, his safety, and his future family: to elude the threat of Esau and to avoid the error of Esau's marriages. As in the matter of the birthright, she does not hesitate to take decisive action:

> *Then Rebecca said to Isaac, "I am weary to death of Hittite [Canaanite] women. If Jacob marries one such as these, what good will life be to me?" Then Isaac called Jacob and blessed him, and charged him, "You shall not marry one of the Canaanite women. Arise, go to Paddan-Aram to the house of Bethuel, your mother's father; and take as wife from there one of the daughters of Laban your mother's*

brother. God Almighty bless you. . . . May he give the blessing of Abraham to you and to your descendants with you, that you take possession of the land of your sojournings which God gave to Abraham!" Thus Isaac sent Jacob away; and he went to Paddan-Aram to Laban, the son of Bethuel the Aramaean, the brother of Jacob's and Esau's mother (27:46—28:2).

In addition to the first blessing that his father, Isaac, gave him (27:28-30), Jacob receives the "blessing of Abraham," which came from God (26:3-5) and which joins inheriting the land to being a blessing to all the nations. The gift of the land is, in fact, conditional upon his becoming a blessing. But that can take place only if the stumbling block of intermarriage with the Canaanites is removed; thus the promise of the land (28:4) is hemmed in fore-and-aft (27:46; 28:6) by the interdiction *You shall not take a wife from among the Canaanite women* (27:46; 28:6).

Despite the parental warning to Jacob, as he departed for distant Paddan-Aram to find a wife, Esau continues his folly. *When Esau saw that the Canaanite women did not please Isaac his father, Esau went to Ishmael and took to wife, unto the wives he had, Mahalat, the daughter of Ishmael . . . the sister of Nebaiot* (28:8, 9). This passage is not without its element of humor. Seeing that his parents sent the favored Jacob to marry within the family, Esau decides to follow suit in his own blundering fashion. Like his brother, Jacob, he too "travels"; but at the end of a journey whose shortness is only the more evident by comparison with that of his brother, Esau marries the daughter of Ishmael, himself the son of an Egyptian mother and the husband of an Egyptian wife! Thus Esau adds an Egyptian to a Canaanite wife, the very two peoples marked by Leviticus 18 as sexually licentious. Scripture wants us to know of a certainty that this daughter of Ishmael was not from a different non-Egyptian mother but from that same Egyptian who we know was the mother of Nebaiot. The midrash wryly comments that "Esau would have done better had he divorced his other wives. Instead, by taking her *unto the wives he had* [italics mine], he added affliction upon affliction [Heb., *mahalah*, his wife's name], confirming the adage: 'A worthless palm tree finds its way to a grove of worthless trees.'"[9]

Under the steady guidance of Rebecca, it is Jacob and not Esau who becomes the inheritor of the covenant, and it is as a result of her actions that he sets off for Haran. His receiving of the covenant, then, is as much at the behest of his mother as it is his own doing. With added years of trial and maturity, he comes more fully into his own acceptance of his role and the weighty responsibility it carries. The two dreams that mold his destiny clearly spell this out: the first in which he envisions the human adventure as a mighty ladder spanning heaven and earth and the second in which he overcomes the awesome angel who changes his name to Israel, a harbinger of the people soon to be born. Tradition once again sees Jacob affirming God of his own volition as did his father and grandfather: "God of Abraham, God of Isaac, and *God of Jacob.*"

Now we understand better why Scripture lavishes so many chapters on Jacob and Joseph, Rachel's husband and son, an accounting that comprises fully half the book of Genesis, as much space as is given to the creation, the deluge, the tower of Babel, and the patriarchs Abraham and Isaac altogether, the entire story of humankind to this point. For if, as we have suggested, the substance of Genesis is the establishment and transmission of the covenant that binds God and Israel and defines both their faith and their history, then the task of handing down is different, and more difficult, for Jacob than it was for his father and grandfather. For Abraham it was enough to succeed with one son, Isaac, and for Isaac to succeed with one son, Jacob. The duty of Jacob, the third and last patriarch, however, was toward all twelve sons. What had hitherto been transmitted from a father to a single son was to be handed down by Jacob not to one son but to twelve, each with his own problems and potentialities. Abraham and Isaac failed with half their male progeny; Jacob must achieve at least a measure of success with his entire dozen, for they were to constitute the nascent nation. Bestriding the crossroad between patriarchal succession of the past and the nation that is yet to come, Jacob stands at a critical point, the bridge between the folk's prehistory, a chronicle of individual lives and family adventures, and the progenitors of the chosen people. In all respects Jacob becomes "Israel."[10]

THE DECISIVE ROLES THAT SARAH AND REBECCA PLAY in the transmission of the covenant have been discussed. But what is Rachel's part? Compelled to accept the bitter fate of sharing her husband, Jacob, with her sister, Leah, Rachel's life is troubled, briefer, and, it would appear, less impressive than that of Sarah. The sages' reading of Sarah's life leaves us with the picture of strength and nobility, the model matriarch who, with Abraham, championed the cause of the one God who desired justice and righteousness from humankind. When Isaiah calls the straying people back to their origins centuries later, it is to both Abraham and Sarah that he refers: "Listen to me, you who pursue justice/ You who seek the Lord/ Look to the quarry you were dug from/ Look back to Abraham your father/ And to Sarah who brought you forth" (Isa 51.1-2). Nor is Rebecca any less formidable. Both fortitude and vision, first revealed in her encounter with Eliezer (Gen 24), are reflected in her determination that the birthright go to Jacob and not Esau. Sarah and Rebecca alike lead long and fruitful lives, one miraculously giving birth in old age. They contend with their husbands, converse with angels, conduct the affairs of their homes with charity and firmness, deal with their sons, and plan their futures.

But what of Rachel? We find no later legend affirming her succession to Rebecca as we did Rebecca's succession to

Sarah. Compared to the sovereign personalities of the first two matriarchs, it is Rachel's femininity that first strikes the reader—beautiful and beloved. For Josephus, while Sarah stands for "wisdom," Rebecca for "patience," and Leah for "beauty of soul," Rachel represents "sense perception."[11] Rachel's capacity for love seems to mark her from her predecessors. However, as the biblical record of her life and the abundance of later legends surrounding her open before us, we shall come to see that it is she, even more than Sarah and Rebecca, whose tender humanity captures our imagination, she alone who continues each year to draw thousands of fervent pilgrims for prayer and communion to a shrine devoted to her memory. Indeed, in present-day Jerusalem, whereas streets are named after the kings and even the prophets of Israel, it was not deemed fitting to make so mundane a use of the esteemed names of the patriarchs or the matriarchs. The single exception was Rachel—in her case, affection overcame veneration. Rules were set aside, and a thoroughfare, on which the common traffic of the city's people passes each day, was named after Jewish history's most beloved woman—"Mother Rachel Street" (*Rehov Rahel Imeynu*).

In the many chapters devoted to the story of Jacob—his youth, ambition, early success, deception of his father, struggles with Esau and Laban, marriages, loss and recovery of Joseph, descent into Egypt—much is told and much remains untold, in the typically veiled charm of the Bible. To understand how Jacob was transformed from a shrewd, ambitious young man to the patriarch Israel, as well as to grasp something of the meaning of human compassion on which the redemption waits, it is to Rachel that we must turn.

We shall find that two themes are central to her life: *succession*—for the matriarchs play as important a role in accepting and handing down the covenant as do the patriarchs—and *love*—for the romance between Jacob and Rachel has no parallel in all the Bible. Succession is the underlying theme in the Jacob-Rachel story, but it is made manifest through love. The perilous task of handing down the covenant that all humankind may find blessing is not to be brought about through divine fiat but by the fidelity of the people Israel. This fidelity is the mystery of their survival in the face of tribulation and exile. Why else should they continue to bring children into a world where earthly rewards were so scant?

For the first chapters of biblical history, however, the entire venture hung upon the birth and loyalty of a single child. Hence the reader's interest in squeezing every drop of meaning out of the sparse tales the Bible records of the patriarchs and matriarchs. In the case of Rachel and Jacob, although the family was again the framework within which the process of succession was worked out, it was a context that, more than with their predecessors, featured love. And love is not without its trials.

Part *II* _____

The Trials of Love

Jacob's Dream
Ilya Schor

Chapter 2

The Journey

Then Isaac called Jacob and blessed him, and charged him, "You shall not marry one of the Canaanite women. Arise, go to Paddan-Aram to the house of Bethuel, your mother's father; and take as wife from there one of the daughters of Laban your mother's brother" (28:1).

The undertaking was both dangerous and doubtful. Jacob was to set out alone across the perilous desert—a journey usually made under the protection of a caravan. He was to seek a wife among people he did not know and then cross the desert again on his return. All this he was to do out of filial obedience in the name of an incredible promise made by his grandfather to him who was called Lord of all the world, the creator of heaven and earth, the one true master of all, who had chosen Abraham and his descendants in whom *all the families of the earth shall be blessed* (12:3). Did Jacob believe the astonishing story of the covenant so far as to brave the perils of the journey? Perhaps he would find a wife among the nomads along the way or some other diversion at an oasis where present prospects might seem preferable to fanciful dreams and incredible promises. What was to prevent so clever and ambitious a young man from veering off the narrow course his parents had set for him once he disappeared into the desert night far from family and home?

When it became necessary for Sarah and Abraham to arrange a marriage for Jacob's father, Isaac, they sent faithful Eliezer to represent them. One wonders if the embassy was not motivated as much by a desire to keep Isaac at home under parental scrutiny as by the perils of the journey and the tradition of delegating a surrogate for so delicate a negotiation. In Jacob's case, however, Esau's rage precluded such ancestral caution. Not daring to remain a moment longer, Jacob was compelled to flee at once, and alone.

All that parents can do for children had been done—the birthright, the blessing, the warning, the escape. But the blessing of the Promised Land was conditional upon Jacob's marriage and return; and even if he overcame that hurdle, would not the rage of his brother, the hunter Esau, stalk him? The temptation to abort the perilous venture must have been powerful. Who knows what doubts and schemes the young wanderer was turning over in his mind. When heaven intervened . . .

Jacob left Beer-sheba, and set out for Haran. He came upon a certain place and stopped there for the night. . . . Taking one of the stones there, he made a pillow for his head and lay down for sleep. He dreamt that he saw a ladder fixed in the earth but whose head reached the heavens, and angels of God were going up and down upon it. And the Lord was standing beside him and said,

"I am the Lord, the God of your father Abraham and the God of Isaac. This ground on which you are lying I will give to you and your descendants. . . . All the families of the earth shall bless themselves by you and your descendants. Remember I am with you: I will protect you wherever you go and will bring you back to this land. . . ."

Jacob awoke from his sleep and said, . . . "How awesome is this place. This is none other than the house of

God, this is the gateway to heaven." Thereupon Jacob made a vow (28:10-17, 20).

THE ENCOUNTER AT BETHEL COMPRISES THREE elements: the vision of the ladder, the presence of God, and the vow of Jacob.

The rungs of a ladder represent the possibility of movement between the point where its base rests and that to which it reaches. The enormous extent of Jacob's ladder, stretching as it does between heaven and earth, has no counterpart in the material world. What, then, may it mean? Could it suggest that apparently remote and conflicting ideas—heaven and earth, holy and profane, time and eternity—are in reality part of a single continuum of spirit, upon which the human and the divine ascend and descend?

The primordial harmony in which all might have dwelt side by side in sublime consonance had been disrupted by the realities of history; now was each the other's enemy, distant and dissident, shattered into innumerable hostile parts. Within the apparent chaos, however, lay the potential to overcome that dissonance, an invisible ladder hidden from the fleshly eye but now and again visible to the spirit in visions of the night. Such is the mystery of creation. The *angels ascending and descending* suggest that the ladder can be mounted. The divine within empowers us to hear the word, if we so wish, and to do the deed, if we so desire. We are not always deaf to the call of heaven, nor must we assume that our cries go unheard; the path between heaven and earth can be turned into a veritable highway. For God is not at war with humankind, nor is the higher world as distant from the lower as "heaven from earth"; rather has God in His loving-kindness built a staircase of the spirit that humans may learn to traverse through His merciful and just commandments. The ladder is a thoroughfare for traffic divine and human: it is the promise of the covenant.

The ladder is also the symbol of man himself. Consider the metaphor once again: like the ladder, we are fixed in the earth, bound as the animals by the laws of nature—birth and death, hunger and sickness, rage and terror. But, like the ladder also, our heads reach the heavens, for man alone of all creatures has a divine soul breathed into him, and he alone has the capacity to transcend himself, to infuse flesh with spirit, to dwell "here" but to live "there." This is the paradox of which the psalmist sang: "O Lord . . . what is man that you are mindful of him and the son of man that you think of him. Yet have you made him but little lower than the angels" (Ps 8:5-6). Deriving the Hebrew *adam* from both *demut* (image) and *adamah* (ground), Abraham Heschel writes that man is both "image and dust . . . a duality of mysterious grandeur and pompous aridity, a vision of God and a mountain of dust. It is because of his being dust that his iniquities may be forgiven, and it is because of his being an image that his righteousness is expected."[1]

In his dream, Jacob hears the heavenly voice telling him he need not fear the expedition across the desert; God will accompany him and bring him back, the land will be his, and all the families of the earth will find blessing in him and his descendants. The journey between heaven and earth is, then, intimately bound up with the journey to Haran to find a wife who can join him in the life of the covenant.

Jacob awakes in fear and trembling. *God is in this place and I knew it not,* he cries. *How full of awe is this place! . . . Surely it is the house of God and the gateway to heaven!* And reaffirming for himself the response of his father and grand-father before him to their divine encounter, he vows to fulfill his task. He will not break that vow. The desert no longer holds any terrors for him. Esau is forgotten, and wayside temptations vanish. Determined now to achieve his goal, Jacob is sent by the vision of the ladder straight as an arrow to distant Haran, without a glance to the right or the left. Through the twenty years with Laban, the image of the ladder and the awe of that place will remain with him;

on his return he will stop at that very spot before continuing homeward.

What Abraham began and Isaac carried on, Jacob vows to continue; what Isaac and Rebecca counsel, the dream at Bethel confirms. Jacob understands now the significance of his father's instructions: his life is not his own; heaven has a claim on it. And to honor that claim Jacob must find a bride who will not thwart the covenant. Jacob can give his heart only to one who would join him in fulfilling the vision of the ladder: love was directed by the charge of succession. And this became a guiding principle of the people Israel. For in the concern of Rebecca and Isaac for a proper mate for their son, we discover the passion of the Jewish parent to protect the child from a marriage that would jeopardize the covenant. The children of Israel were not to marry frivolously; personal feelings must give place to destiny.

What was at stake with Rebecca and Isaac, namely, the abandoning or the maintaining of the covenant through marriage, is precisely what would be at stake a thousand times in every generation. When future generations read of the extraordinary efforts that were taken by the patriarchs and matriarchs to protect the purity of the family, they were strengthened in their own attempts to arrange their lives so that suitable mates would be chosen. The people Israel were destined to take Jacob's lonely road to strange lands countless times, arriving as penniless as he and struggling each time to build once again a community where the covenant might be maintained. The vast majority, alas, were lost, some by persecution, others by choice—forced or persuaded, by the inhabitants of the strange lands in which they settled, to forsake their ancient dream. But some, here and there, remembered the vision of the ladder, felt the Presence, and made the vow to remain loyal to the covenant, which carried within it blessing for all humankind. For enough of them, succession guided love so that the people, their numbers fearfully reduced by the travails of exile, managed to survive.

Jacob and Rachel
Marc Chagall

cAt the Well

*Jacob continued his journey and came to the land of the
eastern tribes. There he saw a well in the open country
and three flocks of sheep lying beside it, for the flocks were
watered from that well. Over its mouth was a huge stone,
and all the herdsmen used to gather there and roll it off
the mouth of the well and water the flocks. . . . He asked
them if they knew Laban the grandson of Nahor. They
answered, "Yes, we do. . . . And here is his daughter
Rachel coming with the flock. . . ."*

*While he was talking to them, Rachel came up with her
father's flock, for she was a shepherdess. When Jacob saw
Rachel, the daughter of Laban, his mother's brother, with
Laban's flock, he stepped forward, rolled the stone off the
mouth of the well and watered Laban's sheep. He kissed
Rachel, and lifted up his voice, and wept (29:1-3, 4-6, 9-11).*

We meet Rachel for the first time at the well. It is an
unforgettable scene. No drama could have improved upon
her entrance onstage. Marked with innocence and impulse,
this moment has fired the imaginations of artists and writers
over the centuries. When Jules Romains wants to express
an idea of feminine beauty, he calls up the image of Rachel
at the well. "That young florist, so pale and so pretty, must

be a Jewess. Rachel standing amid the carnations and the roses."[1] And when Whittier seeks a model of a man and a maid, it is here that he finds it:

I love to hear
Tales of the pure, the good and the wise,
The holy men and maids of old
In the all-sacred pages told,
Of Rachel stopped in Haran's fountains
Amid her father's thirsty flock,
Beautiful to her kinsman seeming,
As the bright angels of his dreaming,
On Padan-aram's holy rock.[2]

The Bible does not speak in syllogisms; it prefers the logic of life. Perhaps that is the secret of its timelessness: the subtleties of the philosophers are for the few, but who does not understand life? To face the inevitability of death, to be trapped by temptation or propelled by greed, to bear a child, to know the love of a parent, a friend, a mate— these are the experiences of humans irrespective of time and place, whether in a tent in ancient Palestine or a towering skyscraper in Manhattan. Philosophy halts at the border of reason's domain, but the Bible penetrates everywhere because it experiences everything, including love.

Biblical love is the love of God for us—"With eternal love have I loved you, O children of Israel" (Jeremiah 31)— which we return to God—"You shall love the Lord your God with all your heart and all your soul and all your might" (Deut 7:5)—and which we share with our fellows— "You shall love your neighbor as yourself" (Lev 19:18). Scripture rarely uses the word *love* between man and woman. We are not told, for example, that Adam "loved" Eve, only that he "knew" her—*And Adam knew Eve his wife, and she conceived and bore Cain* (4:1). Nor are we told that Abraham "loved" Sarah. And although it is written that Isaac loved Rebecca, it is only *after* their marriage!—*He took Rebecca as his wife; and he loved her* (24:67). When, however, the Bible speaks of Jacob and Rachel, it speaks in human terms of love and sacrifice that we understand at once: *Rachel was of beautiful form and fair to look upon. And Jacob loved Rachel; and he said [to Laban] : "I will serve you seven years for Rachel your younger daughter"* (29: 17-18).

The joining of Isaac and Rebecca is not without its oriental charm; there are memorable scenes in the tale of Eliezer, eminent emissary of Abraham and Sarah, nobly garbed and laden with gifts, traveling with a luxurious caravan to a distant land to find the lovely Rebecca for Abraham's only true son, Isaac. Nor is the story without social and legal significance, for Rebecca's assent to Eliezer's proposal provides the scriptural source for the rabbinic ruling that a woman cannot be married without her consent.[3] But moving and detailed though the story is, it is more Eliezer's story than Rebecca's—matchmaking at its most sublime, rather than the exaltation of human love. Nothing is said of Rebecca's feelings before she is wed, nothing of Isaac's. Who can know what was in his heart when he heard of the plans for the trip; when he waited impatiently through the long period of the two journeys, back and forth; and when, at last, seeing her camel approaching, he went out to meet her? Who can know what was in the heart of Rebecca when she first learned of the proposal; when she heard the virtues of Isaac and his family recounted; when she gave her approval; and when, during the long and lonely trip to Canaan, she wondered what her promised husband might be like?[4]

About such things the Bible is silent. Not until the tale of Jacob and Rachel do we read in Scripture a love story in all its richness and pathos. There is no equal to it elsewhere in the Bible and few in the literature of three thousand years afterward.

Jacob's is a tale quite different from that of his father. Unlike the story of Isaac's courtship, there is here no emissary clad in oriental finery at the head of a caravan laden with rich gifts. Fleeing from Esau's wrath over the birthright he lost, Jacob did not have the luxury of an intermediary who would undertake the long journey for him; he had to act for himself. Nor could one who arrived with only his staff offer a delicate bracelet or a silver nose ring. All he could give was himself: spontaneity, vigor, virility, an act of generosity, and an outburst of love. *He stepped forward, rolled the stone off the mouth of the well and watered Laban's sheep. He kissed Rachel, and lifted up his voice and wept* (29:10-11).

The description of their meeting at the well is extraordinary. In quick strokes the canvas is filled, the picture depicting the culmination of Jacob's journey is put before us. The contrasts are stark: the exhausting and extended journey and the immediacy of the meeting, the parched desert and the refreshing well, the lonely anticipation and the joy of communion. A minimum of words, a maximum of meaning; nothing of premeditation, nothing of Eastern circumlocution, no formalities, no gifts, no intermediaries. Jacob's response is impulsive and decisive. How often during the dreary weeks of the journey must he have dwelt on the oft told story of Eliezer's meeting with his mother Rebecca at the well; now he himself approaches a well. Perhaps it is the same well,[5] for he is near Laban's house. Suddenly he sees a lovely young shepherdess approaching with the face and figure of his mother. "From the moment he saw her at the well," says one midrash, "his soul was bound to hers."[6] Another midrash relates that Jacob recited a blessing over her beauty: "For the sages have taught: Upon seeing human creatures of unusual beauty, one should say, Blessed are you, O Lord, Who has such as these in your world! And there was none so fair as Rachel; it was for this that Jacob wanted to marry her."[7] "It was destined that they meet at the well," observes the Zohar, "that Jacob might rivet his eyes and his heart upon Rachel's loveliness."[8] "She surpassed all women in beauty," observed Josephus.[9]

Still, although the simple meaning of the story seems clear, there were those who objected to linking mere physical beauty to such a momentous decision.[10] A leading Hasidic teacher, astonished at the blunt description Scripture gives of the amorous meeting of Jacob and Rachel, as well as the midrash's apparent confirmation of its literal meaning—"It was for her beauty that Jacob embraced her"— explains that physical charm is shown to us in order that we might appreciate and turn to the heavenly source of all beauty. "The true meaning of the lovely shepherdess' meeting at the well is that it alludes to the supernal Rachel [the Shechinah], whom Jacob was drawn to embrace upon confronting [the earthly] Rachel. . . . [Indeed] one is permitted to embrace earthly beauty only if this leads one to espouse heavenly beauty."[11]

Knowing her to be his uncle's daughter and believing her to be his destined one, Jacob finds marvelous new strength—as special young men are wont to do in the presence of special young women—and proceeds to roll back the huge stone, which only the collective might of the shepherds could budge, "as easily as a cork is drawn from a bottle."[12] Surely this was a very different Jacob from the young man Scripture described as *a quiet man, dwelling in tents* (25:27), who, according to the sages, had spent his days since early youth learning Torah in the academy of Shem and Ever, a withdrawn, shy, pallid yeshiva student.[13]

The motif of the stone appears again and again as metaphor and symbol in Jacob's career. There is the stone he removes from the mouth of the well, the stone that was his pillow at Bethel, the stone marker that he sets up after the dream, and the stones he erects as a peace monument between himself and Laban when they part company for the last time. "Jacob is a man who sleeps on stones, speaks in stones, wrestles with stones, contends with the hard yielding nature of things."[14]

He kissed Rachel, and lifted up his voice and wept (29:11).

WHAT A WORLD OF MEANING IS COMPRESSED INTO these seven Hebrew words! Apart from the Song of Songs, which was permitted into the canon only because it was understood as an allegory of the love between God and the people Israel, I cannot think of another example in Scripture of a man and a woman kissing, certainly not before marriage.[15] Brothers kiss: Joseph and Benjamin, Jacob and Esau. Parents and children kiss: Laban and his family, Jacob and his sons. Orpah and her mother-in-law, Naomi, kiss; God kisses Moses at his death, say the sages; and even heaven and earth are said to kiss. Not, however, man and woman. Yet, despite all this, Jacob "kisses" Rachel.

Later rabbinic literature is as empty of parallels as Scripture and indeed reveals a certain embarrassment at the incident. There the dictum is offered that "All kissing is indecent save three: high office, parting, and reunion."[16] Since the case of Jacob and Rachel fits none of these categories, Rabbi Tanhuma offers yet another to account for Jacob's impulsive behavior—"'kisses of kinship,' for it is written that *she was his kinswoman.*"[17] A cautious medieval commentator suggests further that if he kissed her, it was certainly not on the mouth, and the *Shulhan Arukh,* the code of Jewish law, decrees that, apart from parent and child or an infant relative, all kissing is prohibited.[18] Such intimacy was outlandish as well to Christian commentators: the sixteenth-century Protestant theologian John Calvin protests that even kinship cannot excuse Jacob's conduct, since at this point in the story Rachel could not have known of the relationship, Jacob having failed to introduce himself. Calvin concludes that the passage must be ascribed to an error in Moses' redaction of the Torah text![19]

Jacob's act has been understood in quite a different way from these interpretations. The Jewish mystical classic, the Zohar, transcends the plain and even the midrashic meanings of the story by discovering in the kiss of Jacob and Rachel the uniting of the sundered spiritual worlds and the apotheosis of the divine-human encounter. To the mystic the intimate aspect of that encounter is the goal of all religious striving, the heart of faith. It is through the experience of human affection, even the affection between man and woman, that the encounter with the divine and the life of the spiritual worlds is sometimes expressed. How else describe the divine than by means of the most profoundly human? Although God and the people Israel are already seen as lover and beloved, bride and groom, and the embrace and kiss treated as moments of rapture by the prophets and rabbis, it is in the mystical literature, particularly the Zohar, that such symbolism reaches its zenith. In a celebrated passage the kiss of Jacob and Rachel is expounded in conjunction with the words of the Song of Songs, "Let him kiss me with the kisses of his mouth" (1:2), which the rabbis had already taken to be a sign of the divine espousal of the people Israel.

What prompted King Solomon, when recording the praise of love between the upper and lower worlds, to begin with the words, "Let him kiss me with the kisses of his mouth?" The reason is that no other love is like unto the ecstasy of the moment when spirit cleaves to spirit in a kiss, more especially a kiss on the mouth. . . . When mouth meets mouth, the spirits unite, the one with the other; they are one, and love is one. . . . Who is to kiss me? The most hidden and recondite one. . . . And because he is hidden, the Canticle begins in a hidden fashion, "Let 'Him' kiss me" [i.e. in the third person]. . . . If properly consumated, love ascends to a celestial chief . . . who is called Akatriel [Heb., "one who crowns God"], because he [then] wreathes crowns for his Lord.

When the spirit of love enters the palace of love, the love of the supernal kisses is aroused, concerning which it is written: *And Jacob kissed Rachel.* This arousal brings about the kisses of supernal love, which are the beginning of all love, attachment and union above. . . . But if kisses are from there, what need have we of Jacob here?

33

Do not the kisses proceed from Him? The matter is thus: "Let Him kiss me"—that is, Him who is most hidden above. But how [since He is most hidden]? Through that supernal chariot . . . which is Jacob. . . .

[After this exposition], the companions of Rabbi Jose [who gave it] came and kissed him on his head. Rabbi Shimon [the master of the scholars] wept, and said: "I know for a certainty that the Holy Spirit from above has made itself manifest here." Then they all wept with joy. "Blessed is this generation," he continued. "There will be none other like it until King Messiah shall appear. . . ."[20]

Returning to Scripture's altogether earthy tale, we must ask about Rachel's role in all this. If Jacob kissed her, can we not assume that Rachel allowed herself to be kissed? She did not, after all, retire in blushing confusion to her mother's tent after the assault, but proceeded directly to inform her father of his arrival. In order to understand Rachel's forthright behavior, we must give some consideration to the description of her as a *shepherdess*. The role of the shepherdess suggests the quality of mercy, for shepherds must guide and care for their charges. The sages recount that when Moses, a shepherd in Midian, pursued a lost sheep to a perilous cliff and returned it to the flock, heaven marked him as now being worthy to guide the flock of Israel.[21] Just as the creating, ruling, judging God is called "king," so is the compassionate, caring, merciful God called "shepherd." "The Lord is my shepherd, I shall not want" (Ps 23). The young Rachel, who tended her father's flocks in Haran, became in time the legendary shepherdess and mother of all Israel, rising up from her tomb to console the suffering people.

But if tender concern is one characteristic of the shepherdess, modest but sturdy independence is another. The sages, troubled that a young woman as beautiful as Rachel should have had the freedom to roam the pastures alone with other shepherds, offer several suggestions—Laban had no choice but to send her to care for the flock since he was without sons; Rachel had a special way with the animals; the flock had been reduced by disease to a small number. Not satisfied, however, with such explanations, they stress that her virtue was guaranteed by divine protection.[22] In any case, it would seem to Catherine Chalier that Rachel as shepherdess—a rustic, robust outdoor type—is the counter-image to the later, prevailing biblical model of woman as an indoor, secluded, protected person, one whose primary task was to care for her household: "The honor of the princess is in her privacy" (Ps 45:14):

> As if woman's unique, essential, and incomparable mission were to call forth a "place" within space: a place towards which the virility of man could come to gather itself, before embarking on his conquests. As if this were the ontological feminine function: "to illumine the dulled eye, to reveal the origins of all earth's gentleness," to help her husband return to his full self by preparing for him a home, by teaching him the meaning of privacy.[23]

Indeed, the rabbis tell us that "Women are not commonly found in the field" away from home,[24] and, more precisely, that the home *is* the woman.[25]

Chalier points to the gender-specific character of the dichotomy, between "indoor" and "outdoor," associating interiority with the former and exteriority with the latter. Rachel contrasts with the typical image of woman as an "interior" (home or withdrawn) figure. The quality of self-reliance, even audacity, which Rachel as shepherdess represents, continues in her lifetime and in legend after her death. She has the courage to repudiate her father by leaving him and taking his idols. Thomas Mann in his *Joseph the Provider* goes further, suggesting that "The lovely one was a thief and rascal too. Her loveliness was no stranger to stratagems. For love of her husband she stole her gloomy father's images, thrust them into the camel's bedding, and sat on it and said in her beguiling voice: 'I am unwell with my periods and cannot stand up.' But Laban searched in vain, to his own chagrin." Rachel alone among the barren matriarchs protests to her husband that he has not given her children. Leah, keeping from Jacob her pain over her unloved state, remained close to hearth and home and is buried deep in the cave of Machpelah, but Rachel, the outdoor, roaming shepherdess, was destined to serve her people and is laid to rest along the roadside, that she might rise up to console the exiles when they would pass on the way to Babylon.

In contrast to the image of the biblical woman as mistress of the house, in which she bears and raises her children, Scripture also presents us with a number of women who can be called "public" persons. Sarah leaves family and land to join Abraham and brings others to the one God; Rebecca responds *I will go* (24:58), when asked if she will leave her home, even, the sages add, if her family refuses;[26] Esther delivers her people in time of peril; Deborah leads troops into battle. The image of the woman of valor in Proverbs is true to both qualities: she serves the Lord without as well as within her house, planting vineyards, bringing food from afar "like a merchant fleet" (Prov 31:14), and acquiring property. Wisdom, strength, hope, and piety are her virtues.

In the light of this understanding of Rachel's special independence, her behavior on meeting Jacob seems less surprising. Indeed, Josephus resolves his discomfort with Jacob's apparently unpatriarchal actions by simply substituting Rachel for Jacob, so that it is Rachel doing the kissing and the embracing![27]

After kissing Rachel, Jacob *lifted up his voice and wept* (29:12), as if to express ineffable joy. To have found so suddenly and so perfectly what his parents and he had sought when he set out on his long and perilous journey evokes contradictory emotions. Tears and exultation meet together. The tears are the tears of bliss, which bride and groom shed beneath the bridal canopy. The rabbis, still troubled by the kiss, offer three further reasons for Jacob's weeping: because, unlike Eliezer who brought lovely jewelry to Rebecca, he came empty-handed; because he foresaw that he would not be buried with her at Machpelah; or because he noticed people whispering over this "lewdness." For, according to a midrash, the shepherds complained that this stranger, Jacob, had violated the laws of moral action instituted after the flood, which was understood as a punishment for humankind's sexual perversion. Having restrained themselves out of obedience to this new code of conduct from approaching the solitary lovely Rachel in the pasture, they resented Jacob's cavalier behavior.[28]

This last midrash of the rabbis raises a further question. When the sages say that it was sexual perversion that brought about the flood that nearly destroyed the world, they are offering a warning about the ruinous effects of uncontrolled erotic emotion so evident in the contemporary pagan society. The biblical pattern posited marriage first, with love following, and being born out of, marriage. Thus, Isaac *took Rebecca as his wife, and* [that is, afterwards] *he loved her* (24:67). Rachel and Jacob, however, demonstrate the opposite. Their passion is "immediate," unmediated by family or ceremony; it is spontaneous and decisive. When Jacob saw Rachel, surrounded by her sheep, approaching the well, he knew simply that she was the destined one Rebecca had meant for him. Here was a love both instantaneous and certain, complete in a single glance. Immediate as it was, however, it harbored no capriciousness, no lightheartedness, but led rather to a permanent, ever-deepening bond, able to endure great sacrifice.[29]

At THE FATEFUL MEETING BY THE WELL THE ACTORS were Jacob and Rachel, and Jacob and Rachel only. Would that it could have remained so.

Rachel hiding the stolen idols from her father
Gian Battista Tiepolo

*Chapter 4*_____

$\mathcal{L}aban$

THE STORY OF RACHEL AND JACOB IS NOT SIMPLY A story of love, but of love on trial. We have already touched upon the first two of these trials, the trial of the journey and the trial at the well. Now a further test is introduced. With the entrance into the story of Rachel's father, the crafty Laban, whom we remember from his wily treatment of Eliezer, the idyllic vision of romantic bliss that stood above place and time like a Garden of Eden dissolves into the world's crass realities. Paradise ends, as it were, and history begins.

When Laban heard of the arrival of Jacob, his sister Rebecca's son, he *ran to meet him, embraced him and kissed him* (29:13). The sages detect deceit in these words. Refusing to believe that Jacob had really arrived empty-handed, Laban "embraced him" to see how large a money belt he had wrapped around him and "kissed him" to learn whether he had hidden precious jewels in his mouth. But Jacob, fleeing the wrath of his brother, brought nothing of value save his traveling stick. Not finding payment to compensate him for Rachel as he had been compensated for Rebecca, Laban negotiates seven long years of labor from the lovesick Jacob.

To Jacob, however, the years of servitude seem no more difficult than rolling the stone off the well had been. And with good reason:

Rachel was of beautiful form and fair to look upon. And Jacob loved Rachel. And he said: "I will serve you seven years for Rachel."

And they seemed unto him but a few days for the love he had to her (29:18-20).

Unlike the feat at the well, however, Jacob's desire is not merely a show of passion as brief as it is powerful, but an enduring love that outlasts years of servitude to a wretched taskmaster whose concern is only to squeeze whatever profit he can. The trials of love are a popular theme in literature and legend, and Jacob's seven years of quiet labor may seem positively humdrum in contrast to the spectacular adventures of medieval knights who crossed oceans, slew dragons, and conquered vast kingdoms for love. But the passions of medieval chivalry were often fleeting and always adulterous. In contrast, Jacob's love, not at all less passionate than theirs, is marked by that quiet steadfastness that characterizes the permanent commitment of marriage.

Through love Jacob can perform feats of strength. Through love he can offer up the best years of his young life in servitude, resigning himself to Laban's chicanery with hardly a notice for the passage of time; he can sacrifice and not know that he has sacrificed, for with love all things are possible. Psychiatrist Victor Frankl, in his *Man's Search for Meaning*, tells us that what enabled some inmates at his concentration camp to survive while others perished was the obsession with an idea, a purpose, a person, which alone gave meaning to the terrible days. Laban was not a Nazi nor was Haran a concentration camp, but Frankl's observation helps us understand how Jacob's seven years of forced labor could be eased with the vision of Rachel before him.

As with the scene at the well, this biblical description of love overcoming servitude became a literary staple. Heinrich Heine, in his *Rabbi of Bachrach*, describes one such telling of the tale: "The little fellow now put his book on the broad arm-rest of the easy-chair and explained the story of Jacob and Rachel, how Jacob had lifted up his voice and wept aloud when he first saw his cousin Rachel, how he conversed with her so sadly by the well, how he had to serve seven years for Rachel, and how quickly they passed for him, and how he married Rachel and always loved her."[1] Not only the rendering but the very language was common parlance among those who knew the Bible. To cite another writer, "On account of the greatness of our love, the days ever appeared to us to be few."[2] Or yet another who finds here the biblical romantic ideal:

> Heavenly Father, who only art the source of love and the giver of every good gift, we thank thee for the love wherewith the soul of thy servant clave unto this woman as Jacob unto Rachel, which many years have not quenched.[3]

If the story of Jacob and Rachel has entered into the ranks of world literature as a model of love and sacrifice, what was its effect on the classical Jewish writings? In the Bible itself it is one of the few family incidents recounted in the Torah and also mentioned by the prophets. So Hosea centuries later: "And Jacob fled into the field of Aram. And Israel served for a wife. And for a wife he kept sheep" (12:13). In the Talmud a parallel is hinted at in its most famed love story, written more than a thousand years after the biblical one, the tale of another Rachel and her beloved Akiba, who, because of her, achieves notoriety as one of the preeminent Torah scholars of his time.

The Talmud recounts that a young woman named Rachel, the daughter of a wealthy Jerusalemite, found nobility in the soul of Akiba, one of her father's shepherds. Rachel's father promptly disowned his daughter upon her secret marriage to Akiba. Though impoverished, Rachel encouraged the unlettered shepherd to devote himself to the study of Torah, to the point of selling her long, beautiful hair. At her urging, he departed for the great academy in Babylonia and remained there for a number of years. By the time Akiba finally returned to Jerusalem in the company of his admiring students, he had become a celebrated sage. When some of his disciples, ignorant of Rachel's identity, restrained her from pushing through the crowd to embrace Akiba, he surprised them by pointing to the poorly dressed woman and proclaimed: "Let her be, for all that I am, and all that you are, are due to her!"[4]

The parallels between the two stories, biblical and talmudic, are intriguing. Both husbands, Akiba and Jacob, have related names, *AkiBa* and YA'AKoBH; both depart from home in the early periods of their lives to study Torah: Akiba in the Babylonian academy just after marriage and Jacob in the school of Ever just before marriage (according to the midrash); both rise from stations of obscurity to positions of renown; both fathers-in-law, Kalba Sabua and Laban, are unattractive, powerful men who place obstacles in the way of their daughters' marriages; both sets of lovers suffer separation for painful periods of time (which in each case, as the duration is about to run its course, is doubled): in the biblical tale, for the sake of love for the other, in the talmudic narrative, for the sake of love for the Torah; both wives are called Rachel, and both radiate a beauty that is duly noted: the comely appearance of the one and the hair of the other; both make heroic sacrifices: Akiba's Rachel gives up the comfort of her father's house to wed him and forgoes his company to enable him to study Torah, Jacob's Rachel acquiesces in the substitution of her sister for herself as Jacob's first wife; and both are independent personalities: Jacob's Rachel became the legendary defender of her people, and Akiba's Rachel defied rank to marry a shepherd and repudiated status to spur him on to scholarly greatness.[5] Thus it would seem that the most renowned biblical love story of Jacob and Rachel found later some measure of expression in the most renowned talmudic love story of Akiba and Rachel.[6]

ONE WHO READS THE SCRIPTURAL TALE OF THE tribulations of Jacob cannot but conclude that it was the sustaining power of love that enabled him to overcome the years of servitude with which Laban bound him. There were more ordeals to come.

> *Jacob said to Laban, "Give me my wife, for my time is fulfilled. . . ." And Laban gathered all the people of the place and made a feast. When evening came, he took his daughter Leah and brought her to him; and he went in to her. . . . When morning came, there was Leah! So he said to Laban, "What is this you have done to me? I was in your service for Rachel! Why did you deceive me?"* (29:21-25).

"It was for love that Jacob worked seven long years, and for seven more," writes Chauncey Depew, "and I have often wondered what must have been his emotions when on the morning of the eighth year he awoke and found the homely, scrawny, bony Leah instead of the lovely and beautiful presence of his beloved Rachel."[7] What emotions indeed! Anger, surely, and outrage, but with them a dread intuition that Laban perpetrated the crime in the certain knowledge that he could get away with it.

That Laban's deceit was fully in character, the midrash learns from his denomination *Laban the Aramean* (25:10), which it understands to be a moral rather than a geographical referent, taking *Arami* ("Aramean") from *ramai* ("deceiver"), as in "*Lamah rimitani*: Why have you *deceived* me?" (1 Sam 28:12). The midrash further suggests that, fully aware of Laban's notoriety, Jacob's offer to serve him seven

years *for Rachel, your younger daughter* (Gen 29:18)
amounted to a set of conditions such that there could be no
question as to the nature of the agreement. *"Rachel,* and not
Leah; *your daughter,* and not some other woman named
Rachel; your *younger* daughter, and not the older one."[8] In
suggesting a seven-year term he may even have been
appealing to Laban's fear of the magical power of numerol-
ogy: just as the number seven ruled the days of the week
and the years in the Sabbath and Jubilee commemorations,
so was it meant to be the controlling number for his marriage. Seven was also a common factor of the numerical
value (*gematria*) of Jacob and Rachel's Hebrew names
(26×7 and 34×7)—but not of Leah's—suggesting that only
they were destined for one another. To no avail. Laban is
swayed not a hairbreadth from his evil intent by either
words or numbers and turns Jacob's seven years against
him by requiring from him a second term. "Though you tie
down a cheat in every which way, nothing good will come
from him," is the verdict of the midrash.[9]

Laban takes cruel advantage of Jacob's modest circumstances by denying him a dowry and exacting hard labor as
the price for his daughter. Indeed, both girls complain about
the way their father has treated them financially (31:14). But
we see Laban at his shrewdest in the way he mutes Jacob's
outrage at the substitution of Leah, so that Jacob's cry *Why
did you deceive me?* (29:25) is the beginning and the end of
his protest. First, Laban makes sure there is an audience to
the deception: in honor of the wedding *Laban had gathered all the men of the place together and prepared a feast*
(v. 22). In making the community a party to his action,
Laban gave it the sanction of accepted behavior. Laban's
second thrust is the argument he makes for cultural precedent in response to Jacob's complaint: *In our country it is
not right to give the younger sister in marriage before the
elder* (v. 27). Simply taken at face value, Laban's explanation reveals the depths of his deceit. For if he feels himself
so bound by the force of local custom, why did he promise

the younger daughter in the first place? Because it offered a way of extracting seven years' free labor from Jacob, to whom from the outset he never intended to give Rachel, promised or not.

But if Laban's response is a public defense of his action, there is a further, private level of meaning meant for Jacob's ears alone. Like all tricksters, Laban is something of a psychologist, and the assertion of the rights of the elder over the younger child is designed to strike Jacob at his most vulnerable spot. For had not the accuser himself violated this very same law of primogeniture in taking the birthright from his elder brother, Esau? Laban's remark has a taunting tone: although your country may permit lapses in proper conduct—namely, your behavior with Esau—*in "our" country* we respect the traditions of our fathers. The parallel was unavoidable. For what was most precious to Isaac—the birthright—Jacob beguiled Esau; so, for what was most precious to Jacob—Rachel—is he beguiled. How, after this, could Jacob pursue the matter? He may even have had second thoughts as to whether he should have acquired the birthright in the first place. For it was that deception that forced Jacob to flee from Esau's anger to a foreign land where he would invest twenty years of hard labor for an unscrupulous relative. Could that deception of his have caused *this* deception to be practiced upon him?

That it might have should not blind us to the moral force at work behind Jacob's disinheriting of Esau. Time and again in the Bible what has priority in the order of nature is superseded by an ethical imperative. Ishmael, Esau, and Reuben were firstborn children, but, as already noted, because they were not considered worthy of the trust of continuing the covenant, Isaac, Jacob, and Joseph were substituted for them. Here we have an illustration of the biblical rejection of the pagan world, in which nature's gods ruled supreme, in favor of a just and merciful God, who is not nature's instrument but its Lord.[10] Jacob's obtaining the birthright, then, was not simply a matter of fraternal strife or "deception," but the triumph of a new and better scale of value—morality over nature. Although Scripture records Jacob's reaction to the treachery practiced upon him by Laban, it tells us nothing about the mortification Rachel must have felt on being replaced by her sister, other than that Rachel too was taken as a wife to Jacob (in exchange for another seven years of labor!) and that she was loved by Jacob more than was Leah. The midrash, however, does not let the matter rest there, focusing its attention not so much upon Jacob's outburst at Laban's outrageous behavior as upon Rachel's silent acceptance of her shame. Was not such submissive acceptance unusual in the extreme? Would we not expect a cry of betrayal from the bold young woman Rachel reveals herself to be? Instead, denied the promised one for whom she had been forced to wait seven long years, she responds with a silence as astonishing as it is unexpected. But it is in this very silence that the midrash and the mystical writings find the genius of Rachel's character.

Torn between her love for Jacob and her compassion for her sister, she chose not to put her sister to shame. Perhaps she feared that otherwise Leah would be given to the infamous Esau to whom the sages say she had been promised and over which betrothal she had wept such bitter tears that her eyesight had been affected. Some of the sages even propose that Rachel's silence shows that her desire to prevent Leah's humiliation led her to become an accomplice in the deception! One suggests that Rachel knew that Laban was regularly diverting Jacob's gifts for her to Leah. Another implies that Rachel told her sister the private signs—touching Jacob's right toe, thumb, and earlobe, for example—that she and Jacob had agreed upon to prevent any deception[11] and suggests that Leah used these to mislead the tipsy Jacob in the pitch-dark nuptial chamber. Yet another proposes that Rachel went so far as to hide under the bed in order to aid her sister.[12] Support for these contentions is thought to be found in Scripture itself: *In the morning, behold, it was Leah* (29:25), that is to say, "Until the morning it was not Leah; since she knew the signs, Jacob believed her to be Rachel."[13] Only with the breaking daylight did he recognize who lay at his side.

Though the trial of Laban continues all the years that Jacob remains with him, out of the deception at the wedding is born another ordeal that assumes center stage—the trial of Leah.

Detail from the Tomb of Julius II: Leah
Michelangelo

*Chapter 5*_____

Leah

FAMILY TENSION IN THE BIBLE IS TYPICALLY SIBLING
and not oedipal. Indeed we are hard put to find examples
in Genesis of the struggle between parents and children
that is supposedly at the heart of all family stress. Instead
Scripture offers us instance after instance of the rivalry of
brothers—Cain and Abel, Isaac and Ishmael, Jacob and
Esau, Joseph and his brothers.

And of sisters. For distressing though these episodes of
fraternal tension are, the most tragic instance of such sibling
antagonism is that between Rachel and Leah. Here we have
the infinitely compounded woe of sisters who are also
wives of the same husband, a practice so frowned upon
that it was placed on the list of forbidden sexual relations in
Leviticus: "Do not marry a woman as a rival to her sister
and uncover her nakedness in the other's lifetime" (Lev
18:18). In view of this prohibition, the question naturally
arises as to how the marriage of Rachel and Leah to a single
husband could have taken place at all:

> For this Rachel-and-Leah is marriage; which, I have seen
> it,
> Lo, and have known it, is always, and must be, bigamy
> only,

Even in noblest kind a duality, compound, and complex,
One part heavenly-ideal, the other vulgar and earth:
For this Rachel-and-Leah is marriage, and Laban, their
    father,
Circumstance, chance, the world, our uncle and hard
    task-master.[1]

The Rachel-Leah marriage was not simply bigamy, however, but two *sisters* marrying the same husband; and against
this the biblical prohibition is unqualified. Jewish tradition
offers four solutions for the problem. First, the proscription
against such a liaison was said to be not then in effect,
since the giving of the Torah took place only many centuries later. This same reason explains Abraham's serving his
guests meat together with milk (18:8), a combination clearly
contrary to the dietary laws expressed in Exod 23:19. Such
an argument becomes problematic, however, in light of the
rabbinic tradition that the patriarchs observed the laws of
the Torah even before they were given at Mount Sinai.
Some, accordingly, offer a second solution: the patriarchs
did, in fact, keep all the laws when they resided in the land
of Israel, but only a portion of them in such far-off places
as Haran where Jacob married Rachel and Leah. This is
confirmed, it is suggested, by the early death of Rachel
immediately upon entering the Promised Land, when the
full force of the Torah prohibitions came into play. In a
third solution, divine sanction allows violating the law in
Jacob's case because the future progeny of these marriages
would comprise the heads of the twelve tribes of Israel.
Finally, as Nahmanides records, "Since Leah and Rachel
each feared that whichever of them did not marry Jacob
would become the wife of his brother Esau, God decided to
give them both to Jacob."[2]

Whatever the justification for the marriage of two sisters
to one man, it is clear that as co-wives the sisters were
placed in an untenable situation. After all, each loved the
same man, each sought his love, each wished to be the

mother of his children, and each felt envy for the other. Thus, *when Rachel saw that she had borne Jacob no children, she became envious of her sister* (30:1); and Leah complained: *. . . You have taken away my husband* (30:15)! One twentieth-century poet describes the dilemma with sadness and satire:

Rachel

My father came and bid me stay,
Enjoined the women bar my way.

And dumb to all entreaty, led
My sister Leah in my stead,

Where Jacob waited for his bride.
I heard the revelry subside,

The guests depart. I slept alone,
Dreamt Leah slept beneath a stone.

Leah

My father did it to be kind,
And I who knew the dark was blind.

Who loved in silence, hoped, believed,
But Jacob mocked me, Rachel grieved.

And kinsmen turned away in scorn.
I grazed the flock, I shucked the corn.

Fled Jacob's wrath. Fulfilled, reviled,
When autumn came, I bore his child.[3]

In the poem, "Rachel and Leah," the Yiddish writer Itsek Manger describes the tension in his typically irreverent yet penetrating manner:

Rachel stands barefoot in the doorway,
Quietly humming a song,

The Trials of Love

All the swallows flitting by
Are fragrant with blossoms and spring.

Jacob, that radiant person, came
To her in a dream at night,
And from his strenuous labor
Three lovely presents brought.

A *bentsherl*—a blessings-book—
Some patent leather shoes,
And a gold ring! How she loves him!
If the swallows only knew!

She squints her eyes up at the sun
And laughs and laughs and beams,
Because that very same great sun
Shines down in the field, on him.

A breeze nestles at her feet
And ruffles up her hair
And mutters softly in her ear:
"Another five whole years!"

"Rachel!" her sister Leah calls,
"Your coffee's getting cold."
Rachel trembles quietly:
"I'm coming, Leah! Now!"

All of a sudden she grows sad.
She knows that Leah weeps
Every night upon her bed
And she knows what that means . . .

And in her heart she feels a pinch
And hurries into the nook:
"Here, Leah, my dearest sister, take
The shoes and the blessings-book!

And Leah, dearest sister, you
May keep the golden ring,
But leave for me, for me alone,
The one I adore—him."

And from the sisters sharply breathe
Their longing and their grief,
And whoever laughs or mocks them
Is a fool and a thief.⁴

The dramatic development of the Rachel-Leah story suggests the action of a divine pendulum, now swinging toward
the one sister, now toward the other. At first the movement
is toward Rachel, the young, beautiful shepherdess whose
first appearance at the well sparks Jacob's love; then Leah,
who is substituted for Rachel on her wedding night; then
Rachel, whom Jacob insists also be given to him as a wife;
then Leah who, because *the Lord saw she was unloved,
opened her womb* (29:31) to an abundance of sons for
Jacob while Rachel remains barren; then Rachel, whose
chosen handmaid gives two sons to Jacob *that through her
[Rachel] too may have children* (30:3); and then Leah, whose
handmaid also bears sons, as does Leah herself once again.
Finally, the pendulum rests with Rachel, whom *God remembered . . . and opened her womb* (30:22) so that she con-
ceives and, at last, bears her first son, Joseph. In typical
biblical style, this fast-moving drama is tightly condensed
into the fewest verses possible—even more compressed in
Hebrew than in translation—half concealing worlds of hope
and despair that later writers' fantasies expanded in countless retellings of the tale.

THE RACHEL-LEAH CONFLICT CENTERS UPON THE
contest between *love* and *motherhood.* Is there some scale
of priority whereby one can choose between them? On the
one hand, continuation of the covenant between God and
the people requires children; on the other, true marriage
demands love. Is succession so important that it can be
satisfied with loveless children? It would seem so: despairing of bearing children themselves, Abraham's wife Sarah
and Jacob's wife Rachel present their husbands with handmaidens who will bear children in their stead. Conversely,

can a childless love-marriage succeed? Again, it would seem so, for we hear no complaint from Jacob in all the years of Rachel's barrenness (is it because he had children through Leah?). But neither Rachel nor Leah was satisfied with her lot. Each wanted both love *and* motherhood, affection *and* fertility. The struggle between them is nowhere given so clearly as in the names the sister-wives—never the father— give to their natural and surrogate children.

Names in the Bible often express the significance of the lives they denote. Leah, secure in motherhood, seeks Jacob's love; Rachel, beloved, aspires to motherhood. Consider how the names of Leah's sons express her yearning:

- Reuben (from the Hebrew: "see, a son")—*See, God has given me a son. . . . Surely now Jacob will love me.*
- Simeon (from the Hebrew: "to hear")—*The Lord heard that I was unloved and has given me this one also.*
- Levi (from the Hebrew: "to join")—*Now will my husband be joined to me, for I have borne him three sons* (29: 32-34).

Herein lies the tragedy of Leah's life. Could bearing children gain for her the love for which she yearned? Could love be produced by making public its lack in the names of her children? Must not love develop of itself if it is to develop at all? There was little possibility of that in the shadow of Rachel. The love of Rachel and Jacob was a mutual passion: immediate, persistent, "necessarily exclusive."[5] What room, then, could there be for Leah? Had she not been forced upon Jacob by her father's intrigue? And did she not coop- erate in the deception lest, as the sages have it, she be compelled to wed wicked Esau? She would not have Esau; Jacob would not have her. Whom she can have she does not want; whom she wants she cannot have.

What could Leah have reasonably expected from Laban's intrigue? One midrash turns the screw tighter by having her exacerbate Jacob's anger when he discovers the substitution. Leah was said to have rebutted his outrage by pointing out that when she impersonated her sister by deceptively responding to his call for Rachel in the darkness of the nuptial chamber to win him as her husband, she was doing no more than Jacob himself had done in the darkness of Isaac's blindness when Jacob impersonated his brother by deceptively responding to his father's call for Esau to gain the birthright! *He went to his father and said, "Father." And he said, "Yes, which of my sons are you?" Jacob said to his father, "I am Esau your firstborn"* (27:18).

Could Leah hope for love under those circumstances? It is true that heaven took pity and granted her children when Rachel had none and that this must have stirred Jacob. But love? Not according to the underlying meaning of the names she continues to give her children. Indeed, Jacob seems to have all but ignored Leah; not in a single instance does he speak directly to her alone. During the time when Leah is bearing children, when we might most expect Jacob to have been receptive, it was for Rachel that he was toiling a second seven-year stretch! On the occasions that he speaks of his "wife" in the years when Leah alone is still alive, it is always to Rachel that he refers. Under such circumstances, Leah's dogged resolution in naming her children is quite remarkable. With the birth of each child, she continues to express her unrequited affection. *Surely now Jacob will love me* (Reuben), *The Lord heard that I was unloved* (Simeon), *Now will my husband be joined to me* (Levi). Leah's protest points to the difference between maternity and the affection of the heart, the voluntary act of love.

Although the sages make much of Leah's "restraint," finding in it a piety of sorts, there is a protest implied in the naming of her children, a perseverance that is confirmed by Rachel's sharp and imperative reaction after the birth of the fourth son:

When Rachel saw that she had borne Jacob no children, she became envious of her sister; and Rachel said to Jacob,

Give me children or I shall die! Jacob was incensed at Rachel, and said, Can I take the place of God who has denied you fruit of the womb (30:1-2)?

Rachel's brusque demand seems out of character unless we see it as the outburst of a woman who could no longer restrain her pent-up frustration, heightened over years of watching one son after another born to Leah while she had none. How could she be a wife, even if beloved, without being a mother?

Jacob's sharp reply to Rachel's demand seems equally out of character. Why was he not more sympathetic, asks the midrash? Was she not his beloved wife, and was it not natural for her to want children after such a long and vexing wait? Quoting Isaiah—"I have given them, in my house and within my walls, a monument and a name better than sons and daughters" (Isa 56:5)—Isaac Arama (1420–94) defends Jacob, arguing that his annoyance was meant as an affectionate rebuke to Rachel, who appeared to see her relation to her husband solely as the bearer of his children.[6] What Jacob intended by his outburst was that, though he would have wished Rachel to be the mother of his sons, his love for her was unconditional. He would love her even without children: "Am I not more to you than ten sons?" (1 Sam 1:9). For Arama, then, Jacob is arguing a broader understanding of women than their fecundity. "For the two Hebrew nouns with which Scripture denotes the female— *Hava* and *Ishah*—reflect two aspects of her character. (1) *Eve/Hava—the "mother" of all the living* (3:20) [denoting motherhood, the unique quality of her sex]; and (2) *Woman/ Ishah—who was taken from man/Ish* (2:23) [denoting personhood, the universal quality of humanity]. This latter name means that women are equal to whatever moral or intellectual achievement men are capable of."[7]

In contrast to the names of Leah's children, which signal her desire to win Jacob's love, the names of Rachel's surrogate children, born to her handmaiden Bilhah, point to Rachel's unrelenting drive for motherhood. Thus:

- Dan (from the Hebrew: "he vindicated")—*God has vindicated me and given me a son.*
- Naphtali (from the Hebrew: "contester")—*I have waged a contest with my sister, and prevailed* (30:6-7).

In explaining the name she gives to Bilhah's son Naphtali, Rachel herself reveals the protracted conflict with Leah. The tension between the sisters is painfully obvious. For all Rachel's jubilation at the birth of her handmaiden's children, her celebration has as hollow a ring as did Sarah's on the birth of Ishmael to her handmaiden, Hagar. Although Rachel claims and names the boys as her own, quite as she told Jacob she would when she charged him, *Consort with [Bilhah], that she may bear on my knees and that through her I too may have children* (30:13), these children were, after all, born not to her but to a surrogate, leaving her as much an *akarah* (a barren woman) as before.

Rachel's joy in "prevailing" is, in any event, short lived, for Leah, not to be outdone by her sister, follows suit only too quickly by using her handmaid, Zilpah, as surrogate. So Gad and Asher are born. Then, unwilling to wait any longer, perhaps in remembrance of her grandmother, Sarah, who bore Isaac when *Abraham was one hundred years old* (21:5), Rachel begs Leah for the aphrodisiac mandrake that Reuben has brought her. The mysterious power of the plant has long caught the reader's fancy. "Go and catch a falling star," wrote John Donne, "Get with child a mandrake root." So eager was Rachel to possess the mandrake in the hope that it might work its wonders for her, that, in exchange for the magic potion, she allows her sister to return to Jacob's bed. Leah, however, without the mandrake, promptly bears Issachar and Zebulun, and with the naming of Zebulun she lays claim to Jacob's affection yet again. The name is explained: *This time my husband will exalt me for I have given him six sons* (v. 20). As an encore, she produces a daughter, Dinah.

Against Leah's own six sons and a daughter and her handmaid's two sons, Rachel can count only two sons, and those by virtue of Bilhah, her maidservant! The odds weigh more and more heavily on the side of Leah. At this point in the story, when defeat has followed defeat and all hope seems lost, Rachel's heartfelt desire is at long last fulfilled with the birth of a child. Her words upon naming him reflect her deepest feelings: *God has taken away my disgrace. So she named him Joseph, which is to say, May the Lord add another son for me* (vv. 22-24).

Motherhood is Rachel's consuming concern, and the felt disgrace of her barrenness has been removed with the birth of this child. But the name she gives him expresses neither thankfulness for the child nor a reference to her husband as the other names of Jacob's children seem to do. So set is her mind's eye to see beyond this son to the next, holding him who was born only as a forerunner of those who will follow, that she has the name of her son speak not of a past event but of the future alone—Joseph: *May the Lord "add another"* [Heb. *yosef*] *son for me*. The reproach of Rachel's barrenness is indeed gone, but the completion of her task as a mother is, in her eyes, only beginning.[8]

The divine pendulum swings between the sisters for the last time and comes to a rest—pointing toward Rachel.

THERE ARE THOSE, HOWEVER, WHO FIND LEAH THE more worthy of the sisters and support their claim with a variety of arguments. Leah, who was healthy in body and whole in spirit, needed neither the mandrake love potions, for which Rachel bargained, to bear children nor Laban's idols for religion. In addition, they argue, Leah's conversion to Jacob's religion was seen as evidence of a piety superior to Rachel's. Although both sisters took upon themselves the patriarch's faith in the one God, Rachel's act was thought to be tainted by her need to convert in order to marry the promised Jacob, whereas the conversion of Leah had no such flaw; it was truly "for the sake of heaven."[9] Furthermore, far from being a sign of disability, her "weak" eyes were evidence of moral strength. For just as Laban and Isaac's younger children (Rachel and Jacob) were destined to marry each other, so were the older children (Leah and Esau) meant for each other. It was that prescribed liaison with Esau, of whose wickedness she was well aware, that brought Leah to so uncontrollable a weeping that her eyes were affected. Though the marriage had been arranged by divine fiat, such were the passion and pity of Leah's tears that the heavenly decree was annulled. Nor was Leah passive in her substitution for Rachel on Jacob's wedding night. For reasons of piety and not romance—aversion to Esau's evil and attraction to Jacob's goodness—she permitted herself a role in the deception. It was only necessary for the lamp of the bridal chamber to be put out and for Jacob, whose wits had, in any case, been dulled through drinking long and late the night of the wedding feast, to have his every call for "Rachel" answered by Leah. Not until the next day did he awake to the deception: *When morning came, there was Leah* (30:25)![10]

Leah's worthiness is demonstrated even through a tale of the miraculous exchange of embryos! A rabbinic extrapolation of the text tells us that Rachel's first pregnancy was not with Joseph but with Dinah (who was eventually born to Leah); Leah, at the same time, was originally pregnant with Joseph, not Dinah. But Leah had divined that Jacob would ultimately be the father of twelve (male) heads of tribes. Were she to bear yet another son, there would be room for only one more (eleven having already been born, seven from her and two from each of the handmaidens). According to this retelling, Leah felt this would be unjust to Rachel, who, even if she were to be the mother of Jacob's twelfth and final son, would be inferior to the handmaidens, each of whom had two sons. Should this happen, Rachel would never achieve the status of a matriarch. How then could Leah help the sister who had remained silent for her sake on what was to have been Rachel's long-awaited wedding night? Leah prayed that the unborn children (Joseph and Dinah) be switched, seeking thereby to repay Rachel for allowing the switching of the sisters in the bridal chamber. And so it was. *Afterwards* [i.e., after Leah conceived a son and prayed that it be switched] *she gave birth to a daughter and called her name Dinah ["Justice"]. . . . And God remembered Rachel . . . and she gave birth to a son . . . and called his name Joseph* (30:21-24). Leah's entreaties were heard—Leah bore Dinah, and Rachel bore Joseph![11] Thus the substitution motif continues: Jacob for Esau, Leah for Rachel, and now the unborn Joseph for Dinah.

Some of the mystics further suggested the superiority of Leah by contending that whereas Rachel represented the visible stage of the people Israel's task, the worldly and tangible aspect, the *alma d'itgalya*, Leah represented the invisible stage, the spiritual, recondite world, the *alma d'itkasya*. Leah's eyes, though "weak" in natural vision, were thought to have penetrated the mysteries, for she possessed the Holy Spirit, and the Shechinah did not depart from her tent. Taking as our platforms these two stages, the visible and the invisible, it is possible to construct two periods in the patriarch Jacob's life. In the first period, he is devoted to earthly, tangible tasks—contending with Laban, gaining a livelihood, building a family, and facing Esau. During this time Rachel is his mate. The second period begins when his physical conquests are completed and his name has been changed to Israel. Now his labors turn more to the invisible world, and during this time Leah is his only wife, Rachel having died in childbirth.

These two matriarchal roles are further suggested in the burial of the sisters: Rachel, by an open road on the way to Ephrat (35:19), that she might rise up to comfort the exiles who would one day pass by on their trek to Babylon (Jer 31:15); Leah, whose death is shielded from the record, within the hidden recesses of the cave of Machpelah, along-side Jacob, the other patriarchs Abraham and Isaac, and the matriarchs Sarah and Rebecca. Rebecca came to welcome her into her eternal home, for she had earned her place next to Rebecca's son, Jacob. As recompense for the beauty that had been washed away with her tears her portion was with Jacob and not Esau.[12]

WHATEVER THE MERIT OF THE ARGUMENTS FAVORING Leah over Rachel, they cannot stand against contrary opinions in a wide range of Jewish and non-Jewish literature. One midrash observes that *Leah was hated* (29:31) by everyone. When she passed, people would stare and scoff at her mendacity. "What a hypocrite this Leah is. She pretends to a piety that is foreign to her. Otherwise how could she have deceived her sister?" Indeed, after the deception, they say, Jacob wanted to divorce her and was dissuaded only because of her early pregnancy and the children who followed.[13]

Many commentators take issue with the above-mentioned arguments in Leah's favor. The suspicion cast on Rachel for carrying away Laban's idols is dissolved in the interpretation that she was trying to wean her father from idolatry even at the last moment of departure. In the case of the sisters' "conversions," some reason that the same grounds used to favor Leah over her sister—that Leah's conversion could not have been motivated by marriage—can be argued on Rachel's behalf. Once Leah had been substituted for her, Rachel had no knowledge that she would ever become Jacob's wife, and the fact that she did not revert to her unconverted state proves that her conversion was not influenced by the prospect of marriage but was pure in intent. Further, when Scripture says that Rachel was jealous of Leah, it was Leah's piety and not her fertility that she envied.[14]

But the central event in the life of Rachel, on which later writers focus to laud her character in a hundred different ways, is her quite remarkable silence at the time of Leah's substitution for herself in the bridal chamber just when Rachel's dreams of marriage were to be consummated after seven long years of waiting. This restraint is regarded as one of Rachel's noblest features. When "Esther did not reveal her people or her kindred" (Esth 2:10) upon being called into the chamber of King Ahasuerus, "This teaches," observes the midrash, "that she put a ban upon herself like her ancestress Rachel who also put a ban of silence on herself."[15] As the Hasidic master Rabbi Levi Yitzhak of Berditchev writes, "The merit of [Rachel's] selflessness during the substitution of Leah for herself, lest her sister be put to shame, still succors us."[16]

Surely Rachel's decision to remain silent could not have been without anguish then or torment later. But in the brief space within which the tale is told—the more momentous the event the terser the biblical description—we are given no hint as to Rachel's inner feelings. All the more reason for the masters of the midrash to seek them out. Thus the name Rachel gives to one of her handmaid's children, Naphtali ("Wrestling") and the implication recorded in the name—*I struggled [niftalti] with my sister* (30:8)—is turned by the midrash into an *inner* grappling:

> I wrestled mightily with myself over my sister's plight. I had already perfumed the marital bed. Rightfully, I should have been the bride, and could have been, for had I sent a message to Jacob that he was being deceived, would he not have abandoned her on the spot? But I thought to myself: if I am not worthy to build the world, let it be built by my sister.[17]

When Scripture says that *God remembered Rachel . . . and opened her womb* (30:22), the midrash takes it to mean that God remembered "that she was silent when Leah was placed in her stead." But was there not more to be remembered than her silence at the *time* of the marriage? What of all the years *after* the wedding when she did not protest? For she did not. And when Scripture states an apparently contrary idea—*Rachel envied her sister* (30:1)—it is to be understood, according to the midrash, that it intends but to tell us that she envied the piety and the good deeds of her sister, as noted earlier. Thus there is no substance to the claim that Rachel did not deserve to have been rewarded with a child because she was a sinner who violated the prohibition against a second sister's marrying the same husband during her lifetime. For Scripture's justification in forbidding such a marriage—namely, to prevent sisters from becoming *tzarot*, rivals (Lev 18:18)—was not applicable to Rachel because she was never jealous of her sister (except for her piety), either at the time of the marriage or later.[18]

For the mystics too, despite their esteem for Leah, it is Rachel who is victorious. In good measure because of their veneration for the place, Rachel's grave site along the road to Bethlehem became, together with the Western Wall of the temple and the cave of Machpelah, one of the three holiest points of pilgrimage in the Holy Land. Rachel's compassion, explains the Zohar, was such that she "achieved more than any of the patriarchs, for she stationed herself at the crossroads whensoever the world was in need." If Jeremiah turned the grave of Rachel into a sepulcher from which she would arise to comfort the exiles on their way to Babylon a thousand years after her death, the mystics transformed it into a station from which a merciful messenger would emerge from time to time through the centuries to bring solace and hope to the bereft. Indeed, they went so far as to give her name to the Shechinah, the indwelling Presence of God, who accompanies the people Israel in their exiled wandering and shares in their suffering.[19]

The virtue the mystics make of Leah's "invisibility" in the later story of Jacob is intriguing, helping as it does to even the balance between the two sisters. But this disappearance from the narrative is surely one more argument for the primacy of Rachel. After Rachel's death, Leah bears no more children. She is neither recorded among the consolers of Jacob after Joseph's disappearance nor mentioned during Jacob's long residence in Egypt. We do not even read of her death. Indeed, nothing more is said of her apart from two references in chronologies and a brief notice that she had been buried in the cave of Machpelah. The reason for her obscurity has more to do with human feeling than with inscrutable mysteries. For just as the exclusivity of Jacob's love for Rachel left no room for Leah during her sister's lifetime, so after her death did Jacob's inconsolable mourning eclipse Leah and banish her from the scene.[20]

Some sages even found in the fate of Dinah reason to cast aspersion on Leah's character, although other sages refute the charge. The story, another example of the sexual depravity of the land, interrupts Jacob's journey home with his family and possessions. Leah's youngest child, Dinah, is raped by Shechem, the Hivite, upon whose clan her older brothers take bloody vengeance. In this tale of dishonor and wild revenge, Dinah is held partly to blame by the rabbis and Leah partly to blame for Dinah. How so? From the opening words of the story: *And Dinah, the daughter of Leah . . . went out [vateytzey] to visit with the daughters of the land* (34:1). First, the use of *went out* instead of the more common "went" (*vateyleykh*) suggests that she was gadding about, looking for trouble. Second, the phrase *the daughter of Leah*, instead of "daughter of Jacob," suggests that in this respect she acted like her mother. For it is written, *When Jacob came home from the field in the evening, Leah went out [vateytzey] to meet him and said, "You must sleep with me"* (30:16). As the one *went out* immodestly, so did the other. Dinah was a *yatzanit* just like Leah. So the prophet put it: "As the mother so her daughter" (Ezek 16:1). Contrariwise, said a sage:

"One can tell the immorality of the mother from the daughter." "Would you then call mother Leah a harlot?"

64

responded another. "Indeed," countered the first, "for when it says, *She went out to meet him,* it means she went decked out as a harlot." "But if Leah prettied herself, she did it only to fulfill the commandment to have a child with her husband." "Even so, the result was that Dinah was inclined toward immodesty. What Leah did for a worthy purpose, Dinah did for an unworthy one."[21]

A further comparison of the two sisters to Rachel's advantage is found in a tale that seems to reflect Hasidism's uneasiness with the doleful atmosphere surrounding Rachel—her deception, her barrenness, her early death, her weeping for the exiles. Sadness was too close to despair, and despair was a denial of the goodness of creation. The Baal Shem Tov, asked by a young disciple to be taken along on a journey, said to him: "You may join me if you can answer this question: Of the Midnight Lamentations, one is called after Leah and one after Rachel. What is the difference between them?" To which the young man, later to become the famed Nahum of Tchernobyl, responded: "What Leah effects with her tears, Rachel effects with her joy." And the Baal Shem invited him into his carriage.[22] "When Israel returns from the exile," adds the Zohar, commenting on this aspect of Rachel, "they will visit *Kever* Rachel to weep there. Rachel will rise up and turn them to joy and will cause the Shechinah who returns with them to rejoice."[23]

IN CHRISTIAN TRADITION THE FAVORING OF RACHEL over Leah plays a significant symbolic role. Leah and Rachel are seen in light of the story of the sisters Martha and Mary in Luke 10:38-42, where Martha comes to symbolize the active life and Mary the contemplative life. Leah is identified with Martha and Rachel with Mary. As Mary is favored by Jesus, so Rachel is beloved of Jacob. Thus Martha and

Leah stand for the active life and Mary and Rachel, favored by Jesus and Jacob, the contemplative life. Further in this tradition, Leah's dullness of eye comes to represent the synagogue's blindness to the true redeemer, while beloved Rachel points to the victorious church. Leah's early fecundity is overcome by the at first barren Rachel, who becomes the mother of all Israel, as the early synagogue is outdistanced by the later church. The church father Cyril of Alexandria writes:

> Leah, the eldest, surely stands for the Synagogue of the Jews. . . . For the Synagogue came first and begot for God the multitudes of the Jews . . . as it is written, "Israel is my first-born" (Exod 4:22). The barrenness of Rachel, who stands for the Church of the nations, refers to the period preceding the coming of our Saviour. But Isaiah told of the time to come when she would bear and nurture many children: "Sing, O barren. Thou that didst not bear, break forth into song. . . . For more are the children of the desolate than the children of the married wife" (54:1; Gal 4:27). So David when he speaks of God: "Who maketh the barren woman to dwell in her house as a joyful mother of children" (Ps 112:9), and the Lord himself testifies . . . "See they come; some from far away, these from the north and these from the west and those from the land of Syene" (Is 49:12). . . . The Church, having accepted the mystery of Christ . . . became mother to the peoples which so increases that it cannot be counted. . . . So the Church of the nations joins the flocks from Israel.[24]

The images projected by Rachel and Leah find expression in medieval and renaissance art. Thus when the synagogue is depicted in church decoration as a woman bereft of sight, it is, as already mentioned, the image of dull-eyed Leah that stands behind her. And when the contrast of synagogue and church is made in terms of active and contemplative life, it is through Leah and Rachel, as well as Martha and Mary, that the comparison is at times envisioned.

Michelangelo's tomb of Pope Julius II, completed in 1545 after forty-two years of designing and redesigning, included a central statue of Moses and two figures portraying the "active and the contemplative life." In Dante, no doubt, Michelangelo found one of his sources:

> Whoso would ask my name, I'd have him know
> That I am Leah, who for my array
> Twine garlands, weaving white hands to and fro.
>
> To please me at the glass I deck me gay;
> The while my sister Rachel never stirs
> But sits before her mirror all the day,
>
> For on her own bright eyes she still prefers
> To gaze, as I to deck me with my hands;
> Action is my delight, reflection hers.[25]

Michelangelo placed his statues of the sisters on either side of Moses. To his right, dressed as a nun, is Rachel in prayer, symbolizing the contemplative life, and to his left is Leah, symbolizing the active life of good works. Although according to the church both ways are principal avenues in the service of God, it is clear which sister is being favored. "The Rachel [statue] is the more expressive, elongated in prayer and 'with her face and both her hands raised to heaven so that she seems to breathe love in every part,' as Condivi wrote. Michelangelo clearly thought of her as a representation of faith. He spiritualized her in convent garb to the detriment of the stolid, earthy Leah."[26]

The physical contrast drawn in Genesis between the sisters has always been a favorite subject of writers. To quote Chauncey Depew again, "I have often wondered what must have been his emotions when on the morning of the eighth year [Jacob] awoke and found the homely, scrawny, bony Leah instead of the lovely and beautiful presence of his beloved Rachel."[27] Nor should we be surprised that even Robert Browning, who knew the Bible in Hebrew, follows the pattern, most obvious in depictions of Jesus until Rembrandt, of favoring the "Nordic" "Rachel of the blue-eye and golden hair" over the "semitic" visage of "swarthy skinned" Leah in his *The Ring and the Book*.[28] The Jewish sages observed that each sister knew of the one for whom she was destined, and, as the time of their betrothals drew near, the more Leah heard about the wickedness of Esau, the more her tears detracted from her appearance, while the more Rachel heard about the virtues of Jacob, the more beautiful she became.[29]

There is a final argument for the rabbis' favoring Rachel over her sister, not made explicitly but delicately woven into the intrigues of the tale: an argument for monogamy. The struggle for a worthy family is central to the handing down of the covenant, the primary function of the role of the patriarchs and matriarchs. This struggle was the principal reason for avoiding the Canaanites as marital partners; their unacceptable sexual practices are graphically spelled out in Leviticus 18 and treated in the Genesis stories.[30] Monogamy was the marital ideal not only with Adam and Eve in the utopian society of the Garden of Eden but also with the end of paradise and the beginning of "history": Abraham and Sarah, Isaac and Rebecca, Jacob and Rachel. The patriarchs were teamed with single wives and together created the "couple" and the family pattern that was to become the paradigm for humankind.[31] The concubine-handmaidens, suggested and provided to their husbands by Sarah and Rachel when they were confirmed in their barrenness, prove a subtle wrong. This conclusion is borne out not only by the liaison of Rachel's handmaid, Bilhah, with Reuben, the eldest son of Leah, but also by the troubles with Sarah's handmaid, Hagar, *who when she knew she was with child, despised her mistress,* and with her son, Ishmael, *who was like a wild ass whose hand was against every man* (16:4, 11)—all stumbling blocks to monogamy as is Leah herself.[32]

Leah is the single exception to the monogamous pattern among the patriarchs and, at the same time, the strongest argument for it. Her role is anomalous. She is a bearer of children as the handmaidens were, but she is also Jacob's legal wife as was Rachel. It might be argued that in her the Bible makes a case for polygamy among the patriarchs; but the burden of the biblical story is precisely the reverse, for it clearly tells us that this arrangement simply did not work. Despite her legal standing, Leah knows that she is not recognized as an equal to Rachel in Jacob's eyes. Despite Laban's scheme, Rachel's kindness, and Leah's compliance, Jacob would not love Leah. He did not love Leah before the ruse and certainly not afterwards, not after their children were born, not, indeed, to the end of his days. But his love for Rachel was from first to last.

Leah appears an outsider. She is thrust upon Jacob by deceit whereas Rachel is loved and chosen. She is fertile, conceiving often and easily (according to one sage, at the very first encounter), whereas the other matriarchs, Rebecca, Sarah, and Rachel, to each of whom Leah is related by blood (the niece of one, the grandniece of the other, and the sister of the third) were all initially barren. She is the mother of children, but these children, described so unflatteringly by Jacob on his deathbed, are the source of much misery: the brothers' kidnapping of Joseph; the firstborn Reuben's affair with Bilhah (the mother of two of his stepbrothers), for which crime the birthright was given to Joseph; Simeon and Levi's cruel slaughter of the Shechem clan; the defilement of Dinah. In later generations the descendants of the Leah tribes were the central figures in the revolt of Korah, the seduction of Baal Peor, and the blasphemy of the "strange fire."[33]

The separation between love and childbearing was common in antiquity. Polygamous societies accept a multiplicity of mates, but monogamous societies, it is suggested, must contend more with adultery, prostitution, and divorce. Leah and Rachel seem at first to serve the separate polygamous roles of maternity and affection. But neither is willing to settle for that; each demands both. Only Rachel, however, achieves it. The story reflects a kind of monogamy of childbearing, as if it were unseemly for the sisters to give birth at the same time. For they do not: when Leah bears, Rachel is barren; when Rachel's handmaid Bilhah bears, Leah is barren, and so on.[34] When the relationship between God and Israel is compared to a married couple, the model is not the fertile Leah and Jacob (as would have been the case had the religion of Israel been a fertility cult) but the passionate and faithful Rachel and Jacob, whose love is mutual and exclusive but not especially fruitful.

For the reasons set out above, it can be argued that Leah does not fit the mold of the matriarchs. Indeed, Jewish women themselves seem to confirm this view. For when, in the folk prayers they composed over the past four centuries or so, the matriarchs are referred to, it is Sarah, Rebecca, and Rachel who are regularly mentioned, whereas "Leah often received short shrift."[35] Leah's official position as spouse highlights the issue of monogamy, and her lovelessness is its justification. Thus we may understand the tragedy of Leah, not simply as unrequited love or as downright deception, but as an illicit attempt to break the patriarchal pattern, a testing, so to speak, confirming by its failure the monogamous standard—in short, a foil for monogamy. Only by subterfuge is an unwanted wife thrust upon Jacob; who can doubt but that, left to his own devices, he, like his father and grandfather before him, would have chosen a single companion? Through Leah's suffering, we are told that the single-wife–single-husband combination is desirable. Rachel, by this standard too, must be the victor.

THE TENSION BETWEEN THE SISTERS, DESCRIPTION and analysis of which has led us to the opinions of many writers in many ages, fades as tradition decrees that both Rachel and Leah rise to take their places alongside Sarah and Rebecca, as august matriarchs of the Jewish people. From Leah were descended the kings and priests through Judah and Levi. From Rachel came he who won the birthright, Joseph; Ephraim, his son, who became the leader of the ten tribes of the Northern Kingdom; Benjamin, whose tribal borders embraced Jerusalem and the temple; and, later, Joshua, Saul, and Esther. From Joseph's line too will come the "Messiah son of Joseph," whose arrival will herald the end of days and the coming of the "Messiah son of David." Thus the adage: "Only the sons of Rachel can defeat Esau," the archenemy of the people Israel.[36] After the exile of the ten tribes of the Northern Kingdom, only two tribes were left, Benjamin, the child of Rachel, and Judah, the son of Leah.[37]

The mystics too established equal roles for Rachel and Leah in their custom of rising at midnight to lament the destruction of the temple, the exile of the people, and the suffering of the Shechinah. This widely observed practice was formally fixed as a rite by the celebrated sixteenth-century Safed kabbalist Isaac Luria and his followers and was divided into two parts. The first part, the "Rite of Rachel" (*Tikkun Rachel*), contained Psalm 137 ("By the waters of Babylon there we sat down and wept"), the last chapter of Lamentations, and other prayers dealing with the exile and suffering of the Shechinah. The second, the "Rite of Leah" (*Tikkun Leah*), turned from the theme of exile to that of redemption and featured messianic psalms and other hymns. Even the unlearned were urged by the kabbalists to perform this rite featuring both Rachel and Leah.[38]

It is, however, in Hasidic literature, the truest successor of the midrash, that the most startling resolution of the rivalry between Rachel and Leah is proposed. The Hasidic rabbi Levi Yitzhak reflects on Gen 29:30:

Va-ye-ehav gam et Rahel mi-Leah.
He [Jacob] loved Rachel more than Leah.

Interpretations of this passage differ somewhat but agree that Jacob favored Rachel over Leah. Translators, however, are troubled by the Hebrew *gam* or "also." Levi Yitzhak gives us quite an unusual reading, building on the midrash but transcending it in a style typical of Hasidic literature:

He loved Rachel also [i.e., even more] because of Leah.
How does he support this rendition, technically possible but far from obvious?

It is clear that while Jacob's purpose in working for Laban was to marry Rachel, Jacob, in fact, wed Leah. And it was Rachel [by her silence] who was responsible for this. Now Jacob's love for Rachel was twofold: he loved her for herself, but he loved her *also*, i.e., even more (*ahavah yeterah*), because she brought him so pious a wife (*tzadeket*) as Leah. This then is what the verse is telling us: *Jacob loved Rachel "also" (gam et Rachel) "because of" Leah (mi-Leah).* Which is to say, it was because Leah became his wife through the efforts of Rachel that Jacob felt an additional measure of love for [Rachel] over what he felt before.[39]

So the story is turned on its head. No tension between sisters, no clash between motherhood and love, no duped husband's anguish. All family conflict vanishes in the new vision of Levi Yitzhak. To him the matriarchs are models demonstrating how to overcome family unhappiness through the power of love and the example of piety. Far from Rachel's envying Leah, she was responsible for her marriage; far from Jacob's resenting the deception, he only loved Rachel more. Human kindness and nobility of character conquer society's flaws. The tale is no longer one of sibling tragedy but a record of the trial and victory of Leah's piety, Rachel's compassion, and Jacob's respect for the one and love for the other. Here the story resolves itself in an unexpected but, in its way, authentically Jewish conclusion.

Rachel
"God remembered Rachel.
He opened up her womb and gave her a son."
Beatrice Wool

*Chapter 6*_____

Barren

I sit in the synagogue. The time that I have dreaded is
about to arrive. I am prepared, I have done all the crying
beforehand. There can be few tears left. . . . I am an
akarah—a barren woman. After three years of the latest
modern tests and drugs, of artificial inseminations (using
my husband's sperm), of long hours in doctors' offices,
of humiliating tests and frustrated hopes, and of moments
of despair, I am still a barren woman. My husband is
healthy; the problem is mine. We have used much of our
savings, all of our patience. We have a serious operation
to go that gives us a slight chance but may cause a
serious risk to my health. . . . So I sit in the sanctuary as
I hear the words . . . *P'ru ur'vu* [1.22]. God's command to
be fruitful and multiply has been given again to our
people. . . . [And] I feel my emptiness. As my menstrual
period comes each month I mourn what could have
been. . . . I feel the pain of emptiness, the despair of
wanting to carry out the mitzvah [commandment] and not
being able.[1]

So one modern Jewish woman poured out her heart, not
unlike the cry of her ancestor Rachel.

The Lord saw that Leah was unloved and he opened her womb; but Rachel was barren. . . . When Rachel saw that she had borne Jacob no children, she became envious of her sister.

And Rachel said to Jacob, "Give me children or I shall die" (29:30; 30:1).

Why the consuming demand for children when Jacob's love would be there in any case? Was it the maternal instinct—or something more? How ironic that the same Hebrew root, *RHM*, is used for "compassion" (*rahmanut*) and for "womb" (*rehem*), when she who was most compassionate was most barren!

Rachel's barrenness can be understood only in contrast to Leah's fecundity. The trial of barrenness is part of the trial of Leah, but the ordeal of childlessness is so central to an understanding of Rachel that it deserves separate treatment. Some of the material in this chapter will be familiar from the preceding one, but our attention will focus on the single perspective of sterility. Before the question of Rachel's plight can be taken up, however, several larger issues must be addressed.

IN THE WEST BARRENNESS AS A RELIGIOUS IDEAL FINDS its root in the early church. Writing on the notion of virginity in the church, Peter Brown points out that the ideal of celibacy—lifelong abstinence from sexual intercourse—was celebrated by early Christianity as an imitation on earth of the "life of the angels," the vision of an altogether harmonious society "like angels in heaven" (Mark 12:25) not joined by family or marriage. This ideal is the source of the great alternative society of the later monasteries and convents and the monastic orders. The Christian view has its origins in a reading of the biblical account of Adam and Eve that understands them as destined to live a virginal, angelic, harmonious life as seraphim around the heavenly throne.

They were seen as presocial creatures not meant to engage in sexual congress. Only because of the fall did they abandon their angelic status and copulate in the manner of lower creatures. Thus some Christians came to view family life as a falling away from the angelic to the beastly, and, continuing thereafter to judge the institutions of marriage and family from the vantage point of humanly angelic society, they found these institutions sadly wanting.[2]

What was first celebrated as a recalling of the Garden of Eden, and what in later generations became for Christianity an alternative society, was anathema to the Jews (and to many Christians), who believed that Adam and Eve were created not for an angelic society but for marriage and children. Thus they reproached the fourth-century Bishop Aphraat, "For you have received a curse and have multiplied barrenness."[3]

Outside the alternative society fostered by the church, however, barrenness was generally seen as a violation of the law of life, a denial of the divine creative element with which women were blessed. It is only in recent times that barrenness by choice has become an accepted secular option for women. Today birth control, overpopulation, the promise of a career, and feminist aspirations for independence have joined forces to lower the birthrate. Reacting to what they view as restrictive and oppressive aspects of women's traditional role, some feminists have called for a flight from the family and the (in their view) degrading tasks of home.

Betty Friedan argued for a professional career over the "feminine mystique" of wife and mother, portraying the family as incidental to a woman's life and as reflecting her "mere biological" side. Only by escaping the "comfortable concentration camp" atmosphere of home, family, and children, she argued, can women become "strong." Kate Millet, a self-described radical lesbian feminist, attacked masculinity as Friedan did femininity. Men hate women as women hate men. Millet sees the family, where "wives are slaves," as an unredeemable, oppressive patriarchy that "must go." In her thinking, procreation need not be associated with marriage, nor the raising of children with parents. In the Marxist nirvana, children will be raised by the state, the family abolished, and "marriage . . . replaced by voluntary associations." Germaine Greer considers "the plight of mothers as more desperate than that of other women. . . . Most women, because of the assumptions that they have formed about the importance of their role as bearers and socializers of children, would shrink at the notion of leaving husband and children, but this is precisely the case in which brutally clear thinking must be undertaken." The "unfortunate mother-wife," she adds, is a failure: to her husband, a shrew and a sexual bore, and to her children, far inferior to the commune as parent. Happily, however, she records, the dilemma is being resolved in the present dissolution of the family. Nancy Chodorow asserts that "Non-biological mothers, children, and men can parent just as adequately as biological mothers," and cites the glowing examples of Communist Russia, Maoist China, and Castro's Cuba. From "the fact that women mother," she argues, derive the neuroses of masculinity and femininity, which equally shared parenting can heal.[4]

Maggie Gallagher, a young Yale graduate and single, working mother, tells a different story. In her recent *Enemies of Eros,* based upon her own misfortunes, she agrees that modern women are exploited; that they are more likely to have been raped by a date, more likely to be discarded by their husbands, more likely to have to earn a second income to make ends meet (in addition to family responsibilities), more likely not to have been married at all; that boyfriends take up the early years, refuse to commit themselves, and then move on to more youthful partners. Having been told that women should be emotionally and economically independent and that personal growth must be pursued at any cost, "till death do us part" has become till you bore me, till the burdens of parenting and monogamy become unbearable, till I need more space, till my secretary gives me a tumble.

In looking for the causes of the exploitation of women, Gallagher points the finger at a notion of sexual liberation that has "sanctioned selfishness in the name of freedom," and at no-fault divorce that has contributed to the number of children raised in semipoverty. Principally, however, she faults the feminist myth that men and women are psychically the same. She suggests that feminism, without intending to, has contributed to the development of a society that is open season on women, for in an atmosphere as permissive as ours it is women who suffer most.

Against those who argue that "female" characteristics are merely the result of "cultural determinism" and that "the sexes are inherently the same in everything save for the reproductive systems," all available data continue to suggest that mothers' relationships with their children are utterly different from, and incredibly more involved than, those of fathers. The best proof, says Gallagher, is the fact that, despite all the efforts made in recent years to demean and discourage it, their mothering instinct is as strong as ever. Otherwise why should they continue to bear children despite the very real possibility of having to raise them alone under severe hardship?[5]

Of late a decided change in feminist attitudes has been noticeable. The kibbutzim of Israel, for example, long held up as models of egalitarianism, have seen a return to traditional families, with enlarged single-family dwellings rather than "children's houses" and division of labor along more traditionally female-male lines. American women have been choosing to limit careers in favor of marriage and motherhood and are less willing to hand their offspring over to surrogates. As vocational goals are achieved, or not achieved, as the attractions of short-term relationships dim and liaisons become less frequent, less fulfilling, or both, the desire for a child grows. Even among those who reject intimacy with men, some are not averse to impregnation in order to mother children without a "father."

It seems reasonable to conclude, then, that despite the upheavals in women's roles that the twentieth century has witnessed, it is in the order of their nature not only for women to give birth but to want to give birth, certainly as natural as it is for men to want to have children. It may be true that for a considerable portion of human history it seemed to be the *only* order of their nature. Nevertheless, it is around the biological fact of motherhood—the wonder of motherhood—that one crucial meaning of "woman" is to be located: to conceive, to bear, to nurture, to offer a love that is richly returned, and one day, after children have matured and had offspring themselves, to claim those children as well, as grandchildren.

BIBLICAL WOMEN EXPERIENCED THIS "NATURAL" phenomenon in sacred and profound terms. They lived in a world whose holy book gave as its first command to humankind, *Be fruitful and multiply* (1:28), where, as in a Käthe Kollwitz drawing, the sublime image of "a weaned child upon its mother" (Psalm 131) evoked utter faith and utter solace: "As a mother comforts her child, so I will comfort you . . . that you may suck from her breast and draw from her bosom consolation to the full. . . . You shall be carried on shoulders and dandled upon knees" (Isa 66:11-13); where the idyllic scene of the venerated man is one whose "wife shall be like a fruitful vine in the heart of your house; your sons like olive saplings around your table. This is the blessing in store for the man who fears the Lord. May [you] . . . live to see your children's children! Peace be upon Israel!" (Psalm 128).

The failure of the Bible to extend its prohibition against homosexuality to include woman explicitly is not to be equated—as some contemporary writers fantasize—with tacit permission. Quite the contrary. The ban was omitted because it was unthinkable, the "order of creation's" image of woman as wife and mother having become so internalized in Israelite society that such an aberration remained outside the limits of conceivable behavor. Hardly a case is recorded in the entire span of biblical and rabbinic literature. Indeed, to be able to have a child but to decide against doing so was considered by the later sages to be akin to shedding the blood of the unborn. Childless love was thought to be incomplete, and giving birth, "the ability to transcend the self into another."[6]

Tradition expressed a certain heartlessness toward the childless; as the poor, the leper, and the blind are condemned to a living death, so are the barren. And this is derived from Rachel, who pleaded, *Give me children or else I am dead* (30:1).[7] As they are denied earthly pleasures, so too are the childless forbidden the pleasures of heaven— this is the verdict of the Zohar. "The Holy Name does not dwell upon the one . . . who leaves no children. Upon departing this world in a state of incompleteness, they cannot reach the holy name. . . . They are not privileged the vision of the glorious effulgence . . . which radiates from the most sublime region."[8]

Still, the matriarchs, when barren, are not rejected by their husbands. Sarah's role did not diminish after Hagar had given Abraham a child, nor was Rachel disparaged by Jacob. The midrash stresses that, though *akarah* ("barren"), she was nevertheless *ikarah*, the "principal one," the mistress of the house.[9] It is true that the matriarchs lived much before the prophets, psalmists, rabbis, and mystics here cited, but these later traditions represent, in part, the expression and institutionalization of previous patterns of behavior to which the lives of the matriarchs were central and by which they were to some extent confirmed.

To be barren as a woman is one thing, as a Hebrew another, but to be barren as a matriarch adds a further, and special, dimension. The first signifies natural order, the second divine purpose; the third suggests the assurance of the covenant. How so? The covenant God made with Abraham promised blessing to all humanity through the people that would come from Abraham and Sarah. But without a child to continue what Abraham and Sarah began there could be no people, and without the people no blessing for humankind. It was the bearing of a successor-child that represented fulfillment of the matriarchal role.

Barrenness, however, is a characteristic of the matriarchs. Of Sarah it is written, *Shall I in truth bear a child, old as I am* (18:13)? Of Rebecca, *Isaac pleaded with the Lord on behalf of his wife, because she was barren* (25:21). And of Rachel, *The Lord opened Leah's womb . . . but Rachel was barren* (29:31). Why this paradoxical infertility? Could it be to alert us to the precariousness of human birth and the preciousness of the child once born? So fragile was the chain of the covenant in those early years that it might have broken had even one of the matriarchs remained childless. Barrenness, then, drove home the inestimable value of these children, with what care they must be raised, how vital that the right son inherit the birthright, and how indispensable his marriage to a woman who will honor the covenant and wish to continue it—over all of which the matriarchs took great pains. Sometimes they acted with more wisdom than the patriarchs, as with Rebecca's choice of Jacob over Esau for the birthright-blessing against Isaac's intention. Both the forces beyond and within their control—the reality of infertility and the nurturing of the child—are elements in the struggle for succession. Two of the matriarchs, Sarah and Rachel, are so obsessed with the need for a child that they offer their handmaids to their husbands as surrogates to bear an infant in their stead despite the hazard of such an arrangement. When the children are born to the handmaids, Rachel and Leah name and assume responsibility for them. And though the barren matriarchs were the favorites of husbands who never berated them for their state, they continue to berate themselves as incomplete, as fostering a kind of death within life.

Consequently, in the matriarchal families, where concern for succession is paramount, each child is cherished, for only through that child can the blessing of the one become the blessing for all. Something more than womanly instinct is involved in these cases. What other cultures may have expressed philosophically or legally, Scripture teaches by way of narrative. The generous amount of space devoted to the difficulties both in bearing children and in finding proper mates—the search for partners being fraught with as much danger as was their birth—points to the same issue: handing down (*mesorah*) and accepting (*kabbalah*) the covenant. As if to say: "How precious the offspring that issue forth from these! Take them not for granted! Raise them with the utmost care!" One might have expected that these first children of the covenant upon whom so much depended would be born miraculously through a heavenly kiss. Though the divine will is implied in each birth, they are manifestly conceived within the bounds of mortal marital life. Nevertheless, these children will not be like other children. The frank details of their lives will be recorded for all to read and ponder in the most widely and constantly used book of all human history. They will play a role that can be played by no others, and upon the quality of their lives will depend not only the future of this marriage or that family or even the entire people, but of all humankind.[10]

It is against this background of motherhood and matriarchy that Rachel's barrenness must be considered. Hers, however, is a special case. There is no other love story among the matriarchs, or in the entire Bible for that matter, like Rachel's. No other matriarch must contend with the pervading presence of a Leah, who is neither handmaiden nor, worse, second wife, but a first wife, sister, and, exceptional among the matriarchs, bountiful mother of sons. (As mentioned in the last chapter, Leah's fertility is one of the characteristics that set her apart from the matriarchs.) Neither beauty nor love seems to suffice. Rachel was no more comforted for her barrenness by the love of Jacob than her later counterpart, Hannah (the mother of the prophet Samuel), was by her husband's assurance—"Why are you crying and why do you eat nothing? Am I not more devoted to you than ten sons?" (1 Sam 1:8). Rachel wants to be not only a wife but a mother. Driven to jealousy, accusing her husband, and turning to love potions, Rachel felt unfulfilled on all three levels—as a woman, a Hebrew, and a matriarch:

> The Bible [writes Catherine Chalier] cannot conceive of the fullness of love without lineage. The severity of the rabbis on this point, in which they identify sterility with death, finds its roots in the history of the matriarchs, and in their struggle, often dogged and anguished, against such a fate, against the ravages of a temporality of decline, without the possibility of self-transcendence through posterity.
>
> Thus for Rachel, the unbearable proximity of death and barrenness, indeed, of their inseparability, renders null and void love's fullness all the while that fecundity— that by which transcendence of self takes place—is denied. It is as if by lacking this passage to the other-than-oneself, which is childbirth, love could only have eyes for the terrible menace of death, could only perceive the truth of its inevitable mortality, of its incapacity to struggle with the force of this finite destiny. Indeed, Rachel, the beloved, braves the derision of those who, on the frontiers of indecency, wait for manifest proof of justice—for does not the evil of sterility reveal some secret iniquity? A further burden to Rachel's suffering is her confrontation with the envy she feels. Her generosity in giving up her place to Leah is hardly repaid. Rivalry,

wrong when it was a question of marriage, with its hope for happiness, now confounds her magnanimity, and, faced with her sister's pregnancies, mortifies her.[11]

Rachel seeks a child not only to transcend the self, the yearning of every woman (indeed, every person!), but also to secure the covenant, the unique role of the matriarch. Despairing, she complains of Jacob, *Give me children, else I die*. Jacob, who has fathered children with Leah, denies responsibility and responds harshly, *Can I take the place of God who has denied you fruit of the womb?* (30:1-2). Demeaned, Rachel sacrifices her pride and brings him her maidservant *that she bear upon my knees and I also may be builded up through her* (30:3). As with Sarah and her hand-maiden, Hagar, before her, Bilhah will bear children on Rachel's behalf. She names and adopts the two boys; they will be hers although borne by another—Scripture's surrogate mother. Not to be outdone, Leah, who had stopped bearing, brings Jacob her handmaid, who bears two children to counter Bilhah's two sons. Determined to pursue the avenue of fecundity to the end, Leah gives birth to yet another two sons after the discovery of the mandrake elixir, and finally a daughter, Dinah. Rachel still hopes for a child of her own, without which she would have fulfilled her role neither as a wife nor as a matriarch.

At last, *God remembered Rachel and opened her womb, and she conceived and bore a son . . . and called his name Joseph, which is to say, "May the Lord add (Heb. YSF) another son for me"* (30:22-24).

THE CLIMAX TO THE TENSION OF THE TALE IS OVER too quickly for the sages, who, not satisfied with Scripture's brief account of this momentous birth, add tales of their own as to how it came about. Rachel, they say, was granted a child by virtue of her compassion for her sister whom she herself helped disguise in order that Leah not be discovered by Jacob on their wedding night. Leah, they add, joined by Bilhah and Zilpah, assisted Rachel in her supplications for a child.

Petitions for the childless are commonplace in the Bible. Scripture says that *Isaac pleaded with the Lord on behalf of his wife, because she was barren* (25:21), but the sages insist that Rebecca prayed as well.[12] Best known is the prayer of Hannah, who went up to the house of the Lord in Shiloh each year that she might have a child. "In her wretchedness, she prayed to the Lord, weeping all the while. And she made this vow: 'O Lord of Hosts, if you will look upon the suffering of your maidservant and will remember me and . . . grant me a male child, I will dedicate him to the Lord for all the days of his life'" (1 Sam 1:11). Both Isaac's and Hannah's prayers were answered with the birth of Jacob and Samuel.

The most moving exposition on Rachel's prayer, however, is found in a little-known medieval poem from the Jewish New Year liturgy. With the fresh cycle of the calendar year comes the hope of human renewal. Birth and rebirth are recurrent themes. On the first day of the holiday the scriptural readings record the birth of Isaac to Sarah in her old age and the birth of Samuel to Hannah. Further, these children are said to have been conceived on the New Year (as was Joseph), signaling the renewal of creation and the covenant on whose moral law the world rested. Thus human birth pointed to the spiritual rebirth for people as well as for individuals.

Within the liturgy for the New Year are three Hebrew poems by Kalir (570–630), taken from a larger composition dealing with each of the patriarchs and matriarchs. Typical of the style of the time, they are written in a fashion so crammed with wordplay, allusion, and allegory, as well as the poet's own imagination, as to require a highly sophisticated audience or a commentary. The poet takes up the theme of the barrenness of the matriarchs and asks that the merit by virtue of which they were granted children be enlisted in behalf of the needs of the people Israel at the season of the birth of the New Year.

The section on Rachel, however, differs from the others. The merits of Sarah and Rebecca are associated with those of their husbands, Abraham and Isaac, but Rachel is treated alone in her quest for a child. There is no mention at all of Jacob. Not averse to making his own contribution, the poet draws upon a variety of midrashic and biblical sources: the provocation of Leah's sons; the merit of Rachel's silence on her wedding night; the miraculous switching of the sisters' embryos in response to Rachel's prayers rather than to those of Leah as another version has it; the bestowal of matriarchy on Rachel only as a result of Joseph's birth. Jeremiah's picture of Rachel rising from her grave "weeping for her children who are not" (Jer 31:15) (that is, the exiles) is transmuted into Rachel's weeping that she might have children of her own!

The switching of the embryos and the achieving of the matriarchy require elucidation once again. According to rabbinic legend, Leah was pregnant with a boy and Rachel with a girl. But the number of sons to be born to Jacob had been fixed at twelve; were Leah to give birth to a boy, Rachel could have borne only one son thereafter, eleven having already been born: Leah's seven, Bilhah's two, and Zilpah's two. If Rachel had only one son, she would not have been worthy of the matriarchy because she would have borne fewer sons than even the handmaids, Bilhah and Zilpah. Thus the fervor of Rachel's prayer, miraculously granted, that the embryos be switched—giving her a son, Joseph, and Leah a daughter, Dinah—and the hope that the merit of that prayer might redound to the entire people Israel each Rosh Hashanah.

[Confronted by the four sons of Leah,]
Rachel weeps for children of her own.
"Dry your tears," the Lord bids her
—mindful of her kindness to her sister

on her wedding night—
"For you shall yet bear sons."
Then did the master potter,
By whose hands all life is shaped,
Take the female embryo within Rachel
And set it into Leah,
And the male embryo within Leah
He set into Rachel.
For they were already pregnant.
Thus did Leah bear Dinah, and Rachel Joseph.
And she who had been as a stranger in her own home,
While childless,
Now became the center of Jacob's family,
And could be numbered among the matriarchs.

On this Day of Remembrance
Rachel stands and pleads for her descendants.
As she was remembered,
So too may they be remembered.[13]

Some 1,400 years after Kalir's widely used but enigmatic poem, another quite modern one was composed on a similar theme, this by the twentieth-century Yiddish writer Kadya Molodowsky. She was, of course, not the first to treat Kalir's motif of the matriarchs, a motif that appears with great frequency in the Yiddish *tekhineh* literature, folk prayers written by and for women in central and eastern Europe over the past several centuries. Included in Molodowsky's collection, entitled *Froyen-Lider* ("Women's Songs"), is a poem on the matriarchs, marriage, and motherhood with which Rachel is identified.

For poor brides who were servant girls,
Mother Sarah draws forth from dim barrels
pitchers of sparkling wine. . . .
And for street walkers
Dreaming of white wedding shoes
. . . clear honey. . . .

Barren

For high-born brides, now poor,
Who blush to bring patched wash
Before their mothers-in-law,
Mother Rebecca leads camels laden with white linen. . . .

For those whose eyes are tired
From watching the neighbors' children,
And whose hands are thin from yearning
To hold a soft small body
And to rock its cradle,
Mother Rachel brings healing [mandrake] leaves
Discovered on distant mountains,
And comforts them with a quiet word:
At any hour God may open the sealed womb![14]

Detail from the Tomb of Julius II: Rachel
Michelangelo

Chapter 7_____

Death

*And it came to pass that when Rachel had born Joseph,
then Jacob said to Laban: "Send me away that I may go to
my own place and to my own country"* (30:25).

The many years Jacob spent with Laban must have
stretched interminably, devouring his youth and etching
him with early lines of care. Now the final chapter in
Jacob's stay in Haran approaches its close, his mission there
fulfilled. The moment he chooses to announce his departure is suggestive. For Jacob's decision to leave is signaled
not by completing fourteen years of servitude or achieving
financial autonomy. It is the birth to his beloved Rachel of
the child who would one day be his successor, as he had
been Isaac's, and Isaac, Abraham's, that announced his exit.
This is implicit in the syntax of the sentence—*"When"
Rachel had born Joseph, "then" Jacob said to Laban: Send
me away.*[1]

What relief Jacob must have felt now that he believed his
sojourn to be complete; no need any longer to be on guard
against this unpredictable, unscrupulous man who continu-
ally sought to outwit him. His dream of returning and
settling peaceably with his family in the land of his parents
would soon be realized. Jacob's plan, however, is once

again thwarted by Laban. Just as Laban had postponed Jacob's marriage to Rachel, trading it for fourteen lucrative years of service, here too he succeeds in delaying Jacob a further six years into yet another work trap. But he fails to derive the profit he had anticipated from the deal, and things begin to look dark for Jacob. Then, just as at an earlier crucial moment in Jacob's life, a voice intervened:

> *Then the Lord said to Jacob, "Return to the land of your fathers where you were born, and I will be with you." Jacob had Rachel and Leah called to the field, where his flock was, and said to them, "I see that your father's manner toward me is not as it has been in the past. But the God of my father has been with me. As you know, I have served your father with all my might; but your father has cheated me, changing my wages time and again. God, however, would not let him do me harm . . ." (31:3-7).*

THE JOURNEY FROM HARAN TO CANAAN HAD BEEN made in the two preceding generations: by Abraham, in obedience to a similar divine directive, and by Rebecca, when she accompanied Eliezer across the desert to become Isaac's bride. Comparison of this journey with the preceding occasions emphasizes the special importance of Rachel and, to a lesser extent, Leah in the story. When Abraham leaves Haran, we are told that *He took Sarai his wife* (12:5). She is not consulted about the move. In contrast, Jacob's first action is to tell his wives of God's command and to recount the poor treatment he has received at the hands of their father, as if to persuade them of the reasonableness of leaving.

> *Then Rachel and Leah answered him, saying, "Have we still a share in the inheritance of our father's house? Surely, he regards us as outsiders, now that he has sold us*

and has used up our purchase price. Truly, all the wealth that God has taken away from our father belongs to us and to our children. Now then, do just as God has told you" (31:3-6, 14-16).

At the time Eliezer took Rebecca back with him across the desert, she too was asked permission before leaving Laban's house. Rebecca's consent, however, is to a journey made with the approval of her family, including that of her brother, Laban. Here the situation is quite different. If Jacob were simply an indentured servant who had completed his term of service, then he would be free to leave openly. In this case, however, twenty years have passed since Jacob's arrival, and twelve children have been born. Enough time and history have transpired to settle him permanently as part of Laban's family. To depart now was more difficult for Jacob and especially problematic for the daughters of Laban. Yet the wives have no fear in speaking their minds—though we note that the meeting takes place in *the field* near *his flock* (31:4) and out of earshot of others—adding to Jacob's the hurts they themselves suffered from their father: the denial of their rightful possession in being refused dowries and the indignity of being exchanged in return for the decades of Jacob's indentured service. They protest, according to Rashi (31:15), that "Instead of treating us like daughters and giving us a dowry upon marriage, he treated us like strangers and sold us to you in return for your work." The wealth that Jacob has been able to gain despite Laban's machinations Rachel and Leah claim as their own and their children's. As it was the Lord who protected Jacob against the efforts of Laban, so now they bid their husband to hearken to the Lord's word to depart. God does not address them directly, yet they hear the word through him to whom it was addressed. They are not afraid to oppose their father on his own land, affirming the Lord's word against the word of the lord of the place. The dignity of Rachel and Leah is apparent in this episode: we are not presented with a male figure who issues commands and acts alone but with a growing mutuality of husband and wife.

Although *both* women are consulted, it is quite clear that the central figure here is Rachel. It is she who is addressed first and she who responds first. It may even be that it is Rachel alone who is speaking, for the text can be read *Then Rachel replied* (singular), *and Leah* consented (31:14).[2] Despite Leah's many children, whose welfare required that she be consulted and give her approval, it is Rachel who guides the action. For whom but Rachel did Jacob agree to serve Laban all these years? At the birth of whose child but Rachel's does Jacob finally take steps to leave? And who but Rachel shows contempt for Laban by daring to steal his house-gods (*terafim*) and hide them under her skirts (31: 19-35)?[3]

Finally, we note once again the theme that has been central to the life of the covenant: the sundering of human attachments for a divine purpose. In a society where travel was by foot or by camel, there must have been a minimum of moving about. Leaving the family and native land, in all probability never to see them again, must have been rare in those days. Yet that is exactly what the early biblical figures did, ever since Abraham was called to abandon his home for the place God would show him that he might become a universal blessing. Rebecca too abandons family and land, traveling from Haran to far-off Canaan. And now the same breaking of deeply rooted ties of family and place is assented to by Rachel and Leah. Catherine Chalier tells us that they

> were ready to repeat the act of rupture by which Rebecca had already been able to leave Haran, to put an end to natural attachments, because a God quite other than their father's idols commanded it. . . . The capacity to leave is a measure of the clear awareness of the exigencies of their chosen status. If the matriarchs too must hold them-

selves receptive to the voice of God that calls for rupture—whether or not this voice be transmitted through the intermediary of a man—it is really that the Promise, far from being thought of as the privilege of men, remains linked, at every level of its realization, to the advent of the couple, to the hope of its holiness, the very prototype of the fulfillment of the Presence, and thus of meaning. . . . In the story of Genesis, Sarah, Rebecca, Rachel and Leah know, with neither melancholy nor capriciousness, how to give up their moorings in order to enter further into the Covenant, how to keep themselves available to the summonings of a God who chose them even before they had committed themselves to him. This certainly argues for their extreme consciousness of the demands pertaining to the Promise, but also, and jointly, for the necessity of a common receptiveness on the part of man and woman to the urgent solicitations of the holy Word.[4]

Having obtained the assent of his wives, Jacob sets off with family and possessions without informing his uncle. In a last-ditch effort to prevent the loss in work and family he may otherwise suffer, Laban hotly pursues Jacob and accuses him bitterly of underhanded behavior. Jacob grandly replies:

These twenty years I have spent in your service, your ewes and she-goats never miscarried, nor did I feast on rams from your flock. That which was torn by beasts I never brought to you; I myself made good the loss; you exacted it of me, whether snatched by day or snatched by night. Often, scorching heat ravaged me by day and frost by night and sleep fled from my eyes. Of the twenty years that I spent in your household, I served you fourteen years for your two daughters, and six years for your flocks; and you changed my wages time and again. Had not the God of my father been with me, you would have sent me away empty-handed. But God took notice of my plight and the toil of my hands, and he gave judgment last night (31: 38-42).

The final word is with the Lord. It is the Lord who tells Jacob to leave: *Return to the land of your fathers where you were born, and I will be with you* (v. 3). The Lord warns Laban not to meddle with Jacob, as Laban himself testifies: *I [Laban] have it in my power to do you harm; but the God of your father said to me last night, Beware of attempting anything with Jacob* (v. 29). Divine assurance is given twice: that Jacob will survive and that he will prosper.

UPON JACOB'S RETURN TO THE BOSOM OF HIS FAMILY after an absence of twenty years, one obstacle alone hangs over his future like an ominous cloud and stands between him and the comfortable, harmonious domestic life he looks forward to—Esau. Twenty years previously Jacob fled before his brother's murderous threat of revenge for the birthright and the blessing he had lost. Jacob, knowing that he cannot hope to live in peace in his homeland until he resolves this long-simmering conflict, sends messengers before him bearing abundant gifts to humbly announce his coming and prays to God for deliverance. The warrior Esau approaches with what must have seemed a fearsome force. *Looking up, Jacob saw Esau coming, accompanied by four hundred men* (33:1). With the safety of Rachel and Joseph uppermost in his mind, he rearranges his retinue, dividing *the children among Leah, Rachel, and the two maids, putting the maids and their children first, Leah and her children next, and Rachel and Joseph last. He himself went on ahead . . .* (vv. 2, 3). The children are, it should be noted, not grouped together as might be expected, not even the children of a wife and of her maid, though the wives had named the maids' children to make them their own.

Having struggled with the angel in the dead of night and prevailed—*I have seen God face to face* (32:31)—Jacob is emboldened to reach an accommodation with Esau at all costs. The rabbis say that Jacob "prepared himself in three ways: through prayer, by sending gifts, and [should both of these fail] by making ready for battle."⁵ Omitted from this list is Jacob's evident abasement, calling Esau *my Lord* and himself *your servant* and *bowing to the ground seven times as he approached his brother* (33:3). While it helped to save his life, such unctuous servility set the sages on edge. They drew comfort, however, from the verse, "though the righteous man [the zaddik] falls seven times, yet he rises" (Prov 24:16). They pointed out further that, unlike Jacob, Mordecai refused to bow before Haman (Esth 3:2), and when the king's courtiers urged him to comply with the king's command, citing the example of Jacob's obeisance to Esau, he proudly responded, "Yes, that is true. But I am from the tribe of Benjamin who did not prostrate himself before Esau; as my ancestor acted so shall I."⁶ It was for the same reason, they say, that the temple of Jerusalem was built in the territory of Benjamin, and that Saul, the first king of Israel, who fought against Esau's descendants the Amalekites, was not from the royal tribe of Judah but from the tribe of Benjamin.⁷ Benjamin, of course, was the child of Rachel.

So it was that through gifts, prayer, and appeasement Jacob entered into a fragile peace with his brother and, the last hurdle overcome, pushed on to Hebron where his old father, Isaac, still lived.

Now, having put behind him human troubles and conflicts, the time had arrived for Jacob to make heavenly preparations for his homecoming. When twenty years before he had departed from family and country for the distant land of Haran, it was at Bethel that he dreamt of the wondrous ladder binding heaven and earth (28:10-22). The vision of the ladder sustained him through the struggle with

Laban and would yet guide him through the years that lay ahead. On his return home it is at Bethel that he halts and that God appears to him once again (35:1-13). This is the spot where human and divine meet, where men dream dreams and angels descend from heaven. Both visions are of the night, one signaling the exalted task that he pursues, the second the sign of victory and transformation. Both meetings relate to Rachel: the first occurs when Jacob is on his quest to find her, the second when he is bringing her home. At the conclusion of each meeting Jacob builds a pillar and gives the place a divine name. On this second occasion, Jacob too is given a divine name, in recognition of his fidelity to the task laid before him on his outward journey to Haran. After Jacob has instructed his household to remove all strange gods and purify themselves, he builds an altar, and God appears to him.

> *Your name shall no more be Jacob, but Israel shall be your name. So he named him Israel. I am God Almighty. Be fruitful and multiply. . . . The land which I gave to Abraham and Isaac I give to you and to your seed after you . . . (35:12-13).*

We are not altogether certain what the name Israel means. The last two letters of Israel, *EL*, signify "God." The first three letters, *YSR*, however, present a problem. In Gen 32:29, we are told, *Your name shall no longer be Jacob, but Israel, for you have striven with beings divine and human, and have prevailed* (32:29). Israel would then mean "he who strives [Heb. *saritah*, from SRH] with God [or angels]." Two objections to this are that (1) the simple translation of *yisra'el* would be "God strives . . .," not "he who strives . . .," and (2) the verb SRH is otherwise unknown. Hosea 12:5 takes the verb from "dominion" (SRR), which would give us the meaning, "May God have dominion." Isaiah 44:2 (also Deut 32:15; 33:5, 26), reads, "Fear not, my servant Jacob,

Jeshurun whom I have chosen." The synonym here for Jacob-Israel is Jeshurun (Heb. *yeshurun* from YSHR), which means "upright" or "straight," giving us "He acts uprightly with God," or "God is righteous." Thus "rectitude," "sovereignty," "struggling and prevailing" are alternate meanings contained in the name although the precise meaning is not absolutely clear.

However we understand the first part of the word "Israel," there is no question but that it concludes with the divine epithet El. In the change of Abram's name to Abraham, which the Bible explains as *the father of a multitude of nations* (17:5), the midrash sees an allusion to the inserting of God's name, represented by the letter "*H*," into that of Abram's—Abra**H**am. This appears to represent the attempt of a later age to find a precedent for a divine epithet in "Israel" and thereby associate the first with the last of the patriarchs. But among them it is Jacob alone whose new name, Israel, unequivocally includes the name of God.

One talmudic sage offers this parable to explain the inclusion of God's name in the new "Israel": Once there was a mighty king, the great door to whose palace opened with a tiny key. So as not to lose the key, the king attached it to a string. Similarly with the modest people Israel. "Left alone among the nations, they will be lost," says God. "Therefore will I attach my name to guarantee their survival."[8]

Interestingly, the most ancient record of the name *Israel* is in the context of prevailing against great odds. The victory hymn of King Merneptah of Egypt (ca. 1207 B.C.E.) claims that "Israel is laid waste, his seed is not," and some centuries later, on the Moabite stone, King Mesha (ca. 830 B.C.E.) rejoices that "Israel has perished forever." Yet it is these nations themselves that have either disappeared or whose empires have collapsed, and their once mighty monarchs are remembered chiefly because of their relations with the people Israel whose demise they celebrated prematurely.

The change of names from Jacob to Israel signaled the completion of the first part of the patriarch's life. Thus far he had been the son of Isaac and the grandson of Abraham, receiving from them the teachings of the covenant with God, struggling to survive Laban's plots and establish a family and a fortune. Now, as Israel, the time has come for him to advance from the role of recipient to that of transmitter. The young adventurer who lived by his wits will become the wise patriarch who hands down the covenant to his descendants, not, as his father did, to a single one of his two sons but to all twelve, who are destined to become the tribes that will settle the land in fulfillment of the divine promise. The people who are destined to emerge will one day be known by his title, Israel—the "tribes of Israel," the "children of Israel, Israel, in whom I shall be glorified" (Isa 49:3). All this is implied in the new name he acquires in the vision of Bethel.[9]

THE STORY OF JACOB SEEMS TO BE MOVING SWIFTLY toward a contented conclusion. He has parted peacefully from Laban with his family and possessions intact. With the arrival of Rachel's impatiently awaited child, Leah no longer poses a threat to household peace. Even the long-feared Esau has been satisfactorily pacified. The promise of the land and God's blessing have been confirmed in the new name bestowed on Jacob. All seems in readiness: Laban overcome, Esau reconciled, Rachel his wife, Joseph his son, Israel his name, the land promised, God's blessing secured. All is prepared for the joyous meeting with his old father, Isaac. It is at this very moment that there befalls Jacob the darkest tragedy of his life, a tragedy from which he never recovers.

They set out from Bethel; but when they were still some distance short of Ephrat, Rachel was in childbirth, and had hard labor.

When her labor was at its hardest, the midwife said to her, "Have no fear, for it is another boy for you."
But as she breathed her last—for she was dying—she named him Ben-oni; but his father called him Benjamin.
Thus Rachel died.
She was buried on the road to Ephrat—now Bethlehem.
Over her grave Jacob set up a pillar; it is the pillar at Rachel's grave to this day (35:16-20).

The pathos of her death at so young an age is magnified by her lonely burial outside Bethlehem, apart from the other matriarchs and patriarchs who were laid to rest in the family sepulcher in the cave of Machpelah in Hebron, and by the thought that her two boys will be raised without the love and nurturing of their mother. Rachel felt shame in being an *akarah*, a barren wife, unable to give to her beloved Jacob a son to whom the covenant could be handed down. When, after watching with growing apprehension the birth of children to Leah and the surrogate maidservants, her bitter state of sterility was finally lifted and the blessing of fertility granted her at last, she called her son Joseph (Heb. *Yosef,* "Let him add"), as if to say, May the Lord add another, and another, and another. So was she reminded of the name's intent each time she called him, each time she spoke it to others or heard others speak it. Thus the birth of a second son was the partial fulfillment of her deepest aspiration and her death in that second childbirth all the more tragic. The rabbis compare the four matriarchs to the four plants used on Sukkoth—the lulav, etrog, myrtle, and willow. Leah, they said, was as thick with children as the myrtle is with leaves; Rachel, like the withering willow, was the first to fade.[10]

To add to the calamity, Scripture describes a death both painful and protracted. According to medical authorities, a careful study of the text suggests that the birth was in an impacted breech position in which the lower trunk of the infant appears first, with the straightened legs drawn up against the stomach. This possibility would explain how the midwife knew the baby's gender during the birth and why the process was so prolonged and so painful (first, *she was dying* [*meytah*], then, *she died* [*vatamot*]). It would also suggest a plausible cause of death, fatal hemorrhage due presumably to the midwife's tearing of the uterus. Rachel, who above all wanted to give her husband sons, lives only long enough to know that her child was a boy and to name him *Ben-oni*, "son of my suffering," before passing away. Jacob, apparently preferring a more affirmative name, calls him Benjamin, "son of my right hand" (*Ben-yamin*) by which he is henceforth known. It is the only time Jacob names one of his children.[11]

One midrash on the birth of Benjamin provides a remarkable footnote to the tragedy. Removing itself from the pathos of the moment and looking back from the perspective of the centuries, the rabbis review the eminence of Rachel's two sons and audaciously ascribe to her a vicarious joy. They apply to her the verse "He sets the childless woman to dwell in her household as a happy mother of children, Hallelujah!" (Ps 113:9). That Rachel had been a "childless woman" is true, but can we say of her, after her lamentable death, that she was "a happy mother of children"? Yes, responds the midrash, and brings the proof-text *And the children of Rachel were Joseph and Benjamin* (Gen 35:24). It is as if, for Rachel, the act of giving birth itself, regardless of the tragic circumstances that would follow, is sufficient for joy. Despite the teaching that the life of the mother takes precedence over that of the child, the author of this midrash seems to suggest that Rachel would have chosen to give birth to a second child even in the knowledge that it might mean her death![12]

The death of Rachel is the watershed in the life of Jacob. From this point on, Jacob, the bright, ambitious son of Isaac, who matched wits with crafty Laban, won Rachel, beheld the mighty ladder, overcame the angel, received the promise of the Lord and the blessing of Abraham, the brilliant prince who victoriously returns home to enter into his inheritance—this same Jacob, after the death of his darling Rachel, withdraws into virtual oblivion. We read no more of power and wealth or encounters with angels, no more of heroic tales to add to the record of his life. Only sorrow, sorrow so unremitting that it carries him all the way to the grave. Overnight he falls into depression, hardly recognizable, a solitary, morose figure, given over to mourning for his beloved Rachel, concerned only that what she left be preserved. Although capable of fathering children, Jacob has no more with Leah, nor does he take another wife after Rachel's death. Rachel's second child is the last born to him. The rest of the life of this great patriarch is a tale of pathos and sorrow.

From this last trial of Rachel's death, Jacob never recovers.

Part III

The Victory of Rachel

Everything depended upon Rachel.
Therefore, are her descendants called by her name;
And not only by her name,
but by the name of Joseph, her son;
And not only by her son's name,
but by the name of Ephraim, her grandson.
(Gen. R. 71:2)

Chapter 8_____

Joseph

THUS FAR WE HAVE EXAMINED THAT PART OF THE
Rachel story dealing primarily with her life. It was a time of
trials—the journey, the well, Laban, Leah, barrenness, and
death. Sometimes Jacob was tested, sometimes Rachel,
and sometimes both together. Each trial, in time, was overcome except for the trial of Rachel's death. From that
calamity, the record will show, Jacob never revived. This
man of energy and wit, who gained the birthright and stood
against Laban and Esau, who won Rachel and acquired
wealth and power despite years of servitude, now fades
steadily from the scene. But as Jacob's existence without
Rachel becomes a death-in-life, for Rachel there begins the
life-in-death that continues even into the present. For Scripture points unequivocally to the victory of Rachel: in the
glorious ascendancy of Joseph; in the elevation of his sons
Ephraim and Manasseh to the status of tribal heads; in the
gathering power of the tribe of Ephraim, whose name came
to stand for the whole of the Northern Kingdom of Israel;
and finally through the legends of affection and wonder
that surround her grave, a shrine *until this very day* (Gen
35:20).

The triumph of Rachel begins principally with Joseph,
whose story stretches over ten chapters in Genesis. These

chapters comprise one of the richest descriptions we possess of a biblical character, to be compared in abundance of detail only with that of Moses himself. Joseph's rise to glory as the wise viceroy of Egypt gives Rachel's progeny sovereignty in the generation after Jacob, when we see the earliest beginnings of what was to become the people Israel. Though Jacob had twelve sons, it was Rachel's older, Joseph, who captured his heart. Joseph's resemblance to Rachel was such—Scripture uses the same adjectives to describe each of them (27:17; 39:6)—that whenever Jacob beheld the handsome face of his son, he was comforted momentarily for the loss of Rachel.

Although Scripture informs us that Joseph received the birthright because the firstborn Reuben had sinned with Bilhah, Rachel's handmaid (1 Chron 5:1), the Zohar argues that the birthright was intended for Joseph long before. In the darkness of the nuptial chamber, unaware that Leah had been substituted for her sister, "Jacob's mind was centered only upon Rachel, and it was from that intercourse, with that intention, and with that first germ, that Leah conceived. . . . Thus [after the deception became known, Jacob's disappointment was such that the child] did not receive a name of any significance, but was simply called Reuben (*Reu-ben,* 'Behold, a son!'). . . . And the birthright eventually reverted to the eldest child of Rachel [Joseph], as originally intended."[1] By joining the sentence *This is the history of the family of Jacob,* with the first word of the next sentence, *Joseph was feeding the flock . . .* (37:2), the midrash gives us the following reading: "This is the history of the family of Jacob—Joseph!" The passage implies that Jacob travels to Laban, serves him, marries Rachel and Leah, and fathers all his children for Joseph's sake; that Joseph's birth signals the moment of departure; that Joseph brings the family down to Egypt and sustains them there; that for Joseph's sake, the midrash adds, the Red Sea was split and the Jordan parted.[2]

Joseph's ascent to greatness is set in motion by his brothers who, acting on their hatred of him, sell him into slavery in order to be rid of him. The brothers' resentment was stimulated by Joseph's importance to their father as well as by Joseph's own haughtiness. Scripture tells us that *Israel loved Joseph more than all his children, because he was the son of his old age* and that he spoiled him with a *coat of many colors* (37:3). It is clear that Joseph, one of the youngest of Jacob's sons, was treated as the eldest because he was the firstborn of Rachel, whom Jacob alone calls *my wife* (44:27), just as he refers to Joseph as *my son* (42:38), or to Joseph and Benjamin as *my sons* (44:17), as if he had no other wives or children. It must have been clear, even in Joseph's early years, that Jacob considered the son of his beloved Rachel deserving of the birthright. Doing away with him, therefore, would allow the brothers not only to vent their jealousy, but also to strike for a greater share of the inheritance.

Their initial impulse is to slay their brother; instead, however, they cast him into a pit and, later, sell him as a slave to the Ishmaelites. The brothers allow their father to conclude that Joseph has been killed by a wild animal. Perhaps they too came to believe that Joseph was dead, for how long could an Ishmaelite slave survive? They must have expected to profit twice by their actions, once by virtue of the money realized in the sale and again in the enhanced estimation in which Jacob would hold them now that Joseph would be there no longer. But their jealousy has led them into a miscalculation. When the sons tell Jacob that Joseph is dead, Jacob *put sackcloth upon his loins and mourned for his son many days. All his sons and all his daughters rose up to comfort him, but he refused to be comforted. And he said, "No, but I will go down to the grave to my son in mourning." And his father wept for him* (37:34-36).

Jacob's lamentation for his lost child is proposed by a later hand:

O my son Joseph, my son, the fault is mine that this evil has come upon you, for it is I who sent you to inquire after your brothers where wild beasts devoured you. How I grieve, O my son, O how I grieve. How sweet was your life to me, and how bitter is your death! Would to God I had died for you, O Joseph, my son. . . . For now that Joseph is taken from us, the covenant is at an end. . . .[3]

This is the second time Scripture mentions Jacob weeping: once in joy on meeting Rachel and now in grief on separating from Rachel's child. Jacob's mourning for Joseph is part of his mourning for Rachel—Rachel has died, and now Rachel's child has died. The depression into which he had fallen with the loss of Rachel becomes a consuming longing for death. Of his victories and prosperity, of the pleasure he receives from his many children and grandchildren, nothing is heard. Morbidity is now his constant mood and death his steady companion. When Joseph is lost and presumed dead, Jacob wants to die; when it is made known that Joseph lives in renown in Egypt, Jacob's response is, *I will go to see him before I die* (45:28). Even when he descends into that most splendid land and beholds with his own eyes the magnificence of Egypt's viceroy and the life of ease and comfort that awaits him as an aged, honored father, his mind dwells upon the single thought that has followed him from the time of Rachel's death. *Now let me die,* he says to Joseph, *since I have seen your face and you are alive* (45:29). Jacob's mourning is the last of the trials of love, and Jacob's lamentation is the darkest proof of Rachel's compelling presence beyond the grave.

JOSEPH PRESENTS A GRAND SUCCESSOR FIGURE TO Jacob. The efforts of the patriarchs in receiving and handing down the covenant, the momentous task of succession so central to the early biblical epic, culminate in this powerful yet merciful personality, handsome in form, wise in rule, and understanding in judgment. He is raised to a level equal to Abraham, Isaac, and Jacob, a fourth patriarch as it were. Well does dying Jacob name him *nezir ehav—prince among his brethren* (49:26).

Marked for death himself, Joseph rises from the pit to bring life to those around him: to the nations whom he delivers from the dread famine that devastated the ancient Middle East for seven years, to his mourning father who lives in honor in Egypt for seventeen years, and to the brothers who thought to send him to his grave. He from whom life was to be taken becomes the wise life-giver. The sages suggest that Joseph, who "fed the entire world during the years of privation . . . like a ship filled with good things which traveled the seas distributing them," owes his role as provider to Rachel, "who [having once] lamented her barren state" became "like the merchant ships which bring food from afar" (Prov 31:14).[4] Despite achieving limitless power in the mightiest land of the time, Joseph proved true to the covenant of his fathers. He thus became the paradigm for the Jew in exile, especially those who were to achieve fame and fortune in the larger society. Isaac Abrabanel, David Oppenheim, Benjamin Disraeli, and Henry Kissinger have all been measured against Joseph.

Johann Wolfgang von Goethe writes that "When the medley of fable and history, mythology and religion threatened to bewilder me, I liked to take refuge in those Oriental regions, to plunge into the first books of Moses, and to find myself there, amid the scattered shepherd tribes, at the same time in the greatest solitude and the greatest society. . . ." The story of Joseph held a particular attraction for him:

> Joseph, the child of the most passionate wedded love . . . seems to us tranquil and clear, and predicts to himself the advantages which are to elevate him above the family. Cast into misfortune by his brothers, he remains steadfast and upright in slavery, resists the most dangerous temptations, rescues himself by prophecy, and

is elevated according to his deserts to high honors. He shows himself first serviceable and useful to a great kingdom, then to his own kindred. He is like his ancestor Abraham in repose and greatness, his grandfather Isaac in silence and devotedness. The talent for traffic, inherited from his father, he exercises on a large scale. It is no longer flocks which are gained for himself from a father-in-law, but nations, with all their possessions, which he knows how to purchase for a king. Extremely graceful is this natural story, only it appears too short; and one feels called upon to paint it in detail.[5]

What Goethe proposed but never fulfilled was carried out by another European, who in a famed trilogy gave us a masterful, if personal, record of the Joseph saga. For when the rise of fascism in Germany turned Thomas Mann to the Jewish Bible in search of a figure about whom to create a historical fiction, he found Joseph. Mann gave painstaking attention to the social circumstances in which the young adventurer found himself—the ruling class of a civilization devoted to the cultivation of gratification wherever it might be found.

IN LEVITICUS, EGYPT, ALONG WITH CANAAN, IS identified as a land of sexual debauchery: "You shall not copy the [sexual] practices of the land of Egypt where you dwelt, or of the land of Canaan to which I am taking you" (Lev 18.3). The later rabbis of the Talmud and midrash provide their own fiction out of the biblical story, condemning the licentious temper of the land, but partly reflecting as well, no doubt, their own pagan environment. Thus Potiphar was said to have engaged the handsome young Joseph into his service for illicit use. "He purchased him for the purpose of sodomy."[6] And when the brothers come down to Egypt, Judah pleads deferentially with the powerful viceroy of the land to allow their brother Benjamin to leave (in ignorance that it is Joseph to whom he speaks), and refers to himself as *your servant* and to the viceroy as *my lord . . . who are the equal of Pharaoh* (44.18). But he thinks to himself, yes, you are the equal of Pharoah, "as he lusts for males so do you," and that is the reason you want Benjamin.[7] Or, as another midrash has it, "Just as Pharaoh your master hungers for the pleasures of women, so, having seen the comeliness of Benjamin, do you desire him."[8]

But the event in Joseph's career upon which art and literature have focused most sharply, describing, probing, examining, and developing to the limit of human imagination, is his temptation by Potiphar's wife. We will see that the spirit of Rachel is intimately associated with Joseph's successful resistance to her blandishments.

When Joseph was taken down to Egypt, he was bought by Potiphar . . . the chief steward of Pharaoh, who, seeing that Joseph brought him success, entrusted him with all he had. . . . Now Joseph was handsome of form and handsome to the eye, and after a time, his master's wife cast her eyes upon him and said, "Lie with me." But he refused and said to her, "Think of my master. He has entrusted me with all he has save yourself, because you are his wife. How then can I do this most wicked thing and sin against God." And much as she coaxed Joseph day after day, he refused to lie with her. One day he came into the house as usual to do his work when it was empty. She caught hold of his cloak and said, "Lie with me!" But he left his cloak in her hands and fled outside (39:1-13).

Joseph's rejection of Potiphar's wife marks the second time a fall in his fortunes will turn to good account. Falsely accused by her of attempted rape, he is thrown in jail, where he remains for two years. He is taken from the jail to the royal court when Pharaoh, troubled by dreams he cannot understand, hears from his butler of a Hebrew youth who correctly foretold the butler's future from a dream the butler had when himself in jail. It is as a result of Joseph's correct interpretation of Pharaoh's dream that Joseph ultimately becomes Pharaoh's grand viceroy.

Nowhere, however, is it suggested that Joseph knew what the future held in store. Why, then, did he deny himself the delicious pleasures freely offered when a refusal could only incur the wrath of such a powerful woman? Self-interest here dictated indulging the impulse to sensual pleasure. Any ambitious young man, given Joseph's opportunity, should have had no qualms. In succumbing, Joseph would only have been acting as an aspiring opportunist is expected to act, gaining a little power for the moment until someone craftier came along to take it from him, feeding on forbidden delights until another, hungrier and younger, cuckolded him in turn.

But a young man of this type would never have ascended to rulership of Egypt. Such a feat of self-control, for an alien having neither rank nor wealth, argues qualities of a higher order altogether. There must have been in Joseph something of the dogged determination of his father, Jacob; even more, something of the strength of his great-grandfather, who was called *Abraham the Hebrew* (*ivri* from *eyver,* "side") because "Though the entire world was on one side, he was on the other."[9] In short, Joseph still possessed some measure of loyalty to the covenant that the patriarchs had handed down through Jacob to him. Joseph's rejection of his master's wife prepared the way for future events and set in motion the rise of a Hebrew slave to a position second in power only to Pharaoh himself.

But if there was in Joseph something of Jacob, there was also much of Rachel. Joseph is described here as *beautiful of form and beautiful to behold,* the identical language, as noted above, describing his mother, Rachel, at the well (29:17),[10] and suggesting a similarity of appearance that must at once have reminded Jacob of his loss and consoled him for it.[11] If the grace of the child comforted Jacob in Canaan, the strikingly handsome features of the mature young man only served to excite the Egyptian princesses.

They would peek through the courtyard latticework or run to the top of the walls to catch a glimpse of him when he passed, casting bracelets and rings his way in an effort to catch his attention so they might see his face. To no avail, explain the sages, for he "did not lift up his eyes to them."[12] He was called by his father *aley ayin* (49:2), which is read by the sages, *uley ayin,* "one who is immune to the evil eye which leads astray."[13] As a result of Joseph's restraint, it was said that "None of the descendants of Joseph would be ruled by the eye of desire."[14] For this reason, the sages continue, Jacob blesses Joseph's children, Ephraim and Manasseh, that they will *multiply as fish* (48:16), for the evil eye has no power over that which cannot be seen, and the fish in the sea are hidden from sight.[15]

A handsome talmudic sage, Rabbi Johanan, used to station himself outside the *mikveh* or ritual bath, where he would tell the women who emerged, having purified themselves in the waters following their monthly abstinence, to gaze upon him and bear handsome children. "Are you not afraid of the evil eye?" queried the other sages, upset by his indelicate behavior. "Fear not," he replied, "for I am of the seed of Joseph, against which the evil eye of desire has no power."[16]

Sexual modesty characterized Joseph, say the sages, from his earliest youth. When Jacob crossed the Jabbok River to meet Esau, Jacob did not know how he would be received, and so he arranged the order of the company with *the maids and their children first, Leah and her children next, and Rachel and Joseph last* (33:2). A few sentences later, however, the child Joseph seems to precede Rachel (33:7). The midrash explains thus: "'There is none so beautiful as my mother,' thought Joseph, 'and this vile fellow is suspected of immorality.' So he stepped in front of her to block Esau's vision that he not lust after her."[17]

"Who is most to be trusted? A bachelor living among harlots, yet does not sin. None is more trustworthy than he. So with Joseph. Who could be more trusted, for he lived among the Egyptians, 'whose members were like those of asses and whose organs were like those of stallions' (Ez 23:20), and was only seventeen years of age, yet above suspicion and immorality."[18] Upon his deathbed, Jacob called him *firm of bow* (49:24), which is taken to mean that "He kept his passion [*kashiut*, "bow"] under firm control!"[19] "Until the incident with Potiphar's wife, he was not called *zaddik* [virtuous]," says the Zohar, "but after he guarded the sign of the holy covenant, he was called *zaddik,* Joseph the Zaddik."[20]

BUT THIS IS ONLY ONE SIDE OF THE AFFAIR. WAS Joseph's virtue without blemish? Is anyone's? We should not forget that, although the seduction had been carefully planned by Potiphar's wife, who better than Joseph, manager of the family affairs, knew when the servants would be out of the house, leaving his mistress alone? Nor was he unaware of his appeal to women. As with other men graced with good looks, one midrash suggests, Joseph proudly displayed his wares, prancing in the marketplace, painting his eyes, curling his hair. "You behave this way while your father mourns!" heaven warned. "In the end you shall surely suffer at the hands of that bear of a mistress of yours."[21] Criticism of Joseph focuses on the following passage:

> *And Joseph made ready his chariot, and went up to meet Israel his father, to Goshen; and he presented himself to him, and fell on his neck, and wept on his neck a good while* (46:29).

At first sight this record of Joseph's meeting with Jacob when he arrived in Egypt seems straightforward enough. One midrash, however, reflecting perhaps Joseph's failure to contact his father over so many years, suggests that Joseph did not show Jacob full honor. "Why were the years of Joseph shortened? Because he did not descend from his chariot to greet his father but, while still standing in the chariot, *fell upon his neck."* The Targum adds that Joseph was punished because he permitted his father to bow to him first.[22]

A more serious problem in the verse emerges from a comparison with Gen 45:15, in which Joseph kissed all his brethren when he made himself known to them in Egypt; here it would appear he did not kiss his father but only that he *wept on his neck a good while.* Nor is anything said of Jacob's kissing Joseph in return. Rashi quotes a tradition that says that he did not kiss Joseph because Jacob was praying the Shema—"Hear O Israel, the Lord our God, the Lord is one" (Deut 6:4)—at that moment,[23] but the explanation seems forced. Another comment goes to the heart of the matter:

> Jacob did not kiss Joseph because he suspected that Joseph, being so handsome and so distant from home and family for so long, would have been seduced by women. Hence when we are told that *he [Joseph] fell upon his [Jacob's] neck and wept a good while,* it means that Joseph wanted to kiss his father, but [Jacob] would not let him. . . .[24] For Jacob foresaw that Joseph would be inflamed before Potiphar's wife and, therefore, did not permit [his son] to kiss him. . . . How do we know that this happened [to Joseph before Potiphar's wife]? From Jacob's last words to Joseph, *And his bow remained firm* (49:24).[25]

One reason for the perennial popularity of the Bible is its realistic account of human character. But the later midrashic tradition, although frequently engaging in hagiography, is not lacking in the most frank portrayal. The *Midrash Tanhuma,* for example, provides its version of the story in a manner as vivid as any novel:

> *She coaxed him day by day to lie with her, but he would not. One day he came into the house to do his work*

117

(39:10-11). One sage says it was real work; but another insists it was the work of intercourse for which he went in that day, knowing all along that the servants would be at the Nile festival. *She caught hold of his garment and said, "Lie with me"* (39:12). They undressed and laid themselves upon the bed. Suddenly the image of his parent appeared through the window, and his manhood left him, as it says, *There was no man in the house* (39:11-12), and this is alluded to in Jacob's last words to Joseph, that *The vigor of his "bow" relaxed.* He threw himself upon the floor and dug his fingers into the ground until the pain diverted his passion. *The seeds were scattered through his hands* (49:24).[26]

Humans are superior to angels. Angels, possessing no bodily desires, no will, knowing no temptation, act rightly out of compulsion and not by choice. Humans, with the bodies of beasts and the souls of angels, alone possess the agonizing power of moral choice. They hear both the suing of heaven and the song of the devil. Their uniqueness, as well as their glory, lies in their ability to overcome temptation, to subvert the evil impulse within. They therefore are not to be forbidden material pleasure or worldly success but are commanded to transform these into means for the service of God. Something of the agony of Joseph's effort to restrain himself is found in the liturgical rendering of this passage during the Sabbath synagogue service, in which Scripture is chanted according to a system of fixed musical notes. The note for the crucial words *he refused* in the verse *His master's wife cast her eyes upon him, but he refused* is the rarely used *shalshelet,* whose sound is a threefold repetition, trembling and sustained, reflecting at once Joseph's battle with himself and his final decision: the struggle and the victory.

To the Romans, the story of the temptation of Joseph seemed incredible. Roman society, after all, shared many similarities with ours today. "Do you mean," asked one Roman matron of a visiting sage, "that a seventeen-year-old youth in the height of his passion rejected the advances of such a woman?" The sage responded, "If Scripture had no compunction about revealing the liaisons of the sons of Jacob while those sons were still under parental influence— Reuben with Bilhah and Judah with Tamar (38:14-18; 35:22)—why would it conceal the sin of another son when he was in a strange land and far from parental influence?" According to the midrash, the noblewoman acknowledged the truth of his words and of the Torah.[27]

But the Roman woman had a point: where did the young, handsome favorite of the lordly Potiphar find the strength to resist the advances of his master's wife? It would stand to reason that parental influence was minimal, relegated to the distant past in rustic Canaan, far from the glittering land of Egypt where the pursuit of pleasure had been raised to a fine art. As overseer, Joseph had easy access to the house and knew both his master's movements and the servants' schedule. The woman was desirable, desirous, and knowledgeable in the ways of erotic delights. In a land where even incest was practiced by royalty, such liaisons between mistress and servant, common in all ages, must have been a daily occurrence. Furthermore, Joseph surely knew that to spurn her open invitation could ignite a rage in Potiphar's wife that might well ruin him—as it almost did.

In a remarkable attestation to the power of the family, the later tradition insists that Joseph was redeemed by his parents, from whom he drew strength. Of the several versions dealing with this episode, one records that, just as he was about to succumb, the image of his father, Jacob, appeared to Joseph; the other, that it was the image of his mother. These traditions are paradigmatic of communication between the generations. As the child, growing in experience and confidence, leaves the home to enter the adult world of decisions and responsibilities, the nurturing parents appear to recede into the background. When the time of testing comes, as it surely must, will the teaching and example of the parents be sufficient to stave off sin? So with Joseph. Many years have passed since he last saw his father. Perhaps he has not contacted him because he does not want to endanger his new and aggrandized position in Egyptian society with reminders of austere tribal connections. Suddenly he finds himself in crisis, when the flame of passion is set afire and threatens to consume him. Facing such a conflagration, reason is impotent; only a greater fire can quell this one. At that very moment, according to one telling, the image of Jacob, his father, appears to him, and behind Jacob, his father, Isaac, and behind him, Abraham of old, he who had long before cried, "Hineni! Behold, O Lord, I am ready to obey your command, even to the sacrifice of my son!" At that instant Joseph's conscience was flooded with the parental warnings against the abominations of the Canaanite women who were to be avoided though it meant traversing desolate deserts. "Thou shalt not!" was the image Joseph saw.

But in the struggle with passion there is no final victory, only skirmishes along the way, temporary armistices: territory, once conquered, must be conquered again, and again. Joseph, some say, returned to the bedchamber of his mistress a second time. Now all seemed lost, beyond his feeble will or even the help of ghostly parents. Only one could redeem him, and so it was, say the sages. The Lord Himself appeared to Joseph clasping the very foundation stone of the world, the stone upon which the world was established and which was later embedded in the Holy of Holies. Holding it before Joseph, God warned: "If you touch her, I will shatter this stone and with it destroy the world." That is why Jacob, in his final blessing, describes Joseph as *the shepherd, the rock of Israel* (49:24), for it was "through the miracle of resisting Potiphar's wife, that Joseph the shepherd was transformed into the rock of Israel." His power to resist turned hard as stone.[28]

THIS SECOND TIME, THE APPEAL IS DIRECTLY FROM God. But here too Rachel's presence is recognized. For, it is said, the foundation stone of the world had engraved upon it the symbol of mother Rachel![29] She who appeared to Joseph when he was first about to succumb—"He saw the image of his mother Rachel, and it was this which cooled his ardor"[30]—now joins God to deliver her son.

Why Rachel? Because her mastery of desire was even greater than was Jacob's. The seven years' delay in marrying, which Laban imposed, was suffered by Rachel no less than by Jacob. Indeed, during that time they were able to give each other support and look forward beyond the years of waiting to a lifetime of joyous union. Quite different was the terrible challenge that confronted her in her solitude when, on the very day the marriage was to be fulfilled, her father substituted Leah as Jacob's wife. At the time of the deception, Rachel had no way of knowing that later she too would become a wife of Jacob. Whether she would be given to Jacob's brother, Esau, she could not know; at the very least she would lose her beloved Jacob forever. Nevertheless, she subdued her desire for Jacob in silent acquiescence rather than put her sister to shame. In view of the restraint she exhibited, it is understandable why in later times some sages said it was the image of Rachel, not Jacob, that appeared to Joseph when he was about to sin with Potiphar's wife, and why the foundation stone of the world, with which God was said to have confronted Joseph the second time, symbolized Rachel.

"It was by virtue of her power of sexual restraint that Rachel merited that her sons would be known as 'Joseph the Zaddik,' and 'Benjamin the Zaddik,' for, as the Zohar teaches, the title 'Zaddik' is only given to one who masters his sexual impulse."[31]

The full significance of Rachel's silent acquiescence for her sister's sake as a moral force in Joseph's life is the subject of a seventeenth-century Polish scholar's commentary:

What is the meaning of the astonishing midrash: "The people Israel were delivered from Egypt . . . by virtue of the merit of Rachel's relinquishing her marital rights to her sister Leah?"[32]

Let me begin by citing another perplexing midrash: "Joseph told his brothers: You were silent as to the true reason for my disappearance and lied to my father, saying that *an evil beast had devoured him* (37:33). From the fate to which your silence condemned me, I was delivered by the merit of my mother's silence."[33]

How did Rachel's "silence" deliver Joseph? I shall explain.

The *evil beast* that was to have *devoured him* [Joseph] was none other than Potiphar's wife. It was from her that Joseph would be delivered by "the merit of his mother's silence." [For she was silent about the deception Laban perpetrated upon her and even] gave her sister the "signs" by which Jacob would think Leah to be Rachel. For when Joseph was about to give way to temptation, "The image of his mother appeared to him and cooled his ardor." He was able to contain himself, just as she governed herself the night of her wedding. So Joseph was correct when he said that it was his mother's silence that saved him from being devoured by that wild beast, Potiphar's wife. For it was by virtue of the merit of his mother's silence that he saw her image which cooled his ardor and delivered him from that sin.

The above explication enables us to understand the midrash, that the people Israel were delivered from Egypt by virtue of Rachel's relinquishing her marital rights to her sister. Seeing the example of sexual restraint which handsome and powerful Joseph displayed encouraged other Hebrews to stand aloof from the prevailing sexual licentiousness in Egypt. Had this not been the case, the people would surely have been swallowed up among the Egyptians, heaven forbid, and there would have been none to redeem them. Therefore, the midrash correctly says that Israel was redeemed from Egypt because of Rachel's self-discipline, for it was this which enabled Joseph to behold her image and resist, and it was this which encouraged the Israelites to erect a wall against sexual licentiousness, so that they would not disappear among the Egyptians but persist to be redeemed.[34]

Rachel is here affirmed as the centerpiece of the liberation from Egypt. The moral role of Rachel and Joseph recounted by sages of later times was meant as much to speak to the contemporary sexual morality of the Jews amidst pagan, Hellenistic, and Roman surroundings as to explain the biblical narrative. Can we, however, find support for such a grandiose claim for the matriarch and her son? One might argue that though Rachel died when Joseph was young, he could have heard the oft-recounted story of his mother's silent acquiescence in the substitution of Leah on her wedding night; he could, too, have been moved by considering the wondrous self-control this required, especially in view of her love for Jacob and her many years of waiting for him. In that moment of confrontation with Potiphar's wife, who was not less marked by desire than was Rachel for Jacob on her wedding day, the subconscious awareness of Rachel's virtue was said to appear as a vision to Joseph at the very moment of impending disaster, "cooling his ardor"; when he returned a second time, he was said to have imagined that Rachel's restraint acted as the very foundation stone of the world, which would be shattered were he not to follow her example. And if he, the most worldly of all the Israelites and a prince of Egypt, could resist the temptations of the land, then other Israelites, who held him as their heroic model, might do no less. Since, our author argues, it was the enticement of immorality that threatened to sweep the Israelite slaves into the mainstream of Egyptian civilization, restraint meant survival. "Because Joseph hedged himself about against unchastity, all Israel were able to be hedged about." Survival meant readiness for redemption from Egypt, and redemption meant the revelation at Sinai. If the tradition that "Israel was taken out of Egypt by virtue of the purity of their women" is correct, then Rachel must stand at their head.[35]

That the survival of humanity depends upon sexual morality is the argument. This should not surprise students of the ancient Near East, especially of the lands of Egypt and Canaan with which the people Israel were intimately familiar, and which Scripture identifies as lands of sexual "abomination" whose practices, the Bible admonishes, must be rooted out whatever the cost and however long the battle.

In the battle against sexual license, it is Rachel's descendants who are depicted among the chief warriors. Because they are portrayed as the standardbearers of morality, we are told, it is to them that the birthright passes rather than to Jacob's firstborn. Commenting on the passage, *And when the time approached for Israel to die, he summoned his son Joseph* (47:22), the Zohar makes it quite clear that it is because of Joseph's sexual restraint that he merited the birthright: "Joseph is called Jacob's son *par excellence*, because when Potiphar's wife tempted him, he lifted up his eyes and saw the image of his father, and he thereupon resisted and withdrew. Hence it was that when Jacob came to bless his sons he said: *I know, my son, I know* (48:19), as much as to say, 'I know of the time when you proved with your own body that you were my son.'"[36] It is this restraint, the Zohar also records, that wins for Ephraim and Manasseh the blessing that Jacob bestows upon them.[37]

Rachel's other son, Benjamin, and Joseph's younger son, Ephraim, who later inherits the birthright, are both cited by tradition for their sexual morality, although this is not explicit in the biblical text. From an examination of census figures the rabbis conclude that the families of five of the ten sons of Benjamin died in Egypt because they were not worthy of their destined role, but the remaining members were of such moral strength that they were relatively unaffected during the Exodus by the disaster at Shittim when Balak, king of Moab, having failed to destroy Israel through military or magical means, attempted to seduce them into destroying themselves through sexual immorality.[38]

> While Israel stayed at Shittim, the people profaned themselves by whoring with the Moabite women, who invited them to worship their god. Thus Israel attached itself to Baal-Peor, and the Lord was incensed with Israel (Num 25:1-3).

The midrash elaborates: "At the bazaars huts were built for harlots. Old women sat at the doors to drum up business for the girls inside, enticing passers-by to enter by offering discounted merchandise. Once within, after some sweet talk, the Israelite would be encouraged to drink sufficient wine, until Satan burned within him and led him astray. As it is written, 'harlots and wine capture the heart' (Hos 4:1)."[39] This midrashic embellishment of the disaster at Baal Peor, however, scarcely adds to the raw biblical telling of the tale, in which Pinhas, zealously attempting to halt the mortal plague God had brought to punish the people for their sins, takes up a spear and with a single thrust pierces both the Hebrew man and the Midianite woman locked in embrace. While the plague brought death to many Israelites for the sin of Baal Peor, the rabbis claim that the tribe of Benjamin did not transgress and suffered little damage.

The virtue of Ephraim, who received the birthright from Joseph, and who would be the ancestor of the "Messiah from the line of Joseph" (believed to be the forerunner of the true Messiah of the line of David), is likewise affirmed. According to the sages, the city of Shechem, associated with the rape of Jacob's only daughter, Dinah, was allotted to the family of Joseph during Israel's conquest of Canaan and became part of the territory of Ephraim: "Because, said Rabbi Simon, [Joseph] spent [his] manhood between two 'Shechems' [Pharaoh and Potiphar, who were wicked like

Shechem, the ravisher of Dinah], yet [he] did not do their evil deeds. Rabbi Pinhas said, because immorality broke out in Shechem and [Joseph] repaired it. Therefore let Shechem be in his territory."[40] As we have already learned, the evil eye of lust could have no power over Ephraim, who was of the seed of Joseph.

Not only must the Israelites conquer the land, they must conquer the culture as well. Physical triumph was to be paralleled by moral triumph. Even the army might not succumb to the ways of the pagans, looting and raping. "Who is strong? He who controls his desire," counsel the rabbis.[41] In the conquest of the land, military success is intimately bound up with moral integrity, defeat is ascribed to transgression, and victory to rectitude. The occasions of defeat are imputed by Scripture to the Israelites' having veered from the path of God, every man doing what was right in his own eyes (Deut 12:8). Physical victory only brought new challenges: though the land might be vanquished, the "ways" of the land might yet vanquish the vanquishers, as, later, Rome would conquer Greece, only to be conquered by Hellenism. That Israel not suffer spiritual defeat was the constant concern of the prophets.

Joseph, the leader of all Egypt, is, like Moses, tested in the crucible of a corrupt land and found worthy of transmitting the covenant to the descendants of the twelve tribes. In him they saw one who moved among Gentiles on the highest levels without forgetting who he was or the nature of his task, one who resisted the forbidden ways of Egypt. Not only did he obey his father's request to be buried in Hebron, but Joseph insisted that he too be buried in the distant, humble land of his fathers instead of in the grand manner required by his Egyptian station. Fittingly, it is Moses, his successor, who performs for him the service Joseph had performed for Jacob, his father: "Now the Israelites went up armed out of the land of Egypt. And Moses took with them the bones of Joseph" (Exod 13:19).

Of the four qualities of Joseph—virtue, vision, wisdom, and compassion, each of which contributed to the greatness of the man—it was virtue that tradition highlighted as paramount. "Joseph went down to Egypt, and because he hedged himself about against unchastity, all Israel were able to be hedged about." For "the act of hedging themselves about against unchastity was in itself sufficiently meritorious to procure redemption for Israel."[42] And so, the Talmud asserts:

> When the sensuous come before the Heavenly Tribunal for judgment and are about to be condemned for abandoning the Torah, they could defend themselves by claiming that they were overcome by their beauty and led astray by the power of their passions. To which the court would reply: "And were you more beautiful than Joseph, who was subjected to every form of seduction by Potiphar's wife, and yet did not sin?"[43]

Chapter 9

Joseph and Jacob

AFTER A LONG INTERVAL, THE FATE OF THE BROTHERS is once again intertwined with that of Joseph, who, having been appointed Egypt's chief minister for his services to Pharaoh, is now at the highest point of his career. Reacting to the pressure of famine in Canaan, Jacob sends his sons to Egypt, where, under Joseph's wise governance, food is plentiful. Believing Rachel's eldest son to be dead, Jacob refuses to allow Benjamin to make this trip. Thus *Joseph's ten brothers went to buy corn in Egypt. But Benjamin, Joseph's brother, Jacob sent not with his brothers; for he said, "lest mischief befall him"* (42:4).

Joseph recognizes the brothers, but they do not recognize him. How could they? It is a Joseph very different from the conceited stripling they sold into slavery thirteen years earlier. Steeled by adversity, tested in Potiphar's house, he now stands before them as the viceroy of the most powerful king on earth. At such a time, with those who had persecuted him entirely at his mercy, the temptation to revenge must have been strong. Who could have blamed Joseph if he had thrown all his brothers in jail or even had them put to death? Instead, he accuses them of spying, imprisons Simeon, and informs them that they may return only if they bring with them Jacob's youngest son, Benjamin, as evidence that the account they offer of themselves is a true one. Under the persistent strain of mounting circumstances, the brothers reveal what must have weighed on their consciences all these years and confess to their crime against Joseph:

> *And they said one to another: We are verily guilty concerning our brother, in that we saw the anguish of his soul when he besought us, and we would not hear; therefore is this distress come upon us. And Reuben answered them saying, did I not speak to you, saying, do not sin against the child. . . . And they knew not that Joseph understood them; for he spoke unto them by an interpreter (vv. 21, 22).*

This confession of the brothers not only opens the way toward Joseph's forgiveness; it also acts to reconcile the brothers to the special role of Rachel and her two sons. The brothers return to Jacob and explain that Simeon is now being held in jail against their return with Benjamin. Jacob's refusal to send Benjamin speaks eloquently of the special value he places on Rachel's son. His refusal of Reuben's pledge of his own children as surety for the safe return of Benjamin makes it clear that no other child or grandchildren could replace the one remaining son of Rachel. Speaking to the brothers about Benjamin, Jacob does not refer to him by name, but simply as *my son,* as if he did not possess ten others:

> *My son shall not go down with you, for his brother is dead and he alone is left. If harm befalls him on the journey, you will bring down my grey hairs in sorrow to the grave (v. 38).*

The story presses inexorably onward, as hope after hope is removed for Jacob. With the death of Rachel, the brothers

Joseph and Benjamin were left. With the disappearance of Joseph, Benjamin remained. Now Simeon's life requires that Benjamin be taken on the long and dangerous trip to Egypt. What purpose this agony upon agony? Jacob has mourned for Rachel; must he mourn for her children as well? Perhaps we are being told that the transference of the covenant from generation to generation is not dependent alone upon human ventures—other forces are at work. This is one of the readings of the story that must have occurred to later generations of Jews who knew the hopelessness of despair and the frailty of mortal effort. Though Jacob did not know it then, the handing down would surely take place and the birthright would be preserved, even enhanced.

Jacob's refusal gradually gives way to compelling realities. The famine is hard. With each passing day, food reserves diminish, until, at last, he has no choice but to send the brothers once again down into Egypt. They repeat what they had told him before, and what he must have hoped had been forgotten or was somehow no longer the case—that they could not go without Benjamin. *Why did you tell them you had another brother?* Jacob complains. They respond: *Could we know that he would say, "Bring your brother down"?* (43:7). Bowing to the inevitable, Jacob has them take a *double-portion of gifts,* calculated to appease the inscrutable Egyptian potentate and guarantee a safe return. *Take also your brother, and arise, go again to the man* (v. 13). They descend into Egypt as bidden.

The meeting of the brothers and Joseph is one of the supreme moments in the biblical epic: when Joseph saw his brothers, he could not restrain himself but *entered into his chamber and wept there* (v. 30). For the brothers it is an anxious occasion. Brought to the viceroy's home, they are wined and dined for no reason they can surmise. They are also astonished to find themselves placed at table in order of age. But all apparently goes as planned: Simeon is released, and all eleven set off for Canaan laden with food.

Before they have traveled far, however, they are overtaken by Joseph's steward, sent by Joseph to retrieve the silver goblet he had ordered the steward to conceal in Benjamin's sack. The steward challenges them, and the brothers, confident of their innocence, themselves prescribe the death of the brother found to have the cup in his possession. The goblet is revealed. Despairing at the apparent loss of Benjamin, which their father had most feared, the brothers return to Egypt to face Joseph.

MUCH OF THE DRAMA HERE RESTS IN THE OPAQUENESS of the plot. What does Joseph have in mind for his brothers? Is he merely toying with them or actually setting them up so that he may punish them for their treatment of him? Or does he intend only to bring them to full knowledge of their guilt in their treatment of him, with his ultimate intent benevolence and grace? Perhaps all of these were in Joseph's mind during the charade, but because the reader cannot be sure of the outcome, the final reconciliation is all the more moving.

Judah, who had sworn to return Benjamin safe to his father, steps forward to plead before Joseph in a moving address. In this climax of the story, Judah rehearses the events from Joseph's insistence that they not bring Benjamin down to Egypt. His account reveals an understanding of the special relation between Jacob and Rachel's children, which he clearly did not have when he made his callous recommendation to the brothers that they sell Joseph to the Ishmaelites. He also makes it clear that he cannot face the prospect of returning without Benjamin:

> *Now if I come to your servant my father and the boy is not with us—since his own life is so bound up with his— when he sees that the boy is not with us, he will die, and your servants will send the white head of your servant our father down to Sheol in grief* (44:30-31).

He closes by offering himself as a slave in place of Benjamin:

For how can I go back to my father unless the boy is with me? Let me not be a witness to the woe that would overtake my father[1] (44:34).

Joseph can now control himself no longer, and he sends everyone but his brothers out that he may reveal himself to them.

Joseph said to his brothers, "I am Joseph. Is my father still well? . . . Do not be distressed . . . that you sold me hither; it was to save life that God sent me ahead of you. . . . So, it was not you who sent me here, but God; and he has made me a father to Pharaoh, lord of all his household, and ruler over the whole land of Egypt . . . (44:18—45:8).

Joseph's forgiveness is not offered lightly and could not be, considering the immensity of the hurt done to him. It is granted only after a long and painful catharsis. We are reminded of the steadily increasing pressure that Moses applies to Pharaoh through the plagues before the Exodus. Joseph tests his brothers with fear, threats, and hard choices; he pushes them to the very brink of disaster only to wring from them in the end a confession of guilt and love—in short, to break their hearts, for, as the Hasidic saying has it, "There is nothing so whole as a broken heart."

We see the conspiracy that Joseph created to snare his brothers, and we can ponder his motives, mixed most probably. But what enabled him to choose the noblest of them? Ancient holders of power were not renowned for their hesitation in wielding a vindictive sword, even against their own families. Joseph rises above self-interest, because he believes that his "I" is informed by a greater "I," that of God. The egos of self-centered people are the focus of all things; people of faith, however, know that they are but spokes in the wheel of life—God is the center. The former are consumed by a concern for self from which the latter's attachment to the divine frees them. The former worship themselves, the latter, God. Joseph, aware of being part of a divine plan to deliver the people from famine, is able to keep his feelings for revenge under control, allowing the forces of consolation and forgiveness to prevail. The brothers, acting out of selfish motives, had been diverted from slaying Joseph only by the accident of a passing caravan. Joseph, with heaven's guidance, succeeds in overcoming the impulse to violence, much as earlier when tempted by Potiphar's wife he was able to "cool his ardor," because the image of his parent suddenly appeared before him:

And now, do not be troubled, nor let it be disturbing in your eyes that you have sold me into this place, for God sent me before you in order to preserve life (45:5).

Revenge is a matter of moral discord, a conflict of the heart more than of the mind. How oppose such an elemental compulsion? Feeble are the forces of the mind pitted against the passion of the heart. The only way to dampen the flame of impulse, as with the wife of Potiphar, is with a greater fire. The elaborate plot Joseph manufactures for his brothers is the product of his mind, to be sure, but faith in God's providence is an affair of the heart. And it is Joseph's faith in that providence, his vision that his brothers' actions had their place in a scheme of things larger than they know, that enable his compassion for them to prevail in the end. That compassion reveals him as a true son of Rachel, whose loftiest virtue this was, first for her sister, Leah, and later for the exiles on their way to Babylon.

JOSEPH'S DEVOTION TO HIS MOTHER, WHO WAITED through years of servitude for Jacob and then through more years of painful barrenness for Joseph only to die in his youth, is spelled out in a midrash. Legend has it that, a captive on the way down to Egypt, Joseph passed by Ephrat, Rachel's burial place. Upon seeing the grave, he ran to the spot, flung himself upon it, and cried out:

"O mother, mother who bore me, arise and behold how your son has been sold into slavery with none to take pity upon him. Arise from your sleep, O mother, and behold the cruelty of my brothers who tore me from my father and sold me into slavery. . . . Arise, O mother, awaken from your sleep and comfort my father whose spirit ever broods over me." So Joseph lamented at the grave of his mother, until, spent, he lay there sobbing, immovable. Suddenly, from deep within the earth was heard a tearful voice: "Joseph, my son, my son Joseph. I heard your cry; I saw your tears; I felt your grief. My son, trust in the Lord and wait upon him. Do not fear, for the Lord is with you, and he will deliver you from all evil. Go down to Egypt, my son. Fear not, for the Lord is with you, O my son."[2]

Joseph instructs his brothers to return to Canaan and tell Jacob that his son lives and to instruct him to come down into Egypt with all his family.

They went up from Egypt and came to their father Jacob in the land of Canaan. And they told him, Joseph is still alive; yes, he is ruler over the whole land of Egypt. His heart went numb, for he did not believe them. But when they recounted all that Joseph had said to them, and when he saw the wagons that Joseph had sent to transport him, the spirit of their father Jacob revived. "Enough!" said Israel. "My son Joseph is still alive! I must go and see him before I die" (45:25-28).

Perhaps the most startling thing about Jacob's response is that the revelation that Joseph is still alive does not turn

Jacob's thoughts from the contemplation of death that has been his constant companion since Rachel's demise. Even the living Joseph could not erase Jacob's mourning for Rachel. To be sure, he rejoices over Joseph's success; in his heart, however, must have lurked the thought, If Rachel could only have lived to see this day!

But why, one wonders, did Joseph refrain so long from informing his father that he was alive? Perhaps he was fearful of the grief that the disclosure of the brothers' treachery would have caused. Certainly the news had a strong effect on Jacob, whose *heart went numb*. The midrash goes to great lengths in explaining the care that was taken to find a way to inform Jacob that Joseph still lived. One sage points out that it was only *when he saw the wagons which Joseph sent* (45:27) that Jacob was convinced the report of the brothers was true; Joseph had burned the original wagons Pharaoh had prepared, out of concern lest the idols engraved upon them might offend. Playing on the similarity between the Hebrew word for wagon (*agalah*) and that for heifer (*eglah*), the midrash suggests that Joseph "told his brothers: 'If he believes you [that I am alive], good; but if not, say to him [in my name]: "When I left you, were we not studying the chapter about the heifer (*eglah*)?" Hence it says, *And when he saw the agalot.*'" Only then did Jacob believe that Joseph was still alive. The point of the midrash is not simply to confirm to Jacob that Joseph was living but to testify to the quality of that life, namely, his loyalty, even after many years of fortune in a strange and alluring culture, to the Torah of his father. Jacob, at first skeptical of the brothers' report, sees the wagons, understands their message, and cries out, *Enough, my son still lives* (v. 28). This is why Scripture is careful to tell us that they were *the wagons which Joseph [and not Pharaoh] sent*. Jacob is thus assured, the rabbis are saying, that the covenant is still intact and the birthright validated.[3]

Another midrash stresses the delicacy necessary to the task. So fragile had Jacob become from the depression brought on by his multiple sorrows—the loss of both Rachel and Joseph and the danger of the loss of Benjamin—that Joseph and his brothers sought for the gentlest way to inform their father that he was still alive. Joseph's last words to his brothers, as he turned back at the Egypt-Canaan border to which point he had accompanied them upon their return, were that they not reveal the matter to Jacob "suddenly." When discussing how to resolve the dilemma, they came upon their niece, Serah, the daughter of their brother Asher, and greeted her. Known for her goodness and wisdom, she approached and kissed them. They understood then that providence had provided the answer in this lovely grandchild and gave her the task of informing Jacob.

How did Serah fulfill it? According to one version, she waited until Jacob was standing at prayer, tranquil of spirit, and whispered the news to him. Before he finished his worship, he saw the laden wagons that Joseph had sent, confirming what she had told him, and accepted the report. A second version tells us that Serah went to her grandfather and began to play her harp, as she was wont to do from time to time to ease his grief. On this occasion, as she played, she uttered these words sweetly and gently, "My uncle Joseph is not dead; he lives; he is the ruler of Egypt." As Jacob heard the astounding news, which she repeated a second and third time, he accepted its truth, joy filled his heart, and the divine Presence rested upon him. "My child," he said to her, "continue your song. For as you have revived my life, so may your life be eternal." And it is told that Serah was one of the handful who entered paradise alive.[4]

Jacob descends to Egypt with all his family, stopping at Beersheba to worship *the God of his father Isaac,* where the Lord appears to him once again in a vision of the night:

"Jacob! Jacob!"
"I am here," he answered,
And he said, "I am God, the God of your fathers. Fear not to go down to Egypt, for I will make you there into a great

nation. I myself will go down with you to Egypt, and I myself will also bring you back; and Joseph's hand shall close your eyes" (46:2-4).

When Jacob arrives, Joseph comes out from the city to meet him: *He embraced him and wept on his neck a good while. Then Israel said to Joseph, "Now I can die, having seen for myself that you are still alive"* (vv. 29, 30).

BUT JACOB DOES NOT DIE. GOD GIVES HIM SEVENTEEN years of life during which he lives in grand style, surrounded by his large family of children and grandchildren, his every need provided for. All of Egypt honors him; Pharaoh himself seeks the patriarch's blessing. This was surely more than he could have anticipated for his old age, and we may imagine that he would have rested in sweet satisfaction at the crowning rewards he reaps in these last years of life, savoring present successes rather than bemoaning past tragedies. But if this is so, there is no evidence of it in the Bible, which hastens through these years with hardly a mention, as if they had never been. The Bible focuses instead upon the patriarch's approaching death, and in these last moments his thoughts are clouded with memories of Rachel.

At the news that Jacob is dying, Joseph brings his two sons (reminiscent of Rachel's two sons) to his father's bed for a final blessing. Jacob sits up and recounts the past, telling Joseph that God appeared to him in Canaan and blessed him with the blessing of the land and the blessing of children. Then he says a surprising thing to Joseph:

Now, your two sons . . . Ephraim and Manasseh, shall be mine no less than Reuben and Simeon (48:5).

Jacob fulfills the implication of this remark in his declaration *I give you one portion more than your brothers* (48:21), invoking the law of the birthright that calls for a double portion of the inheritance (Deut 21:16-18). This act is the consequence of Reuben's intercourse with Bilhah, Rachel's handmaid, for "When he defiled his father's bed, his birthright was given to the sons of Joseph" (1 Chron 5:1). The two sons of Joseph were thereby raised to the status of tribal heads, representing the double portion that the new owner of the birthright, Joseph, receives. The grandsons of Rachel would thus inherit the land as equals with the sons of Leah and the handmaids. Replacing the tribe of Joseph will henceforth be the two tribes of Joseph's sons, Ephraim and Manasseh. The status of Joseph himself is consequently altered for he is being raised from the rank of tribal head, equal with the rest of his brothers, to the status of *father* of tribal heads, a position comparable to Jacob's. We might even infer that Jacob means to give Joseph a rank equal to his own so that Joseph could take his place in the semblance of a fourth patriarch.

There is a further special significance relating to Rachel in Jacob's elevation of Ephraim and Manasseh. For in doing so, Jacob implies that the blessing of fruitfulness that God gave to him (35:11) means fruitfulness principally through Rachel. By elevating the children of Joseph to the level of his own children, Jacob, in effect, enlarged Rachel's progeny from two to four, seeking thereby to recompense his barren Rachel who bore only in hardship and then in death.

Having requited Rachel for her years of waiting and her brief period of childbearing by granting her a third and fourth child, Jacob now fixes his mind upon Rachel herself and wanders into a last reverie. He recalls their relationship—his long-unrequited love for her, their brief marriage, the two sons she bore, and her tragic death—and he says:

When I came from Paddan, Rachel, to my sorrow, died in

the land of Canaan on the way, when there was still some distance to Ephrat; and I buried her there on the way to Ephrat, which is Bethlehem (48:7).

The Hebrew reads *alai—Rachel died "unto me"*—by which the rabbis understand, "I above all miss her, for I had no delight other than through her"; his suffering from the death of Rachel was unceasing.[5]

Emerging from his reverie, he becomes conscious of Joseph and the two boys whom only a moment ago he had raised into heads of tribes. *Noticing Joseph's sons, Israel asked, "Who are these?" And Joseph said to his father, "They are my sons, whom God has given me here"* (vv. 8-9). Some commentators are confused by the interruption in the narrative. Gerhard von Rad, for example, observes that "The reference to Rachel's death has no recognizable relation to what follows or precedes."[6] The passage is indeed an interruption but a necessary and integral one. The best proof is Jacob's confusion as to who his grandsons are. How could Jacob not have recognized them? It is the reference to Rachel's death that explains how Jacob could have forgotten about the beloved grandchildren whom he had just been discussing. In compensating Rachel at last for her failure to mother many children by increasing her sons' inheritance, Jacob's thoughts had wandered far away, away from Egypt and Joseph, into the most private world of memory and sorrow, longing and loneliness, a world into which he slipped more and more often in his waning years, a world often his only companion, despite his being among his large family in Goshen. His mind at that moment was with his beloved Rachel. Recovering from his reverie, still in that in-between stage of semi-awareness when we are not sure of even familiar surroundings, he looks at the sons of Joseph, whom he has just adopted as his own and who are surely familiar to him, and for a moment does not recognize them. In that intense instant of yearning to be with

Rachel, weak and dim of sight, he fails to make out his own grandsons. *Who are these?* Jacob asks.

Though he mentions Rachel by name only fleetingly in these final moments so carefully recorded in Scripture, and then apparently only as an aside, it is not until we appreciate his consuming concern for Rachel that we fully grasp what transpires at his departure. Quite apart from this specific reference, tributes to Rachel abound in this final meeting. Both the granting of Ephraim and Manasseh equal inheritance with Joseph's brothers and the blessing they receive are direct homage to Rachel, their grandmother. Only if we are blind to the fact that the entire episode is filled with allusions to Rachel can we say that Jacob's reference to her death is out of place here.

An altogether different issue is raised by the rabbis concerning Jacob's question, *Who are these?* Joseph ruled as the viceroy of a land where, presumably, there were few if any Hebrews before the arrival of his family. Who then was the wife of Joseph and who, indeed, are these children? Are they Israelites at all? Two responses are found in the midrash. According to one, Jacob, concerned with the birthright, wanted to be sure of the boys' legal status. For consistent with a later law, the child follows the faith of the mother and not the father. "Are these your legal children?" he was asking Joseph. Did you marry according to the laws of *kiddushin* (the Jewish marriage laws)? Did you give your wife a *ketubah* (marriage contract)? Another midrash, however, presents a contrary view. Not only is there no insistence on legal requirements, which came into effect only many centuries later with the receiving of the Torah, but the midrash goes out of its way to accept these children born to an Egyptian woman and raised in a foreign culture. According to this tradition, Jacob puts Joseph's mind to rest in regard to the legitimacy of the children. "I know that you are afraid that I may reject your children, because you married an Egyptian woman. Know, then, that I will not reject them. On the contrary, I will befriend them and love them even more. For I shall raise them to the rank of my own children." It is tempting to see in these divergent attitudes the later talmudic divisions between the house of Hillel and the house of Shammai, or, still later, the divisions between the Hasidim and their opponents.[7]

When Jacob is told that the boys are the sons of Joseph and, therefore, the grandchildren of Rachel, he asks that they be brought close that he may bless them, much as he, Isaac's younger son, had received the principal blessing from his father. The blessing that Jacob sought from Isaac, that went back to Abraham and came from heaven itself— that is the blessing that old Jacob, dim of sight as was Isaac before him, will give to Joseph's sons. While embracing and kissing them, the old man turns to Joseph:

> *I never expected to see you again, and here God has let me see your children as well. Joseph then removed them from his knees, and bowed low with his face to the ground. Joseph took the two of them, Ephraim with the right hand—to Israel's left—and Manasseh with the left hand—to Israel's right—and brought them close to him. But Israel stretched out his right hand and laid it on Ephraim's head—thus crossing his hands—although Manasseh was the first-born* (48:11, 12-14).

Though Joseph presents them so that the younger will be on Jacob's left and the elder on his right, Jacob crosses his hands; and when Joseph reminds him to place his right hand on the head of the firstborn, Jacob replies, *I know, my son, I know. He too shall become a people, and he too shall be great. Yet his younger brother shall be greater than he* (48:19). Jacob does here what had been done before him, following character rather than birth, or, within the larger context of Israel's struggle with paganism, ethics rather than nature. It is a consistent pattern: Abraham chooses Isaac over Ishmael, Isaac chooses Jacob over Esau, and Jacob chooses Joseph over Reuben. In each case the law of primogeniture is violated: character outranks seniority, morality supersedes birth. As we have noted, biological inheritance must give way to the perpetuation of the covenant.

Why Ephraim, the younger son, was deemed more worthy than Manasseh, the Bible does not make clear, though it does record that Ephraim was the most powerful of the tribes of the Northern Kingdom, the kingdom of Israel (that is, the kingdom of Jacob). The sages tell us that whereas Manasseh, marked by worldly wisdom, was Joseph's interpreter in the court, Ephraim sat at his grandfather Jacob's feet for all the years they were in Egypt and learned Torah. The divine Spirit was said to have guided Jacob's hands in the blessing, so that the right one, the sign of the birthright, would rest upon Ephraim. The midrash remarks:

> With this crown was Ephraim crowned by Jacob our father at the time when he departed to his eternal abode: "Ephraim, head of the tribes, chief of the academy, the most excellent of my children will be called after your name. . . ."[8]

Among these are Joshua, Deborah, Barak, Samuel, Jereboam, David, and Messiah son of Joseph, that is, of the tribe of Joseph, or, to be more precise, the tribe of Ephraim. Who was Messiah son of Joseph? He was to die in the struggle against God's enemies to make way for Messiah son of David who would himself be called Ephraim![9]

And Jacob blessed Joseph, saying,

> *"The God in whose ways my fathers Abraham and Isaac walked, the God who has been my shepherd from my birth to this day—the Angel who has redeemed me from all harm—bless the boys. In them may my name be recalled,*

and the names of my fathers Abraham and Isaac. . . ." So
he blessed them that day, saying, "Your names will be
used when they pronounce a blessing in Israel, saying,
God make you like Ephraim and Manasseh," thus setting
Ephraim before Manasseh. Then Israel said to Joseph, "I
am dying. God will be with you and will bring you back
to the land of your fathers" (48:11-16, 20-22).

RACHEL IS VINDICATED, HER SONS ARE INCREASED,
the birthright is preserved, first with Joseph and then with
Ephraim. But in these words of the patriarch we move
beyond children and grandchildren into the centuries ahead
and into the many lands where this people will wander.
What we touch here is not the division of inheritance, the
traditional content of birthright blessings, but something
highly personal, intimate, a blessing in the spirit of mother
Rachel who, after all, was not a conqueror of the land but
a consoler, a source not of power but of compassion. It is a
blessing different from the blessings of the other patriarchs
to their sons in that it provides a model of blessing for all
parents forever afterward. Jacob, standing between the line
of individual fathers and the twelve tribes who represent
the people Israel, now establishes a transmission of blessing
through his grandsons that will stand for future ages. The
blessing of Ephraim and Manasseh is the very blessing that
will be given millennially by parents to their sons on Sabbath
and holiday, when they place their hands upon their children's heads, as the patriarch did, and say, "God make you
as Ephraim and Manasseh." And for daughters there is the
parallel blessing, "God make you as Sarah, Rebecca, Rachel,
and Leah." (Notice that the name Rachel precedes Leah.)
Contained in the parents' blessing of their sons is not only
the blessing of Jacob-Israel, the blessing of Isaac, and the
blessing of Abraham, but the blessing of Rachel too, for
Ephraim and Manasseh were her grandchildren and not

Leah's. Thus her barrenness is requited still again, on the grandest scale but in the most personal manner, through the generations.

This too is a triumph for Rachel.

> *And Jacob called to his sons. . . . Assemble yourselves . . .*
> *and hearken to Israel your father* (49:1-2).

The story of Joseph draws to a close at almost the same point as the death of his father. After Jacob concludes his meeting with Joseph and his sons, in which the blessing is bestowed, the elevation of Rachel's grandchildren into tribal leaders is accomplished, and the burial of the patriarch in the sepulcher of Abraham and Isaac in Hebron is promised, a full gathering of all the sons is convened in which Jacob-Israel, the last of the patriarchs, takes his last leave.

In this final farewell we find no lofty dreams, no fine platitudes, but rather the blunt truth from one who loves his sons but knows them too well. The old patriarch does not mince words; there is little sentimentality in these final remarks. Each son is addressed individually, his character boldly etched. He wants them to know themselves, their failings and prospects, the better to conquer the one and nourish the other in the trying days ahead. For though they have caused him much grief, these sons are destined to be the heads of the tribes of the people Israel, the frail human carriers of God's covenant.

Reuben is described as *unstable as water* because of his conduct with Bilhah; Simeon's and Levi's vengeance upon the men of Shechem for abusing Dinah is *cursed*, for they *slay men* and *maim oxen; from Judah*, the sire of kings, *the scepter will not depart;* Zebulun will work the sea and Issachar the land; Dan and Gad will defend their portions; Asher will have abundance, Naphtali grace, and Benjamin ferocity.

Joseph alone receives the bounty. *Joseph is a fruitful vine . . . the elect among his brothers; the God of your father helps you and Shaddai blesses you . . . with the blessings of heavens above and the deep below, with blessings of breast and womb. . . . The mighty one of Jacob, the shepherd, the rock of Israel will succor you* (vv. 22-26). The sages are careful to point out that implicit in these high words of praise for the loyal son, the forgiving brother, the incorruptible servant, and the deliverer of Egypt is the patriarch's reminder that all credit goes to Rachel. The *blessings of breast and womb* (v. 25) are understood to refer not to abundant rain, fertile earth, plentiful crops and cattle, but to his mother: "See how greatly Jacob loved Rachel. When he blessed her son, he did so as if Joseph were but an appendage to her, saying, Blessed be the breasts that suckled you and the womb from whence you issued."[10] Jacob gives Joseph a new name, *ben porat—a fruitful vine* (v. 22)—which is taken to mean "son of the most beautiful of women [*hamefoeret, porat*], namely, Rachel."[11]

By contrast to Joseph, the other brothers, even Benjamin, receive a terse mixture of farewells. The rabbis, however, do not permit them to depart from Jacob on such a mixed, cold, even baleful, note, no matter how true it may ring. They insist that such a momentous parting contain, as well, the sounds of hope and faith. According to the sages, the sons, conscious of Jacob's doubts as to their capacity to continue the covenant bequeathed to them, pledge their faithfulness with the words which were to become the Shema, the watchword of their people—*Hear O Israel, the Lord our God, the Lord is one!*

> When our father Jacob [Israel] was about to depart from this world, he gathered his sons together and said,
> "Perhaps when I am removed from this earth, you will abandon your faith and worship another god."
> They replied:
> "*Shema Yisrael, Adonoy Eloheynu, Adonoy Ehad*
> HEAR, O ISRAEL [our father], THE LORD OUR GOD, THE LORD IS ONE.

Even as in your heart there is only one, so in our heart there is only one."

Then the patriarch responded,

"Barukh Shem kevod malkhuto leolam va-ed:

BLESSED BE HIS GLORIOUS KINGDOM FOREVER AND EVER."[12]

Rachel Weeping
Jacob Steinhart

*Chapter 10*_____

Ephraim

CHAPTER 31 OF JEREMIAH IS ONE OF THOSE PASSAGES
of the Bible in which, like the holiness chapter of Leviticus
(19) or the fortieth chapter of Isaiah, we seem to touch the
bedrock of biblical faith. In Jeremiah 31, the character and
meaning of Rachel find classic expression. Not only is the
single scriptural passage for which Rachel is best known
found here; her presence permeates the entire chapter. In
selecting it as the prophetical reading for the second day of
the New Year, Rosh Hashanah, in incorporating parts of it
into the main prayers for both days of that holiday, and in
including several verses from it in the daily evening service,
Jewish tradition has given it considerable prominence.

As Abraham Heschel points out in his masterful work on
the prophets, God is not "wholly-other," unconcerned with
the fate of humankind, nor is alienation from God our
primary state. It is the "divine pathos, the fact of God's
participation in the human predicament, which is the
elemental fact." The essence of prophecy is empathizing
with and giving expression to that divine pathos, having
concern for God's concern. In the face of injustice, "Prophecy is the voice that God has lent to the silent agony, a
voice to the plundered poor, to the profaned riches of the
world. . . . God is raging in the prophet's words."[1] Jere-

149

miah, who lived during that watershed of biblical history
that included the destruction of the temple and the exile to
Babylonia in 587/586 B.C.E., was the mightiest voice in the
land, condemning the people's transgressions and calling
upon them to repent that the impending calamity might be
averted. The destruction that followed, he claimed, was the
consequence of their refusal. God raged in Jeremiah's words:

> O land, land, land; hear the word of the Lord! . . . Will
> you steal, murder, commit adultery, swear falsely, and
> offer to Baal, and come and stand before me in this
> House? . . . How can I pardon you? Your children have
> forsaken me, have sworn by those who are no gods.
> When I fed them to the full, they committed adultery and
> trooped to the houses of harlots. They were well-fed
> stallions, each neighing for his neighbor's wife. Shall I
> not punish them for these things, says the Lord? Shall
> I not avenge myself on a nation such as this? . . . They
> judge not with justice the cause of the fatherless. . . .
> They do not defend the rights of the needy. Shall I not
> punish them for these things, says the Lord? Shall I
> not avenge myself on a nation such as this? . . . Behold
> the storm of the Lord! Wrath has gone forth, a whirling
> tempest which will burst upon the head of the wicked.
> The anger of the Lord will not be turned back. . . . Hear,
> O women, the word of the Lord . . . and teach your
> daughters wailing. . . . For death has climbed through
> our windows, has entered our fortresses, to cut off babes
> from the streets, young men from the squares. . . . The
> carcasses of men shall lie like dung upon the fields, like
> sheaves behind the reaper, with none to pick them up
> (22:29; 7:9-12; 5:7-9, 28-29; 9:8-9; 23:19-20; 9:19-21).

The same Jeremiah, who denounces the crimes of the
people and predicts their punishment with such ferocity
that the baleful record of Jerusalem's destruction, Lamenta-

tions, was ascribed to him, is capable of the most moving sympathy:

> How can I bear my sorrow? I am sick at heart. Hark, the cry of my people from a distant land. . . . Harvest is past, summer is over, and we are not saved. I am wounded at the sight of my people's wound. I go like a mourner, overcome with horror. Is there no balm in Gilead, no physician there? . . . Would that my head were all water, my eyes a fountain of tears, that I might weep day and night for my people's dead (8:18—9:1)!

Thus the prophet of doom and destruction before the catastrophe becomes the people's source of solace afterward. Although the preponderance of the prophet's message is in the former category, chapters 30 to 33 are so special an exception that they have been called the "Book of Consolation." Chapter 31 is the centerpiece of this hopeful mood, and central to it is the symbol of Rachel, lamenting the exile of her people and receiving the divine promise of return to their land. It is because her plea evokes the divine response that it is read in the synagogue on New Year, when the people Israel pray in the hope of such a response:

> Thus said the Lord:
> Hark, a cry is heard in Ramah,
> Lamentation and bitter weeping,
> Rachel weeping for her children.
> She refuses to be comforted for her children,
> Because they are gone (v. 15).

This image of Rachel, and the scene at the well, are perhaps the most memorable of her in Jewish history. The contrast between the two is startling. No longer the young shepherdess for whom Israel-Jacob must lift the stone off the well, but the protector of all Israel; no longer the brimming bride-to-be of amorous Jacob, but the ghost of one long dead risen from the grave; no longer the barren wife, but the matriarch of an entire people, then and forever after. If Jacob cried at Joseph's bloodstained death-cloak and refused to be comforted for a single child, Rachel grieved inconsolably for all the children of Israel.[2] The Zohar tells us that Rachel wept not merely for those who went into exile then; she weeps each time Israel suffers banishment. As Israel's mother, she laments so long as the anguish of the exile persists.[3]

Why do the Bible and the later literature deal so movingly with the tears Rachel sheds for her people, but ignore the tears of Leah? Surely Leah, the mother of six tribes, had many more to weep over! Was it because Leah, fearful of being married to Esau, cried only for herself? Or because of her harsh way with her children, which one sage suggested was the reason for her being entombed in the cave of Machpelah, whereas Rachel, who died so young, so unfulfilled yet so selfless, was buried along the open roadside where she could rise up and weep for the exiles as they passed?

There were two reasons for the prophet's choice of Rachel as his model: because she was a mother, and because she was a special mother. A mother, during long months of carrying, bearing, and nursing her child, establishes a bond of which no father is capable. I shall never forget the distraught wailing of the mother at the grave of an eighteen-year-old war hero. In the face of such a loss, no consolation would ease the mother's pain. It is this pain of the inconsolable mother that has the power to move God's pity. But Rachel is a special mother. Sarah and Rebecca were barren and bemoaned their fate, but only Rachel named a firstborn "Yosef"—*May the Lord add another son to me* (Gen 30:24)—and only Rachel died in the flower of life, giving birth to her second child. It is the total selflessness of the grieving mother, the single-minded zeal for her children, that calls forth the divine compassion.

Who could match her advocacy? Rachel's plea is unconditional. She does not ask for a confession of sin, an admission of guilt, an affirmation of change. Hers is the spontaneous cry of a mother for a suffering child, and her weeping, the prophet affirms, is hearkened to on high:[4]

> Thus said the Lord:
> Cease your weeping,
> Shed no more tears;
> There is a reward for your toil.
> They will return from the land of the enemy.
> There is hope for your future.
> Your children will return to their land (Jer 31:16-17).[5]

This picture of Rachel rising from a humble grave on the road to Ephrat, weeping for the exiles on their dreary way, and praying for their return—this image Jeremiah bequeaths us for all time. His was a sure choice and true, confirmed by the love with which the people sealed that image in their soul ever after.[6]

AND NOT ALONE THE PEOPLE ISRAEL. AS A THEME IN world literature, the earlier scene of Rachel at the well is rivaled only by Jeremiah's portrayal of Rachel's compassion for her lost children. When, for example, Albert Camus wants to describe the sadness Jesus might have felt for the "innocents" of Judaea who died for him (Matt 2:16-18), he writes:

> And as for that sadness that can be felt in his every act, wasn't it the incurable melancholy of a man who heard night after night the voice of Rachel weeping for her children and refusing all comfort? The lamentation would

rend the night, Rachel would call her children who had been killed for him, and he was still alive![7]

And Dante Alighieri:

Lucia, the enemy of all cruelty,
  arose and came to where I was
  seated by the ancient Rachel.
She said, "Beatrice, true praise of God,
  why do you not help him . . . ?
Do you not hear the pity of his cries?"[8]

Perhaps the most powerful use of the Jeremiah passage in English literature appears in *Moby Dick,* a work drenched in biblical symbolism and considered by some the noblest product of American fiction. Why Herman Melville gives the name *Rachel* to a whaling ship becomes clear later in the book, when her captain boards the *Pequod* and pleads for help in searching for his lost sailors, among them his own son, only to be ordered from the ship by the austere Ahab. The whalers part and proceed on their separate ways, the *Rachel* lurching and heaving on the heavy seas:

By her still halting course and winding, woeful way, you plainly saw that this ship that so wept with spray, still remained without comfort. She was Rachel, weeping for her children, because they were not.

Having recounted the sinking of the *Pequod* in the final chapter, the epilogue concludes by describing how Ishmael, the sole survivor and teller of the tale, is miraculously saved:

So, floating on the margin of the ensuing scene, and in full sight of it, when the half-spent suction of the sunk ship reached me, I was then, but slowly, drawn towards the closing vortex. . . . Till . . . the coffin life-buoy shot lengthwise from the sea, fell over, and floated by my side. Buoyed up by that coffin, for almost one whole day and night, I floated on a soft and dirge-like main. The unharming sharks, they glided by as if with padlocks on their mouths; the savage sea-hawks sailed with sheathed beaks. On the second day, a sail drew near, nearer, and picked me up at last. It was the devious-cruising *Rachel,* that in her retracing search after her missing children, only found another orphan.[9]

Where did Jeremiah get the moving vision of Rachel rising from her grave? It is not found in Genesis, which tells only that she died in childbirth and was buried on the road to Ephrat. Did the prophet draw upon the legendary ante-cedents of the later midrash, which explained that Jacob buried her beside the road to Ephrat because the exiles would pass there and she would rise up to weep for them? Or did Jeremiah himself create the picture of weeping Rachel that gave rise to the midrash? Although the midrash was compiled almost one thousand years after Jeremiah, the oral tradition could have gone back much earlier, to about a century and a half, let us say, before Jeremiah, when the destruction of the Northern Kingdom of Israel (commonly called Ephraim) and the first exile occurred. For if the oral tradition interpreted and expanded the legal parts of the Torah in accordance with changing conditions, why not the narrative parts as well?[10] In our present state of knowledge, it is impossible to be certain which came first. But in view of the references to it in Scripture, we can assume that legends about the grave sprang up from earli-est times. Consider Jacob's retelling of the death and burial just before his own death (48:7); the unusual concluding words that are added in the description of the stone Jacob sets at Rachel's grave: *It is the pillar at Rachel's grave "to this day"* (35:20); and the mention of the grave some centuries later in Samuel (1 Sam 10:2). Now, centuries after Rachel's death, Jeremiah gives it a dramatic meaning that has become its classic expression and has itself given rise to a whole literature of legend over the centuries.

Among ancient and modern peoples, great personalities or symbolic moments are memorialized in monuments whose grandeur evokes the towering spirit of their subject. Not so Judaism. Rachel's grave, marked by a pillar, received no very considerable adornment until the tomb erected by Moses Montefiore in the middle of the last century, and this, impressive in its way, would have drawn little attention in Rome. What would Michelangelo have done with such a project? The sculptor who fashioned the monumental image of the youthful David that stunned the world might have been moved by the vision of grieving Rachel to erect a colossus bestriding the road to Ephrat, a pyramid, or a ziggurat, any one of which could have been seen, and marveled at, by travelers for miles around in that barren country, as a graphic reminder of the compassion of Rachel, the mother of all Israel.

From its very origins when Abraham broke the idols of his father, Judaism has been iconoclastic. Jews did not create statues, but feared the ways and powers of the idolatrous cults. The God of Israel was infinite spirit, not to be captured by an image regardless of its magnificence lest the symbol supplant the symbolized. "I am the Lord your God. . . . You shall have no other gods besides me. You shall not make a graven image" (Exod 20:2-4). Nor could human beings, who breathed the spirit of God, be frozen in stone. The greater the person, the stricter the prohibition. Thus the resting place of the noblest of the Israelites, Moses, went unmarked, lest such preeminence be worshiped as divine.

At a time when the three-dimensional image was the primary artistic vehicle of religious expression, such an attitude no doubt inhibited Israel's artistic development. The level of material civilization was higher among the Assyrians, the Egyptians, even the Canaanites, and to build the temple in Jerusalem, it was necessary to import artisans from Phoenicia. Beauty, whether natural or fashioned by humans, was admired but never "idolized" by the Israelites. The prophets did not hesitate to denounce the most dazzling splendor if it was built at the cost of human decency; thus Amos cursed the showy ivory palaces of Samaria. The second commandment, far from being a disparagement of the aesthetic dimension, was quite the reverse: art's very splendor made it a threat to religion.

The ancient Hebrews were, nevertheless, sublime masters of art, but art of a different sort—the art of words. Instead of sculpting a statue, the psalmist sang a lyric, the prophet recorded a vision, the narrator told a story. For words spoke to will and will spoke to deed as no image could. This was the genius of the people Israel—to transform what they heard from on high and from within into words. So too with Jeremiah. To capture the mighty vision of Rachel, the prophet set down a line or two.

Such art lacks the statue's awesome shape and substance, its line and strength. By the same token, however, it is free of the stone's restraints and open to the expanse of human understanding and imagination. The statue is located in a fixed place; the word is portable, accompanying us wherever we may wander. Although the statue suffers the travail of time, the word soars aloft in our consciousness, requiring little baggage with which to travel, handed over from teacher to student, studied, reflected upon, repeated, and embellished. As from a hammer on the rock, sparks from those words kindled new words, and they in their turn set the consciousness aflame. The supreme "word" of Israel is the Bible, but it is not the final word. "There is," as Abraham Heschel reminds us, "no final word."

JEREMIAH'S VISION OF RACHEL BECOMES THE centerpiece for an unforgettable fantasy of the later rabbis, found in the midrash to Lamentations, which tradition ascribed to Jeremiah. In that midrash, God, grieving over the destruction of the temple and the exile of the people, calls the chronicler of the destruction, Jeremiah, to bring Moses and the patriarchs from their graves to bewail:

> The angels, with Jeremiah at their head, join the Lord to view the destruction of the Temple. Upon seeing the ruins, the Holy One, blessed be he, wept and said, "Woe is me for my house! My children, where are you? My priests, where are you? My beloved, where are you? I am like one whose only son died under the wedding canopy I prepared for him. Jeremiah, feel you no anguish for me or my children? Go, summon Abraham, Isaac, Jacob, and Moses from their graves, for they know how to weep."
>
> "But I know not where Moses is buried, O master of the world," answered Jeremiah.
>
> "Go and stand by the bank of the Jordan," said the Lord, "and cry out, 'Son of Amram, son of Amram, arise and behold thy sheep which the enemy has devoured.'"
>
> Then Jeremiah went to the cave of Machpelah and said to the patriarchs: "Arise, for the time has come when the Lord requires you."
>
> "For what purpose?" they asked.
>
> "I know not," he answered. For he was afraid lest they accuse him: "How has such a thing happened to our children in your lifetime?!"
>
> Then Jeremiah went to the bank of the Jordan and called: "Son of Amram, son of Amram, arise, the time has come when the Lord requires you."
>
> "For what purpose?"
>
> "I know not," he answered.
>
> Then Moses put the same question to the angels whom he remembered from the time of the giving of the Torah.
>
> They said, "Son of Amram, know you not that the Temple is destroyed and Israel gone into exile?"

He shrieked and went wailing to the patriarchs, who rent their garments, held their heads and, weeping, arrived at the gates of the Temple. When the Holy One, blessed be he, saw them, "In that day did the Lord, the God of hosts, call to weeping and to lamentation" (Isa 22:12). Sobbing, they moved from one gate to another like a man whose dead is lying before him, and the Holy One, blessed be he, lamented, saying, "Woe to the king who succeeded in his youth, but failed in his old age!"

Abraham came weeping before the Holy One, blessed be he, plucking his beard, tearing the hair of his head, striking his face, rending his garments, with ashes upon his head, and traversed the Temple, bemoaning and bewailing. Abraham approached the Lord:

"Why have you exiled my children and delivered them to heathen nations who have slaughtered them and destroyed the Temple, the place where I offered my son Isaac as a burnt-offering before you?"

"Because your children have transgressed the Torah," replied the Lord. "Sovereign of the universe," said Abraham, "when I was a hundred years old, you gave me a son, and when he was a young man, you ordered me to offer him as a sacrifice. I steeled my heart against him; I had no compassion; I myself bound him. Will you not remember this on my behalf and have mercy on my children?"

Then Isaac spoke:

"Lord of the world, I did not protest but willingly let myself be bound on the altar and even stretched out my neck beneath the knife. Will you not remember this on my behalf and have mercy on my children?"

Then Jacob said:

"Lord of the world, did I not give twenty years of my life in servitude to Laban? And when I left, did I not risk my life to save my children from Esau? Now the children of my children, for whom I sacrificed greatly, are delivered into the hands of their enemies like sheep to the slaughter. Will you not remember this on my behalf and have mercy upon my children?"

Moses thereupon called upon Jeremiah to take him to the exiles that he might return them to their land. They traveled on roads strewn with dead bodies and finally arrived at the rivers of Babylon. The exiles rejoiced, "The son of Amram approaches from his grave to redeem us from our adversaries." But a heavenly voice declared, "It is my decree that they remain in captivity." At which Moses informed them that they could not return for the present but that the All-Present would redeem them soon. Whereupon they raised their voices until their cry ascended above, as it is written, "By the waters of Babylon, there we sat down, and we wept" (Ps 137:1).

"What did the enemy do to our children?" the patriarchs asked Moses when he returned. "Some they killed," he answered; "Others were fettered in chains; others were stripped naked; others died on the way, their carcasses left as prey for birds and animals." At this recitation, they broke into weeping: "Woe for what has befallen our children! How have they become like homeless orphans!" Moses spoke further: "O Lord, You have written in your Torah, 'Whether it be a cow or ewe, you shall not kill it and its young both in one day' (Lev 22:28); but have they not slaughtered many, many mothers and sons, and you are silent!"

Then our mother Rachel stood up before the Lord and spoke: "You know that Jacob, your servant, loved me with a special love, and that he served my father because of me for seven years. But when the seven years were over and the time of my wedding was at hand, my father determined to give him my sister in my place. I suffered unbearable torment. For I had been aware of his plan, had informed Jacob of it and had given him signs by which he could distinguish me from my sister and, thereby, frustrate my father's scheme. But the pity I felt for my sister, and my desire not to put her to shame, brought me to regret what I had done, and gave me the strength to control my longing for Jacob. So that evening when my sister was substituted for me, I confided to her the secret signs I had given Jacob. Further, I hid myself under their nuptial bed and spoke to him in her place, responding to his every word, so that he might not recognize my sister's voice.

"And if I who am but flesh and blood was not jealous of my rival, and did not shame her, but acted toward her with love, why should you, Eternal King, loving and merciful one, be jealous of idols which are as naught, and deliver your children into exile and let them be slain by the sword and suffer their enemies to inflict upon them inhuman suffering?"

So was the compassion of the Lord stirred, and he said: "For thy sake, Rachel, will I restore Israel to their land."

A cry is heard in Ramah,
Wailing and bitter weeping,
Rachel weeping for her children
She refuses to be comforted,
Because they are gone.
Thus said the Lord,
"Refrain your voice from weeping,
And your eyes from tears,
For your work shall be rewarded
And they shall return again from the land of the enemy.
There is hope for your future;
Your children will return to their country" (Jer 31: 15-17).[11]

What was not wrought by the patriarchs, who established the nation, nor by the prophet, who declaimed the divine word, nor by Moses himself, who led the people from Egypt to Sinai and then to the Promised Land, is achieved by a young mother, Rachel. The appeals of the others are rejected. But from Rachel's silent selflessness on Leah's behalf in the biblical story, she emerges in apocalyptic legend as the deliverer of her people.

GOD'S PROMISE TO FORGIVE THE PEOPLE AND return them to their land is spelled out in the remainder of Jeremiah 31, in which the unspoken presence of Rachel is everywhere felt. One of the keys to understanding this passage is the usage of Ephraim:

> Is not *Ephraim* a precious child to me?
> I am a father to Israel, *Ephraim* is my first-born.
> I [the Lord] listened; *Ephraim* was rocking with remorse (vv. 20, 8, 18).

To whom does the name *Ephraim* refer here? Because the Northern Kingdom of Israel was also called Ephraim after the most powerful of its tribes, the suffering of Ephraim could refer to the Assyrian defeat and exile of this kingdom. The date, however, was 722 B.C.E., a full century and more before the time of Jeremiah. It seems more likely that the original referent of the tribe, Ephraim, extended to encompass the Northern Kingdom, was expanded further by the prophet to include the people Israel in its defeated entirety: the tribes of the Northern Kingdom taken captive earlier, but particularly those of the Southern Kingdom (Judah), which fell in 587 B.C.E. and whose inhabitants were taken to captivity in Babylonia. It is this later conquest that is the subject of the book of Jeremiah, and it is in this larger sense, referring to all of Israel, that Jeremiah uses the name Ephraim here, as he does in verse 9, "For I am a father to Israel, Ephraim is my first-born."[12] To follow the development of the usage of the name Ephraim, then, is to trace a line of continuous expansion through much of biblical history: son of Joseph and grandson of Rachel; tribal head; most powerful tribe of the Northern Kingdom; the Northern Kingdom itself; the entire people. To this name, as we shall see, the later rabbis add a crowning, apocalyptic meaning.

The eminence of Rachel that continues through Joseph to Ephraim is summarized by the midrash that, cited earlier (pp. 1, 105), is here given in its entirety and warrants clarification.

Rabbi Shimon ben Yohai said:

"Everything depended upon Rachel. Therefore, her descendants are called by her name, as it is written, 'Rachel weeping for her children'" (Jer 31:15).

"And not only by her name, but by the name of her son, as it is written, 'Perhaps the Lord God of hosts will be gracious to the remnant of Joseph'" (Amos 5:15);

"And not only by her son's name, but by the name of her grandson, as it is written, 'Is not Ephraim my precious child?'" (Jer 31:20).[13]

The opening words, "Everything depended upon Rachel" allude to the events of Jacob's life—his departure for Haran, his indenture to Laban, even his marriage to Leah—all of which revolve around his beloved Rachel. She becomes the mistress (*ikarah*) of the household, the mother not only of her own children, Joseph and Benjamin, but of Jacob's entire family and of their lineage. For when the prophet speaks of "Rachel weeping for her children," he refers to all the descendants of Jacob who have been exiled. Rachel is their mother by virtue of that boundless grief and limitless love, which move heaven to promise their return. When Jeremiah utters these words, Rachel had been dead for a thousand years, during which time, but surely later, the midrash suggests, she takes on the likeness of the spirit of the people itself: they "are called by her name." It is Rachel, the mother of all Israel, who weeps for the exiles.

As Rachel's name embraces her descendants, so does that of her son Joseph. For he too was their protector, their savior in a strange land, the prototype of Jewish leadership for future ages; his name deserved to be associated with the people. So when Amos speaks of the "remnant of Joseph" (5:15), it is to "the house of Israel" that he refers (vv. 1, 3, 4).[14]

Finally, the spirit of Rachel lives on in her grandson Ephraim, the subject of this chapter, for the people are called by his name as well. When Jeremiah says "Is not Ephraim my precious child?" it is the people of Israel that he intends. And the children of that people are reminded again and again that they too are precious children of the Lord, when, on each holy day, with family gathered about the festive table, they hear the words of the parental blessing bestowed upon them: "May you be as Ephraim. . . ." "May you be as Rachel. . . ." As "Joseph" the people are cued to their protector in the distant land of the pharaohs, and as "Ephraim" the disheartened exiles are succored by the promise given their grandmother. Both Joseph and Ephraim are of the seed of Rachel.

Much can be said about the eminence of the tribe Ephraim in biblical history. The sons of Leah, Judah and Levi, will later provide the monarchy and the priesthood, but they, along with their elder brothers, Reuben and Simeon, play only minor roles in the conquest and apportionment of the land. Reuben, Leah's firstborn, isolated east of the Jordan, was involved in the rebellion against Moses and is rebuked by Deborah for the tribe's failure to share the defense of the land. Neither Simeon, the secondborn, nor Judah is mentioned in the blessing of Moses or in the song of Deborah. Levi receives no territory at all, nor is the tribe's later character suggested during Levi's life.[15] Ephraim, however, is destined for greatness as the chief tribe of the north, just as Benjamin, the other son of Rachel, is a leading tribe in the south, containing within its borders the holy city of Jerusalem and the temple. Geographically, the tribes of

Rachel's child (Benjamin) and grandchildren (Ephraim and Manasseh) border upon one another. On the journey to the Promised Land, these three tribes march together with Ephraim at their lead, as "chief of the Rachelites," carrying the standard for them all.[16] From Ephraim was descended Joshua, successor to Moses and the conqueror of the land, as well as Jeroboam, Saul, Esther, and the Messiah of Joseph's line, herald of the Messiah ben David, who was likewise an Ephraimite. Suitably then, although the flags of the other tribes have emblems of lions, gazelles, and the like, Ephraim's has a human figure—a young woman, (Rachel?) (Num 2:18-20).[17]

Detailing the history of the name and tribe Ephraim does not, however, explain why Jeremiah chooses to use it so often in the thirty-first chapter, rather than "the children of Israel" or "the house of Israel," formulas the prophet uses elsewhere. The reason becomes clear, however, when we take note of something not previously remarked: the employment of Ephraim as an endearing term for the people is *limited* to chapter 31. Of the nine times Ephraim is used in Jeremiah, six are in this chapter. Further, of the three outside this chapter, two uses are geographical— "Mount Ephraim" (4:15; 50:19)—and one is an imprecation: "I will cast you [Judah, the Southern Kingdom] out of my sight as I have cast out all your brethren, the whole seed of Ephraim" (7:15). Thus every loving mention of Ephraim in Jeremiah is found in this thirty-first chapter, where Rachel is the dominant presence.

The prominence of Ephraim in chapter 31 points to the centrality of Rachel in Jewish history. We see that the precedence given to Ephraim—in the list of the generations, in the allotment of territory in the Holy Land, in the places of the camps and their standards on the march across the wilderness, in the dedication of the tabernacle—is linked with the place of Rachel in the tradition.[18]

One further connection between Rachel and Ephraim: A native of the land of Ephraim is called in Hebrew *Efrati,* literally "one who comes from Ephrat." And it was *on the way to Ephrat* that Rachel was buried.

WITH THIS UNDERSTANDING OF THE SIGNIFICANCE of Ephraim, we can return to a closer look at the thirty-first chapter of Jeremiah.

> I [the Lord] listened;
> Ephraim was rocking with remorse:
> "You have trained me to the yoke like an unbroken calf,
> And now I am trained;
> Help me to return, that I may return,
> For You, Lord, are my God.
> Though I broke loose, I have repented;
> After I came to my senses, I beat my breast,
> In shame and remorse,
> For I bear the disgrace of my youth" (vv. 18-19).[19]

The Lord will have mercy upon the exiles and return them to their land, because they have taken their suffering to heart and repented. Repentance precedes forgiveness. The punishment the people suffer is neither easily given nor unreflectingly received. It is purposeful, and the people recognize it as such. For they know that "The Lord reproves whom He loves, as a father the son in whom He delights" (Prov 3:11-12).

Were people judged by the scales of justice, measure for measure, our lives would be short indeed. According to this reckoning, Israel, a "stiff-necked people," did not deserve to survive. When Israel worshiped the golden calf at the scene of the revelation at Sinai, God wanted to destroy them and make for Moses a new chosen people. But wrath passed and compassion prevailed. The divine balance tipped in favor of the sinner. In time of exile Jeremiah pleads not for the judgment of the sovereign but the mercy of the parent:

Is not Ephraim a precious child to me:
For as often as I speak against him,
I do remember him still.
Therefore, my heart yearns for him;
And I must deal with him in boundless compassion
(v. 20).

"Boundless compassion"—words that describe a grieving mother—is the response of the Lord. At the very moment of alienation, Ephraim remains God's "precious child" (*yeled shashuim*). That is why Jeremiah speaks of God's love as eternal, never ending: "I have loved you with an everlasting love" (*ahavat olam*) (v. 3), and that is why these words begin the second blessing of the Jewish evening service—"With everlasting love have I loved you, O house of Israel." Israel—sinful, straying, fretful—must be assured again and again that God's love is eternal, persisting despite transgression within and oppression without, lest the people be tempted to forsake the covenant. The pathos of divine wrath is fleeting, but the pathos of divine mercy is eternal. Indeed, in the very moment of anger, love prevails.[20] The people suffer because they have sinned, but God will forgive them not only because they repent but because God's affection for them is beyond reason and justice, as is a mother's for a cherished child. God's love is from everlasting to everlasting.

MORE THAN GUIDANCE AND FORGIVENESS, GOD'S boundless love for Israel contains within it the secret of the final deliverance. It is not surprising, then, that this passage, so central to the prophetic message and to the Jewish psyche, is cited by the sages to point to that redemption by identifying the savior. Taking the name of Rachel's favored grandson beyond the biblical scope of a single person, an entire tribe, the Northern Kingdom, even beyond that of the

collective nation, one singular and memorable midrash—
whose authenticity is questioned but which fits into our
portrayal of the final victory of Rachel—uses Ephraim to
mark the redeemer!

> The Holy One, blessed be he . . . hid the light of the
> Messiah under his throne until the time of the generation
> in which he will appear.
>
> Satan asked: Master of the universe, for whom is the
> light which is put away under thy throne of glory?
>
> God replied: For him who will put thee to utter shame.
>
> Satan said: Master of universe, show him to me.
>
> God replied: Come and see him. And when he saw
> him, Satan fell upon his face and said: Surely, this is the
> Messiah who will cause me and the princes of the earth
> to be swallowed up in Gehenna. . . .
>
> Then the princes will say: Master of the universe, who
> is this through whose power we are to be swallowed up?
> What is his name?
>
> The Holy One, blessed be he, will reply: He is the
> Messiah, and his name is Ephraim, my true Messiah. . . .
>
> [At the time of Messiah's creation], the Holy One will
> tell him what will befall him [and inquire,] Art thou will-
> ing to endure such things?
>
> The Messiah will say: Master of the universe, with joy
> in my soul and gladness in my heart I take this suffering
> upon myself. . . .
>
> During the ordeal . . . , the Holy One will say: Ephraim,
> my true Messiah, long ago . . . thou didst take this ordeal
> upon thyself. At this moment, thy pain is like my pain.
> [For with the destruction of the temple and the exile of
> my children] I have not been able to sit upon my throne.
>
> At these words, the Messiah will reply. . . : Thy servant
> is content to be like his master. . . .
>
> Then . . . the Holy One, blessed be he, will lift the
> Messiah up to the heaven of heavens, and will cloak him
> in something of the splendor of his own glory as protec-

tion against the nations. . . . He will be told: Ephraim, our true Messiah . . . the nations would long since have destroyed thee had not God's mercies been exceedingly mighty in thy behalf, as is said "Is not Ephraim a precious child to me? . . . My heart yearneth for him. And I must deal with him in boundless compassion."[21]

Behold the road,
The same path on which you went forth!
Return, maiden Israel,
Return to those cities of yours! (21)
How long will you waver,
O wandering daughter?
For the Lord has created something new in the land,
A woman enfolds a man (22).[22]

Writes Bernard Anderson of this passage of Jeremiah:

Feminine language is dominant throughout the poem. The image shifts from Mother Israel . . . to . . . Virgin/ Daughter [maiden]. Portrayed as a Woman, Israel is summoned to return in the double meaning that has now become apparent in the poem: to return in a geographical sense from exile to the homeland along a well-marked highway, and to return in the deeper sense of coming home to the covenant relationship. . . . Whereas Rachel, the Mother of Israel, was formerly deprived of her sons, she will have a posterity . . . and therefore a future in the land promised to Israel's ancestors. . . . The Woman will enfold a man (a son) as a sign of [the Lord's] gracious gift of new life in the land.[23] . . . In a miracle of divine grace, Rachel will receive her son back. The new life in the land, there, will be a gift of God, a new creation. As the Lord had opened the womb to provide a future for man at creation [and as he opened Rachel's womb to provide a future for Israel], so now the people are given new life by being restored to their land and being promised a posterity. . . . The old age, symbolized by Rachel weeping for her lost sons, will be superseded by a new age . . . in which the Woman will be the agent of new . . . hope. . . . [*The symbol of that] Woman is Rachel* [italics mine].[24]

Rachel, so desirous of children that she named her first, "Yoseph"—*May God add another*—but who died at the birth of her second, becomes the grieving matriarch for all the lost children of the people Israel and the guarantor of their return; the creator of this image, Jeremiah, was himself a Benjaminite, the tribe whose ancestress was our matriarch.

The biblical kingdom had divided into two, the northern ten tribes becoming Israel (or Ephraim) and the south named Judah and Benjamin. Israel had been taken captive by Assyria in 722 B.C.E., and here Jeremiah describes the fall of the Southern Kingdom to Babylonia in 587 B.C.E. The land is despoiled and the people taken as slaves into exile. But a future reconciliation will come, Jeremiah promises, between the Northern and Southern Kingdoms and between all of them and God:

I shall become God of all the families of Israel,
And they shall be my people.
The people that escaped from the sword,
Found favor in the wilderness,
When Israel journeyed homeward.
The Lord revealed himself to them as of old.
Yea, I have loved you with an everlasting love.
Therefore will I ever be gracious to you.
Again will I build you, and you shall be built,
O virgin of Israel.
Again shall you take up your timbrels
And go forth to the rhythm of the dancers.
Again you shall plant vineyards
On the hills of Samaria.

For the day is coming when watchmen
Shall proclaim on the heights of Ephraim:
Come let us go up to Zion,
To the Lord our God (vv. 1-6).

Forgiveness and healing characterize the exiles' return: a return to the land that will revive under their care and a return to the oneness of God that will restore the wholeness of the people. For when they are joined to God, the warring Hebrew tribes will unite. The innocent piety of the idealized days of Israel's youth is recalled, when those who survived the "sword" of Egypt followed the Lord through the travail of the wilderness as a faithful bride her beloved. To this bride the Lord declares everlasting love. It is this love that makes possible the rebuilding of the land and the forgiveness of the people, who have strayed from the path and violated the covenantal vow. Again the name of Ephraim occurs.

Behold, I will bring them from the north country,
And gather them from the uttermost parts of the earth,
And with them the blind and the lame,
The women with child and her that travaileth
with child together;
A great company shall they return hither.
They shall come with weeping,
And with kindness will I lead them;
I will lead them to streams of water,
By a level road where they will not stumble.
For I am ever a father to Israel,
Ephraim is my first-born.
I will turn their mourning into joy,
And comfort and cheer them in their grief . . . (vv. 8-13).

Rachel died on the way as she travailed with child, but there will be a time when on that very road "women with child and her that travaileth with child" will return. Those who passed Rachel's grave went weeping, in hunger and chains, but there will be a time when they will return on "a level road . . . by streams of water . . . with shouts of joy. Their captors were brutish and grim, but there will be a time when but God will "lead them back with kindness":[25]

> Behold, the days come, said the Lord, that I will make a new covenant with the house of Israel, and with the house of Judah; not according to the covenant that I made with their fathers in the day that I took them by the hand to bring them out of the land of Egypt; forasmuch as they broke my covenant, so that I rejected them. . . . But this is the covenant that I will make with the house of Israel after these days. . . . I will put my teaching into their inmost being and inscribe it upon their hearts. Then I will be their God, and they shall be my people. . . . These are the words of the Lord, who gave the sun for a light by day and the moon and stars for a light by night, who cleft the sea and its waves roared; the Lord of hosts is his name: If this fixed order could vanish out of my sight . . . then the people of Israel could cease for evermore to be a nation in my sight. . . . If any man could measure the heaven above or fathom the depths of the earth beneath, then could I cast off the whole seed of Israel because of all they have done. This is the very word of the Lord (vv. 31-37).

The victory that God promised Rachel will be proclaimed far and wide. All are to know of the remnant's return and of the miraculous revival of the people and the land as beneficiaries of God's never-ending love. The prophet calls for a new covenant: not a repudiation of the covenant at Sinai, but a recalling and renewal of it—a covenant that will be permanent and not contingent. It is the covenant that Moses had already spoken of, "And the Lord your God will circumcise your heart, and the heart of your seed, to love the Lord your God with all your heart, and with all your soul, that you may live" (Deut 30:6). Israel, punished with exile, repents, and God, whose love for them is as a mother for her children, forgives them. Compassion overcomes justice in the promise of eternal salvation. As everlasting as the laws of nature, so will be the people Israel. It is the final vindication of Rachel and her people, their eternal life in the love of God.

Rachel's Tomb
Herman Struck

Chapter 11

Kever Rachel

THE VICTORY OF RACHEL REACHES BEYOND CLAN AND epoch. It is not limited to the spectacular successes of her son Joseph and Joseph's son Ephraim, who along with his brother, Manasseh, was raised to the rank of leader of one of the twelve tribes of Israel, and who became the most influential of them all. Rachel's eminence moves beyond her immediate descendants, beyond her era and the boundaries of her land. Her prominence in Jewish history and legend as a figure in her own right is unique. Rachel stands alone, unequaled despite her brief life. She endures as no other woman in Scripture. One of the most revealing avenues to this larger, postbiblical Rachel is through the memorable chronicles of her famous grave. What greater vindication could there be for the name given to the Jewish cemetery— *Bet Hayim*, "House of Life"—than the resting place of Rachel? For this cradle of death brimmed with vitality from the moment of her burial.

Tradition refers to her grave simply as *Kever* Rachel. Where is it? How does it differ from other biblical graves? Why was Rachel not buried with the other matriarchs at Hebron, in the cave of Machpelah? For answers to these questions we must once again turn to Jacob's consuming concern with his own burial as he faced approaching death.

Jacob lived seventeen years in the land of Egypt, so that the span of Jacob's life came to one hundred and forty-seven years. And when the time approached for Israel to die, he summoned his son Joseph and said to him, "Promise . . . that you will not bury me in Egypt. But when I sleep with my fathers, carry me up from Egypt and bury me in their burying place." He replied, "I will do as you have spoken." And he said, "Swear to me." And he swore to him. Then Israel bowed at the head of the bed (47: 28-31).

A poignant scene, and apparently a straightforward one: the last of the patriarchs, dying after a long life of travail in the peace of a reunited family, requests that his son bury him in his native land. But if we attend carefully, we shall see that Scripture plunges us with the bare minimum of words into the recesses of Joseph's and Jacob's minds.

Of course Joseph promises to bury his father in Canaan, but his heart is troubled. How can Jacob ask that his body be transported to Hebron from far-distant Egypt when he did not take Rachel's body the short distance to the cave of Machpelah, the ancestral burial place? If Jacob truly loved Joseph's mother and lamented her loss, why did he not give her as honorable a burial as he now demands for himself in the family sepulcher alongside the other matriarchs and the patriarchs? If Jacob favored Rachel over Leah, how explain that he did not show Rachel the same *hesed ve'emet—kindness and truth* (47:29) that he now asks from Joseph, by burying her with the honor she above all women deserved instead of digging her grave in so demeaning a fashion at the very spot where she died? How must Joseph, who had risen to the head of the family as well as the state, have turned these questions over in his mind, weighing their every side?

According to the sages, Jacob feared Joseph might put this very query to him, and this may be the reason why only a few verses later the dying patriarch mumbles, seemingly out of context, almost to himself, but also to Joseph: *When I came from Paddan, Rachel, to my sorrow, died in the land of Canaan on the way, when there was still some distance to Ephrat: and I buried her there on the way to Ephrat, which is Bethlehem* (48:7-9). Reflected in this verse is the brooding memory that must have troubled Jacob during these last days as he contemplated his own burial apart from Rachel, and that he felt must trouble Joseph on hearing his request. He utters what he knew was in Joseph's mind to anticipate any criticism from this noblest of all his sons, the prime vehicle of the covenant.[1]

Modern scholars give the passage short shrift. It seems to interrupt the flow of the narrative, and so they rule it out of place—a later insertion or an incomplete text. Classical Jewish commentators, on the other hand, treat it seriously, some with fascination, seeing in it Jacob's attempt to anticipate the query forming in Joseph's keen mind, perhaps betrayed in his eyes: "Why, then," the sages formulate Joseph's thought, "did he not bury my mother, Rachel, in that same burial place, instead of alone where she died on the wayside near Bethlehem, when Hebron was not far away; or, at the very least, in the city of Bethlehem itself?"[2]

A series of answers to Joseph's implicit question, ranging from the naive to the most profound, are put into Jacob's mouth by the commentators:

- The road was in a state of disrepair;
- Jacob was too burdened by his children and flocks;
- The weather was oppressive;
- A woman's honor requires that she be buried where she dies;
- Two wives, Leah and Rachel, should not be buried together;[3]
- No physicians were present to embalm her: though it was only a twelve-hour journey to Hebron, the size of the large company would delay the trip a number of days. That the company was anyway delayed may be

calculated from the lapse of time between Rachel's death and Jacob's arrival in Hebron to see his father, Isaac;[4]

- Nearby Bethlehem was bypassed for the burial because it would later become part of the territory of the tribe of Judah, Leah's son, whereas the spot where Rachel died would become part of her son Benjamin's territory;[5]

- Grief immobilized Jacob at Rachel's death. His words, *Meytah alai—To me, she died* (48:7), imply "Only I knew the fullness of this sorrow." So stark was his agony that he was simply unable to act. "Jacob was frozen by grief, incapable of taking her even to near-by Bethlehem. From that time on his heart was empty, all desire to beget children having left him, and, indeed, no more were born to him."[6]

Each of these reasons has a measure of appeal, the last perhaps the most. But there is yet another explanation. Jacob, they say, accounted for his action thus:

Joseph, my son, I know that you feel resentment toward me. How can I trouble you to take me for burial into the land of Canaan when I did not seem to take similar trouble for your mother, who was buried where she died by the roadside on the way to Ephrat? Pay no attention to the reasons for my action that you may have heard. For it was not because of broken roads or oppressive weather, the burden of other cares, or the absence of physicians to embalm her. Such obstacles could have been overcome. And what dishonor would it be to move her if, by doing so, she would rest with Sarah and Rebecca and at my side? Nor was I afraid of burying two wives in the same sepulcher. Did I not make my peace and live with them all those years and, for that matter, with two additional servant-wives though my only affection was for Rachel, your mother? And it is surely with her alone that I would have preferred to be interred in Machpelah. True, I was immobilized by the shock of your mother's death, but that too would have passed in the face of the divine requirement (mitzvah) of burial. For surely I wanted your mother, whom I loved more than life itself, put to final rest with all honor due her. Have I not marked her grave in a manner that later generations will not forget?

But the choice was not mine. It was taken from my hands. I buried her there on the road to Ephrat not for any of these reasons or for any other like explanation, but only because it was the dictate of heaven! For there was revealed to me that the day will come when the children of Israel will go off into captivity to Babylon, and as they pass along the road, bound, beaten, ragged, and forlorn, your mother will rise up from her grave to comfort them and pray for their return.[7]

A cry is heard in Ramah, the sound of bitter weeping. Rachel weeping for her children. She refuseth to be comforted, for they are gone. And the Lord replies, Restrain your voice from weeping, and your eyes from shedding tears. For there is reward for your labor. They shall return from the enemy's land. And there is hope for your future (Jer 31:15-16).

This passage from Jeremiah is, as we have seen, remarkable testimony to the living image of Rachel within the Bible some one thousand years after she died. The other matriarchs are scarcely mentioned in later Scripture, Rebecca not at all, Leah once in Ruth 4:11, only in conjunction with and preceded by Rachel, and Sarah, in association with Abraham, in Isa 51:2—"Look back to Abraham your father, and to Sarah who brought you forth." In Jeremiah, however, Rachel is her own person, compared to no other, joined neither to her husband, Jacob, last of the patriarchs, nor to her celebrated son Joseph, deliverer of his generation. She is the compassionate mother of her people, and she appears in a contemporary setting as though she were still invested with life.

Already in the Bible itself the legend of Rachel has taken

shape; she develops from a lovely shepherdess to the merciful mother of an entire people. Though the sins of the people will bring tragedy upon them, it will be a time for solace and not censure. Therefore, Leah was hidden away in the cave of Machpelah, but Rachel, mother of utter compassion, was laid to rest by the open way, destined to comfort the exiles as they pass by on the long, bloodstained trek to Babylon. Her grave became a shrine for all the generations to come, for exile was to become the permanent condition of the people. More than fiery words from the prophets, they would need the gentle balm of mercy and one to plead their cause on high.

It is in this role that the image of Rachel that Jeremiah gives is broadened and embellished in the postbiblical literature, whose dates are often obscure but whose origins certainly go back to much earlier times. Two examples are noteworthy. The Aramaic translation and interpretation of Jeremiah known as *Targum Jonathan*, whose approximate date is the first century, provides the following version of our Jeremiah passage:

> A cry is heard *"in the heights of the world, the house of Israel* is lamenting and moaning. . . ."* Jerusalem* is weeping for her children. She refuseth to be comforted, for they are not (Jer 31:15).

"Ramah" is now no longer a single earthly spot but "the heights of the world," while the personage of Rachel has been allegorized into "the house of Israel" and "Jerusalem."[8] In a later midrash we find a further vision reminiscent of Rachel. There Jeremiah reports that on his return from pursuing the survivors of the destruction of Jerusalem who are being led into exile, "I lifted my eyes and saw at the top of a mountain a woman seated, clothed in black, her hair disheveled, crying and pleading for someone to comfort her. . . . I replied, saying, 'You are not more deserving of comfort than mother Zion, who has been devastated into a pasture for the beasts of the field.' 'Do you not recognize me?' she said. . . . 'I am thy Mother Zion.'"[9]

That the Zohar (3.29b) takes the name of Rachel to allude to the collective soul of the nation—"The spiritual community of Israel (*Keneset Israel*) is called Rachel"—is not surprising. We have already seen that the people in their bodily sense are designated by her name, as are the names of her son Joseph, and her grandson Ephraim. To this list must be added Jacob himself, the father of the twelve tribes, who became Israel and after whom the people were most often called—"the children of Israel," "the house of Israel," "the people of Israel," or just "Israel." Thus, of the very few other biblical persons (Judah, for example) whose statures were such that their names could serve to represent the entire nation, three are focal figures of the trials and victory of Rachel: her husband, son, and grandson. Is it altogether accidental that such identification with the people should be peculiar to each of the central members of three generations of the Rachel clan? In any case, the uniqueness of mother Rachel's concern for the fate of her people is strengthened by the way the Bible was drawn to use the names of her chief family members in so collective a fashion.

The Zohar, however, assigns Rachel a yet larger role. It associates her compassion with the Shechinah herself, the divine Indwelling thought to accompany the people into exile, suffering with them and offering them sympathy. The Talmud had already explained the verse "I shall be with him" (Israel) "in time of trouble" (Ps 91:15), to mean that the Shechinah went into exile with the people and would remain there until the final redemption. The mystics, taking a further step, taught that God is in exile from Himself. God is, of course, one in essence, but in reality only "in that day will he be one and his name one" (Zech 14:9). Thus, the illustrious mystic of Safed, Isaac Luria (1534–1572), introduced the widely observed practice of reciting these words before fulfilling a commandment: "I perform this mitzvah to join the Shechinah with the Holy One, blessed be he." This repeated exercise was meant to fix into the consciousness of the Jew each day the notion that every mitzvah, every good deed, if carried out with the proper intention, could advance the overcoming of cosmic and human disharmony. The movement from harmony to disharmony to harmony once again is axiomatic in Jewish consciousness. In the kabbalah's scheme of primordial unity shattered by the "breaking of the vessels," the overcoming of which through the process of *tikkun* or "mending" was seen to be the focal purpose of Jewish existence, we can recognize the biblical time frame of paradise—history—messianic age.

The era of divine-human harmony is followed by a second era, that of contention between good and evil, followed in its turn by a third blissful epoch in which the original harmony will be restored. So too with the people Israel. Once at home on their land, then exiled from it, they will eventually return. Elohim, the god of justice, who measures them against the plumb line of the absolute and accordingly sends the prophets to rebuke them—"You alone have I singled out from among all the families upon the earth. Therefore will I punish you for all your sins" (Amos 3:2)—is the same Adonai, the lord of mercy, who forsakes not the people in their time of suffering but brings tidings of hope and consolation, as the prophets likewise taught. This comfort is symbolically expressed in the image of the Shechinah proceeding into exile with the children of Israel and suffering with them. The mystics, fascinated by Rachel's image as merciful mother of the people, extended her task as long as the exile would last, associating her with the Shechinah herself. Jeremiah found her weeping for those exiled to Babylon centuries after her burial; the mystics envision her weeping for all the exiles ever after.[10]

The Zohar tells us that "the Shechinah never departed from the tent of Rachel," for Rachel was one of the names of the Shechinah:

To Abraham [the Shechinah] appeared as "Lord" as it is written, *And the Lord appeared to him in the plains of Mamre* (18:1). . . . She is called "Lord" when she rests upon the two cherubim. . . . When she first appeared to Moses, she was called "angel." . . . For she is called "angel" when she is a messenger from on high . . . blessed by the father and mother, who say to her: Daughter, go, attend to thy house: go and feed them, go to the lower world where thy household wait for sustenance from thee. Then she is called "angel." . . . But to Jacob she appeared only under the figure of Rachel, as it is written, *And Rachel came with the sheep.*[11]

One passage that supports the Zohar's account and that exploits the philological resources of Rachel's name, can be found in the *Tana deBe Eliyahu,* a midrash the time of whose composition is uncertain (fifth to ninth centuries C.E.) but which considerably predates the Zohar and the writings of the Safed mystics. It retells the famed legend recounted in Chapter 10 above, but with a different and remarkable ending. We recall that entreaties are made to God by Moses, Jeremiah, and the patriarchs that the exiles be returned from Babylon, all of which are rejected:

It was not the Holy One's intention to restore them to their own place, until Rachel stood up in entreaty before the Holy One, saying to him: Master of the universe, let it be remembered to my credit that I did not mind the wife who was my rival. Nay more! Let it be remembered for my sake that though my husband worked for seven years to wed me, yet when I was about to enter the bridal chamber, my sister Leah took my place. I refrained then from saying anything to Jacob, so that he would not be able to tell my voice from my sister's voice. If I, who am mortal, did not mind the wife who was my rival, will you mind the rival who is no more than an idol? Of such as it,

Scripture declares, "Eyes have they, but they see not; they have ears, but they hear not" (Ps 115:5-6). At once the Holy One's compassion crested like a wave, and he swore to Rachel that he would restore Israel to their place, as it is said, "Thus saith the Lord: A voice is heard in Ramah, lamentation, and bitter weeping, Rachel weeping for her children," etc. (Jer 31:14). Read not Rachel weeping for her children, but *RuaH EL*—the spirit of God—weeping for her children.

In the concluding sentence the Hebrew letters of Rachel, *RHL*, are used to make the words *RuaH EL;* manipulation of the letters of a word for the purpose of teaching a further lesson was a common literary fashion among Hebrew writers. Here it is suggested that Rachel "caused" the spirit of God to weep, or, more precisely, "The spirit of God (thus appealed to by Rachel) joined (her) in weeping for her children." In identifying Rachel with the Shechinah, however, the mystics are careful not to identify the human with the divine, a subject that Jewish writers had to handle with some delicacy. They posit two Rachels: the earthly Rachel, who rose from her grave to lament her suffering children, the people Israel; and the heavenly Rachel, the *Ruab El* or Spirit of God, who responds to the earthly Rachel. It is the tears of the earthly Rachel that rouse her heavenly counterpart.[12]

Over her grave Jacob set a pillar; it is the pillar at Rachel's grave to this day (35:20).[13]

The pillar is located about one mile north of Bethlehem and four miles south of Jerusalem.[14] The persistence of the Rachel pillar is attested to in Genesis itself by the unusual phrase *to this day*, as if to alert the reader to the timeless quality of the grave. Indeed, it is one of the very few burial sites whose prominence is confirmed throughout history, beginning with the Bible itself. Three thousand years ago, the book of Samuel records it as a well-known landmark: "And Samuel said to Saul, when you leave me today, you will find two men near the tomb of Rachel in the territory of Benjamin" (1 Sam 10:2). By the time of the famous passage from Jeremiah, who lived centuries after Samuel, venerable legends about the spot abounded.

A much later account tells of Joseph stopping to pray at his mother's grave on being taken captive to Egypt. The church father Eusebius of Caesarea (ca. 260–ca. 339 C.E.) refers to the grave; a Genizah (fragment) of the tenth century makes the first Jewish postbiblical-rabbinic mention of it; the Jewish traveler Benjamin of Tudela (in Spain) described it in some detail in 1170. It is said that in 1622, when the celebrated thinker Rabbi Isaiah Horovitz (*SHeLaH*) was in the Holy Land, he gained permission to erect walls around the grave site; the stone building over the grave, which the English philanthropist Moses Montefiore built in 1841, still stands and was featured on a stamp issued by the British from 1927 to 1948 when they held the mandate over Palestine. In 1864 *haMaggid,* a European Hebrew journal, carried the report of a Sephardic sage that a well had been dug near the grave of Rachel for the convenience of visitors theretofore compelled to carry their own water for the journey. Most recently, the Yeshiva of the Shelter (*Ohel*) of Our Mother Rachel was established nearby. *Kever* Rachel has never lapsed into a mere "antiquity," despite its ancient origins. Perhaps the words *to this day* were taken by later generations as an admonition to maintain and renew the grave, as has been done from generation to generation. The remarkable three-thousand-year history of the grave suggests that Rachel's selfless compassion for her "children" commanded an enduring response.[15]

What did the grave look like? Tradition is rich in legend. One suggests that each of the sons, except for Benjamin, put a stone on the grave, another, that the entire collection fused miraculously into a single rock. A further legend

185

records: "On the grave of Rachel Jacob set eleven stones for the eleven tribes, for since Benjamin was born only through her death, no stone was set for him. The stones were all of marble. At the top was a stone larger than all the others in memory of Jacob whose name was inscribed upon it. Lifting that stone into position required all the strength of Jacob's men. A mile from them was encamped a group of Bedouins who stole the great stone to use it for the foundation of a building they were erecting. However, when they arose the next day, they found the grave as it had originally been with the great stone in place. They took it again and still again, but each time it was mysteriously returned."[16]

Though visitors were constant throughout the year, the pious would make special visits on the fourteenth day of the month of Heshvan, according to tradition, the day of Rachel's death, and at the beginning of the month of Elul, in preparation for the High Holidays. Some made a point of visiting just before the blowing of the shofar, the ram's horn, on Rosh Hashanah. Pinhas of Koretz, a friend of the Baal Shem Tov, said that were he to visit the land of Israel, he would spend the days at the Western Wall and the evenings at *Kever* Rachel, "for it is good to be found beneath the mother's apron." When the Maid of Ludimir, who developed a following among Hasidim, settled in the Holy Land, it was said that her spirit traveled from Jerusalem to *Kever* Rachel to visit with Israel's mother.[17]

When, after having been proscribed for centuries, Hebrew books began to be printed by Jews in the Holy Land in the nineteenth century, one of the most common illustrations, along with the temple, the Western Wall, and the tomb of the patriarchs and the matriarchs in Hebron, was the grave of Rachel. Pictures of *Kever* Rachel were—and are—used to decorate holy places and holy articles such as wooden handles and mantles for the Torah, windows and walls of synagogues, mezuzah cases, Sukkot decorations, charity boxes, amulets, and memorial lamps, as well as articles for daily use such as maps, rings, pipes, dishes, carpets, paintings, and pictures. Packets of earth taken from near the grave were distributed to all the communities of the exile so that they could be placed in graves under the heads of the deceased. *Kever* Rachel is frequently mentioned in the writings of those who, longing to return to the land of Israel, were reminded by countless tales that Rachel too wept and prayed for their return; on the first day of each New Year chapter 31 of Jeremiah was publicly read in the synagogue.

Over the years, a number of manuals for meditation to be recited at the *Kever* Rachel have been published, as well as a slender volume of passages from the Zohar. The fervor of these prayers makes apparent the preciousness of this spot to the people Israel. All the prayers reflect the longing to return, which burned in the hearts of those scattered through the distant lands of the exile:

> Peace to you mother Rachel, rock from whence we were hewn and pit from which we were digged. Peace to you and to your pure soul which ever laments in the shadow of the most high. Thy loving children send their greetings from all parts of the earth. O how they yearn to be near thy grave and to pour out their tears for your beauty which wastes in the ground. But the roads are too onerous and the oceans too mighty to traverse. Nevertheless, we who come from a distant land have made the trip to humble ourselves upon thy grave in which reposes the body of one as pure as heaven itself. Though we have traveled many roads and crossed many waters on the long trip, our love, as children for their mother, has not been quenched. Just as the mother rejoices when her children come to visit her grave, so do we give praise to God that we have been worthy of this visit, and the tears of our eyes which flow into yours are tears of joy, that we be worthy to visit your grave which has been digged for you in the Holy Land. Happy are you and happy your pure soul, and woe to us who have been exiled from our Holy Land because of our sins, preventing us from visit-

ing you each year and humbling ourselves upon your grave.[18]

Although while this prayer expresses only the desire to visit the resting place of Rachel, such litanies usually include a request, a plea, a call for intercession. What is the history of this custom of pleading for the intercession of the dead? The Talmud seems wary of the power of the grave in the case of Moses and suggests that Scripture tells us that "No one knows his burial place to this day" (Deut 34:5) in order to forestall his being worshiped as a divinity. However, it was permissible, it would seem, to invoke the aid of the saint. To the Talmud's question, "What is the reason for visitation at the graves?" Rabbi Hanina responds: "So that the dead can pray for us."[19] The Zohar explains the custom in its own way, providing a *raison d'être* for those who followed the mystical path:

> The Lord fashioned three locations for the souls of zaddikim [the holy ones]. One is for their *nefesh* [that third part of the soul] which does not depart this world. . . . Those who suffer misfortune and require compassion pray over their graves. The zaddikim then inform the sleepers of Hebron [the patriarchs] who awaken and enter the earthly garden of eden where the *ruah* [a higher part of the soul] of the deceased zaddikim wear their crowns of light. After consultation, a decree is issued. The Holy One accepts it and acts mercifully. The *nefesh* of the deceased zaddikim remains in this world to defend the living.[20]

The *Shulhan Arukh*, the most popular code of Jewish law, refutes the suggestion that this practice constitutes praying to the dead, forbidden in the Bible. It is argued that the souls of the deceased are still alive, and that prayers recited at their graves are made in fact to God, who is the more ready to accept them because they are joined with the prayers of the zaddikim. "For through the zaddik, who shares the suffering of others, God has mercy on them." The practice of visiting the graves of saints, though common among their followers, the Hasidim of eastern Europe from the eighteenth century on, had already reached its height among the mystics of Safed in the sixteenth century, when graves were visited not only to beseech the Lord but to receive divine revelations as well.[21]

TWO MORE PRAYERS EVINCE THE POWER OF RACHEL as a successful pleader with the Almighty when invoked in times of trouble:

> O MOTHER, MOTHER, go quickly before the throne of glory of our Father in Heaven and pour out your heart for the helpless children scattered to the four corners of the earth. Know you not, O most beautiful of women, that our honor is of little worth among the nations, that the bitter yoke of exile weighs heavy upon us, and that the blood of your children is poured out as water among the peoples. You who gave us birth, cry out for our fate, for to whom of the saints should we turn if not to you, Rachel, our holy and pure mother. Therefore go quickly and plead our cause, that the Lord break the yoke of the exile from our necks, and gather up the scattered of Israel to Jerusalem the holy city, with blessing and length of days, until Messiah comes, speedily and in our days. Amen.[22]

> PEACE BE TO YOU, O our mother Rachel. May your soul dwell with the Lord and be bound up in the bond of life. Peace be to you and to your resting place!

> "Happy were you in this world and it is well with you in the world to come." In this world, where you walked in the ways of the Lord; and in the world to come, where

you have been called and where you dwell with the holy angels. May the Merciful One revive you that we may behold your face which shines as the brightness of heaven. May your merit protect us and all Israel, that peace be with us.

O King, full of mercy, I come this day to prostrate myself on the grave of Rachel, our mother. Just as you remembered her when she was barren and opened her womb, as it is written *and God remembered Rachel and opened her womb* (30:22), because of the compassion she showed her sister in not revealing her identity and causing her shame when on her wedding night the deceitful Laban substituted Leah for Rachel, so too, by virtue of Rachel's merit, remember us and the whole house of Israel. Accept our prayers and hearken to our supplications. Look upon the desolation of thy city and how we have been made a mockery by the nations who taunt us to despair. How long will thy people suffer in captivity? For our sages have taught us that Jacob did not bring our mother Rachel to Bethlehem but buried her by the roadside that she might comfort the exiles on their way to Babylon, as it is written, "A voice is heard in Ramah, the bitter wailing of Rachel who weeps for her children. She refuseth to be comforted for her children, because they are gone." And you O Lord answered her, as it is written, Thus said the Lord: Cease your weeping, shed no more tears; your toil will be rewarded. They will return from the land of the enemy. There is hope for your future. Your children will return to their land (Jer 31:15-17).

What shall we say and how shall we speak? If, because of the first exile which lasted but seventy years, Rachel stormed the very heights, what of this bitter exile which we have endured these nineteen hundred years, and which is marked by one catastrophe after another, scattering us to the four corners of the earth and bringing upon us unbearable suffering? O mother Rachel, how can you rest in your grave? Awake and rouse up those who sleep in Hebron together with all the other saints. Plead our cause before the Lord in behalf of the remnant of your afflicted people. How long must evil ones exult and your people be turned into a mockery? How long will you fail to take pity upon us, upon your land and upon Jerusalem your city, where strangers tread the holy places? And if it is because of our sins that all this has come upon us, are you not the master of mercy? Will you cast us off forever?

So do we bow before you broken in heart and humbled in spirit, that you recall the merit of our holy patriarchs and matriarchs and the merit of that saintly one, our mother Rachel. Forgive us our sins and help us turn to you. Lengthen our days in well-being in the Holy Land. Remove all obstacles to our study of the holy books and the carrying out of the mitzvot [commandments]. Give us health to serve you day and night. May we be able to earn a livelihood. May the rain fall in its season and our crops be bountiful. May our children find worthy partners. And may we deserve to see the redemption in which the exiles will be gathered. May it come speedily and in our days. Amen. Selah.[23]

These prayers assume that the matriarch possesses a certain power—sometimes called the "merit of Rachel"—which could be called upon in times of trouble. What is being referred to? It is the doctrine of the "merit of the fathers" (*z'khut avot*), a teaching that goes back to the earliest rabbinic writings. The covenant made with the patriarchs because of their righteous deeds protects the children of Israel from annihilation even when they have sinned and secures their future redemption. What is noteworthy here is that the redeeming power of the patriarchs' virtue ("the merit of the fathers") is consigned to a woman, to Rachel. And it is the famous passage, from Jeremiah 31, of Rachel pleading for her people, which the Lord acknowledges and agrees to, that is cited as the evidence of her merit. Thus, the old midrash tells us, when the Lord recognized the needs of the exiled people by allowing them prophets even outside the land of Israel, "He did so only because of the merits of the fathers. For thus it is said: 'A voice is heard in Ramah, lamentation and bitter weeping, Rachel weeping for her children.'"[24] In other words, the rabbis understood Jeremiah to be saying that when Rachel cried to God about her children who were exiled, He promised to return them to their own land, and, consequently, that it was because of Rachel that God spoke to the prophets in the Babylonian Exile, informing them of Israel's return, to ease the despair their suffering had brought. This "merit of Rachel"—examples of which have been discussed above in Chapters 6 and 10 in regard to the prayer for the New Year written by Kalir and the later midrash to Lamentations, where, after the failure of the prophets and patriarchs to intercede for the exiled people, Rachel's plea is heard along with the citation of Jeremiah's words—became the common possession of the people who come as supplicants at her grave to this day.[25]

RACHEL'S GRAVE WAS ALSO A PLACE WHERE WONDERS took place. We are told by the grandson of the zaddik Rabbi Shlomo of Radomsk that his grandfather was struck down in 1864 by an illness that left him at the point of death. The Hasidic masters of the time, among them the rabbi of Zanz, took it upon themselves to pray for Rabbi Shlomo. When he recovered, he made a joyous feast of thanksgiving at which he sang the mystical hymn *El Mistater*—"Oh Hiding God." Soon afterward this letter arrived for Rabbi Shlomo from a friend in Jerusalem, the Hasid Pinhas, son of Hayim of Radom:

Iyar 6, 1864

On the eve of the first day of Iyar, about sixteen of us went to the grave of our mother Rachel. We recited the afternoon and evening service, ate and drank in good fellowship, and rose up at midnight for the prayers of *Hazot* and *Tikkun Rachel*, as is our custom. Suddenly I began to weep so uncontrollably that I fell into a stupor, during which I heard a roaring noise and saw before me Pinhas, the son of Rabbi Meir of Apt. "Know you not," he said, "that Shlomele Radomsker is deathly ill?" Whereupon I broke into such bitter tears that my soul almost departed my body. Seeing this from the other world, my mother, may she rest in peace, came to console me. "Cry not, my child," she said, taking my hand. "The worst has passed, thank God. I shall show you where the holy one from Radomsk sits." I followed her to a small room and, behold, there he was, the Master of Radomsk, may he be blessed with many more years of life, sitting on his chair, his face so aflame with light that I could scarcely look upon him, surrounded by Hasidim, and singing "Who is like unto thee, O Lord?" in a melody that haunts me still. And I was revived.

All this I have seen in my dream.

The unworthy Pinhas, son of Hayim, of Jerusalem, may it be rebuilt soon and in our days.

When Rabbi Shlomo visited Zanz, he took this letter with him and showed it to the holy one of Zanz as evidence of the miracle he had experienced.[26]

Rachel's role as helper in time of trouble extended to wherever there was unrest, injustice, or privation. In her mysterious interference in human affairs as a messenger for good, she bears striking resemblance to Elijah the prophet. Even within the Bible the presence of both goes beyond their death, and both are linked to the final redemption of the people. Malachi tells us that "Elijah will come before the great and terrible day of the Lord" (Mal 3:23); in Jeremiah,

Rachel elicits a divine promise that "There is hope" in the people's "future" and that they "will return from the enemy's land" (Jer 31:16-17). About both Elijah and Rachel tales are told of miraculous acts of kindness for the poor, the suffering, and the forlorn. The midrash goes so far to identify the roles of the prophet and that of the youngest matriarch and to suggest their kinship: "One time the sages sat and inquired from whose seed Elijah came. Some said: From the seed of Rachel. Some said: From the seed of Leah. As they sat discussing the matter, Elijah himself entered and stood before them. 'My masters,' he declared to settle the matter, 'I come from the seed of Rachel!'"[27]

Compared to the tales of Elijah, however, those of Rachel are hardly known and apparently have not as yet been compiled. Here is just one.

The holy master, Mordecai, the Maggid of Tchernobyl (d. 1837), was well known for the mitzvah of *pidyon shevuyim*, that is, of redeeming Jews who were often imprisoned in those days under false or harsh charges, or for blackmail. This activity of his led to controversies with the ruling powers and to his own imprisonment. Though the attempts of his followers to have him released failed, they did gain permission to supply his vital needs such as *talit* (prayer shawl) and tefilin (phylacteries), kosher food, and the like, and even to provide him with funds so that he could continue his regular practice of dispensing charity. Thus those poor, who each Thursday received a donation from him to help them prepare for the coming Sabbath, would continue to receive it through the small window to his cell. In the case of women, modesty required that he leave on the window ledge coins that they would then pick up.

One day a woman he did not recognize approached the window. He was about to put down a coin when she told him that she had not come for money but to ask a *she'elah*, a legal question.

"Ask, my child," he said.

She began by citing a story from the Talmud whereby the

daughter of Rabbi Nehuniah ben Kaneh, who was himself famed for digging wells so that pilgrims could drink from them, fell into a well. Told of the tragedy, Rabbi Nehuniah took no action either the first hour or the second. When it seemed she was near death and the people came to inform him a third time, he replied that there was no need to worry; she was safe and had already emerged from the well. And so it was. Now Rashi, in commenting on this passage, asks how it is possible for the child, whose father performs the good deed of digging wells for the welfare of others, to suffer so. In the same fashion, the woman expressed astonishment that the Maggid of Tchernobyl, son of the famed Rabbi Nahum of Tchernobyl (who had engaged in the mitzvah of redeeming captives as did his son) should be held captive in a prison!

"What shall I say to you," responded the rabbi, "for your question troubles me as well."

Then she herself gave the answer.

"It is the will of heaven that you be held captive and the bitter suffering of imprisonment enter your bones, so that you will understand even more the magnitude of the mitzvah of *pidyon shevuyim*. Now that you have achieved this understanding, you will be released. And I send my blessings to all those who are freed from such captivity."

And she vanished.

While the rabbi was puzzling over the strange incident and trying to grasp what manner of woman would dare to speak so directly to him, the prison warden arrived to order that he be released and taken home. The warden could not explain the reason for the release except that a woman had demanded it of him.

The rabbi of Tchernobyl knew that something more was involved here than a simple release from prison, but he could not fathom what it was. After exhausting human inquiry, he turned in prayer for divine help until at last it was revealed to him.

The woman was none other than our mother Rachel,

who had come with the force of the Talmud to storm heaven for his release.

CARING FOR *KEVER* RACHEL WAS ENTRUSTED ONLY TO the most worthy. There were two caretakers, one representing the Sephardi community (of Middle Eastern descent) and one the Ashkenazi (of European descent). For sixty years the Sephardi caretaker, who died in 1929, was Joshua Burla, father of the novelist Judah Burla. Overlapping some of his term was the Ashkenazi caretaker, Solomon Freiman. He was born in the old city of Jerusalem in 1902, a fifth-generation Jerusalemite, the son of Jacob, the *shamash* or beadle of the ancient Hurvah synagogue and former Ashkenzi caretaker of *Kever* Rachel, to which position his son succeeded. Solomon's period of service spanned the two world wars, the Turkish and British rule, and the 1929 massacre in nearby Hebron, concluding with the rise of the state of Israel.

Solomon Freiman relates that during World War I, a week before General Allenby entered Jerusalem and ended the harsh Turkish reign, a group of kabbalists came to the hospital where Freiman was recovering from an illness and asked for the key to the grave. When he told them that the opening of the gate was a guarded secret, they carried him out of the hospital and toward Rachel's grave through a strong wind and rain, miraculously avoiding or placating the Turkish soldiers they met on the way. "It is difficult to describe," Freiman records, "the self-sacrifice of those kabbalists who walked to that holy place in such a time of danger to pray for the people of Israel and particularly Jerusalem." In the Second World War, when General Erwin Rommel was on the outskirts of Palestine, the leader of the Jerusalem kabbalists brought a group of followers to the grave every Thursday evening to pray through the night.

During the darkest time of the Yom Kippur War of 1973, when it seemed that the sudden Arab attack might overrun

Israel, the venerable head of the Mir Yeshiva, Rabbi Hayim Shmulevitch, made his way to the grave of Rachel late one night, and prayed:

O Lord! You said to Rachel: "Restrain your voice from weeping" (Jer 31:16). But I say: Weep, Mama, weep!

Ribbono shel Olam! Du sogt zu Rachel: Mini koleykh mibekhi. Ober ikh zog, veyn, Mama, veyn!

To maintain the Jewish claim to the grave, Freiman would keep it open whenever possible, though during the time of disturbances he was forced to abandon the Arab bus that served the Jerusalem-Bethlehem route and make his way there by other means. The Arabs too honored the grave and prayed there. Freiman, who spoke Arabic fluently, respected their piety and was on good terms with them. They referred to him as "the honorable Solomon, son of the *shamash*" and may have saved his life by warning him not to return to the grave on the day when the Arab attack commencing the 1948 War of Independence would take place.

A glance at a few additional items found in the simple diary Freiman left, which begins in 1932, is instructive:

1.21.36

Two pilgrims came today, one a Jew, the other a Muslim. The Jew prayed fervently and shed tears over the exile. The Muslim too wept and prayed according to his custom. Both lit candles and went on their way.

8.2.42

A woman came at 4:00 P.M., requesting the key [a good omen for childbirth]. I gave it to her and later visited the hospital where I remained until she gave birth at 10:00 P.M. Both baby and mother were doing well. She wanted to reward me but I would not accept the money.

8.3.42

A Jew come from Tel Aviv requesting the key. I traveled with him for four hours to Tel Aviv. A son was born to him.

2.12.44

[A visitor had left a piece of paper in the early morning near the door while it was still closed.]

"O our mother! The door to your grave was bolted, but not my heart. My yearnings and words will yet reach you. So too may the walls which prevent your pleas from reaching the throne of glory be torn down, that the children may return to their land. Then the clouds will disperse, a new light shine upon Zion, and the name of our Lord will be magnified and sanctified in our days!"

10.16.44

A Jew came requesting the key to Rachel's grave for two women. . . . At six he returned, elated: one had borne a boy, the other twins.

10.22.44

Today I went to the *Vaad Haleumi* [the Jewish government under British rule] and answered questions about the grave.

11.14.44

The grave was open all night commemorating the anniversary of Rachel's death. About fifty people were present: Hasidim, kabbalists, Sephardim, westerners [Ashkenazim], Kurdim, and Bukharim. They wept and prayed for the welfare of the people Israel in exile. . . . They organized groups to pray at other holy graves: that of the matriarchs and patriarchs in Hebron, of Joseph in Nablus, and of Rabbi Simon bar Yohai in Safed. . . . The Bratzlav Hasidim sent a minyan [quorum]. . . . They prayed all night, recited the midnight vigil (*tikkun hatzot*), psalms, *selihot* [penitential prayers], and blew the shofar [ram's horn] until six in the morning.

11.25.44

Busloads of American soldiers and a guide. Among them was a Jew who wanted to light a candle. All day buses with soldiers pass, but only if there is a Jew among them are they allowed to visit.

1.15.45

A black soldier, Joseph son of Moses of Johannesburg, visited the grave of our mother Rachel a second time. Yesterday he came with a group of Christian black soldiers and bought three books of psalms, a mezuzah, and a packet of earth [to be placed in a person's grave, so that the person, wherever buried, is also, as it were, buried in the Holy Land], but did not reveal that he was a Jew. Today he returned alone and wanted to light a candle for a blessing for himself and his family. I gave him a booklet with the ten commandments and a mezuzah as a gift. Tears stood in his eyes as I blessed him with the hope that he might live to see the rebirth of our land together with all the people Israel. . . . He understood many Hebrew words. I had no time to find him a Jewish family to spend the Sabbath with, as he had requested, before he departed Jerusalem.

5.3.45

Four Egyptian Arabs and one woman measured the grave with string for an omen. One recited psalms and other prayers in Arabic.

5.8.45

Germany has been defeated! . . . About seventy Jews . . . sang and danced, praised the Lord for His mercy and asked for deliverance for the people Israel who wait impatiently for the time when "The children will return to their land" (Jer 31).

6.17.45

From six in the morning until five in the evening several hundred Arabs mourned the death of their sheik, whose body was placed in the outer court for several hours where the lamentation was fearful. I have never seen its like.

6.4.46

Bratslav Hasidim were here overnight.

3.5.46

A German Jewess survivor came and prayed. She requested permission to stay the night that she might pray for herself and for the Jews in exile. . . . I locked the grave and told her I would return at 6:30 in the morning. At that time I found her spirits raised, indeed altogether exalted, for she had been able to worship in solitude in this holy place. She told me that she had prayed until 10:15 in the evening, after which she slept until twelve. At 12:15 she rose to recite psalms and other devotions which she knew by heart. With the dawn she said the morning service. At 7:30 she left on foot for Jerusalem.

4.29.46

A child of five cried at the grave: "O mother Rachel, when will you return and halt our tears?"

6.4.46

Survivors [from the Holocaust] who have arrived in the past months pray at the grave of our mother Rachel. Our brothers from the exile pour out their hearts before the mother of the Jewish people. Their prayers and tears are indescribable. They recount the terrible happenings which befell them and with pleas that tear the heart beg the Lord to have mercy on the remnant of Israel.

10.13.46

A group that survived Buchenwald visited the grave of Rachel and lit a candle for the souls of those who had perished in the exile, and blessed those who had survived.

11.7.46

A recent arrival, who had visited a week earlier with a group, returned. Weeping and lamenting, she cried: "Where will the tattered survivors who remain go? There is no place other than the land of Israel. Rachel, Rachel, how long will we be without a land of our own? . . .

Only the land of Israel. Six million have perished. It is enough, enough!"

Freiman died in 1949, after spending eight months in a hospital recovering from an injury incurred during the War of Independence. Under Jordanian rule, *Kever* Rachel was closed to Jews for nineteen years until it was liberated during the Six Day War in 1967, when the chief chaplain opened its gates once again. Since then, it has been available to all.[28]

IN THE REESTABLISHED STATE OF ISRAEL, *KEVER* RACHEL has achieved a new vitality, with thousands of pilgrims from near and far frequenting it yearly. No doubt the destruction wrought by the Holocaust has contributed to its importance. After the devastation wrought by Hitler's hordes in Eastern Europe, which saints' graves could people make pilgrimage to, commune with, and pray over? Scattered sepulchers in Europe escaped the machines of destruction, a very few of which are still marked and some visited: of these, uncared for in the strange absence of a reverent population, most are accessible only with difficulty. The devout longing once expressed at these European graves, and now revived to an extent with the Hasidic upsurge and the fall of the Soviet state, has shifted in some measure to those sages and mystics buried in the Holy Land: Akiba, Maimonides, and Rabbi Nahman of Horodenka at Tiberias, the Ari in Safed, Shimon ben Yohai in Meron, and, of course, the graves of the patriarchs and matriarchs at Hebron. None, however, is visited more frequently or fervently than the tomb of Rachel.

Although both men and women come to the *Kever* Rachel, it is especially popular among women, who find here as in few other places a feeling of sisterhood. One pious woman at the shrine explained that Rachel's deeds

were marvelous: in order to shield her sister from embarrassment when Laban substituted Leah in her stead, she
handed over to her sister the "signs" that would identify her
as Rachel to Jacob. "After all," she explained, "Rachel was
just flesh and blood like us. Yet she was so selfless."[29]

The favored place of women at the tomb is clearly evident. The room in which the tomb is located is separated
into men's and women's sections with separate doors for
each, but the main entrance leads to the women's section.
The men use a side door, and their section is smaller and
barren of furniture. The women's section has couches
and chairs. Here, in addition to fulfilling their religious
needs, women may also relax among friends and sit and
chat for extended periods of time.[30] When they pray, they
face the tomb itself rather than following the normal practice of facing Jerusalem.

There is a pattern that most of the women who visit the
shrine follow. Upon entering the courtyard surrounding
the shrine, they first wash their hands, kiss the mezuzah on
the door, and approach the tomb, which they touch much
as the stones of the Western Wall are touched by the faithful. Then a prayerbook or a book of Psalms is taken for
worship, following which the tomb is often touched again—
when the pilgrim may wish to commune directly with
Rachel—after which the book is kissed and returned. Upon
leaving, the women perform an act of charity by putting
some coins into one or more of the many boxes that represent different needy causes; finally, they again kiss the
mezuzah.

The question "Why do you come to Rachel's tomb?" was
put to a number of women at the grave. Most answered,
"To pray." Some said, "To cry." So common is it to shed
tears there that the Hebrew dictionary cites "to weep at
Rachel's tomb" as idiomatic for the excessive display of
emotion. If today, when public weeping is frowned upon
and people are taught to keep their feelings under control,
it appears bizarre to travel to a place simply to cry, let us

remember that heartfelt emotional expression in worship was once a common sight. Rachel herself is the model. Rachel, whose tears for her exiled children could not be halted and whose weeping was said to have moved heaven itself—"when the gates of prayer are closed," says the Talmud, "the gates of tears remain open"—continues to unlock the tears of Jewish women who visit her grave.

Although the shrine is a special place for women to pour out their hearts, especially prominent are prayers for fertility, for Rachel is the emblem of barrenness overcome. This practice has given rise to a curious custom whereby those who are having difficulty conceiving wear a red string that has first been wrapped around the tomb seven times as a talisman for pregnancy. When a woman is in labor, especially in difficult labor, the great key to the massive lock of the metal-covered door to the inner room is put beneath her head; then, so it is said, the birth will go smoothly. The child born after such procedures is often brought, in thanksgiving, as an infant to Rachel's grave.[31]

TODAY *KEVER* RACHEL PLAYS A UNIQUE ROLE. HERE, amidst a throng of pilgrims and worshipers, Hasidim, Sephardim, yeshiva students, pious women, and travelers from all parts of the world, something of the accumulated folk piety, called forth by people's affection for this most beloved of the matriarchs, is felt. Jacob mourned, Joseph and Ephraim remembered, the Lord responded to Rachel's entreaty. Today, many centuries later, the enormous vitality of *Kever* Rachel's stubborn endurance testifies to the people's everlasting devotion. Rachel lives on in the inner sanctuary of the Jewish heart. Indeed, the special quality of the grave is beginning to rouse interest among modern Jewish women, whose new feminine awareness has sent them searching for appropriate modes of expression and will doubtless lead them into new ways to approach the uniqueness of *Kever* Rachel.

As Rachel's grave has been central to the millennial exile of the Jewish people, so too, according to the Zohar, will her grave be focal to the final redemption, when, at the end of days, as blasted hope will have almost given way to mute despair, Messiah will of a sudden appear at last to engage in the final conquest:

In paradise Messiah will lift up his eyes and behold the patriarchs visiting the ruins of God's sanctuary. He will see mother Rachel with tears upon her face, refusing to be comforted by the Holy One, blessed be he. Then will Messiah raise his voice and weep, the Garden of Eden quake, and the righteous and the saints lament with him.

Pangs of travail will overtake the people Israel, and all nations will rage against her. A pillar of fire, visible to all the nations, will be suspended from heaven to earth for forty days. Then Messiah will descend from the Garden of Eden. And on that day the whole world will be shaken and all the the children of men will seek refuge in caves and rocky places. For it is written, "And they shall go into the holes of the rocks and into the caves of the earth, for fear of the Lord and for the glory of his majesty, when he ariseth to shake terribly the earth" (Isa 2:19). Thereupon Messiah will begin to war against the nations. After forty days, during which the pillar shall have stood between heaven and earth, and Messiah shall have manifested himself, a dazzling multi-colored star will come forth from the East. Seven other stars shall surround it in battle. The one star shall engage the seven with rays of fire flashing on every side, smiting them into darkness. After twelve months of battle, Messiah will be carried up to heaven in that pillar of fire. When he descends, the pillar of fire will again be visible to the eyes of the world, and Messiah will reveal himself.

Then a voice will break forth from paradise: "Rise up, O ye saints and stand ye before the Messiah!" And all the saints from above will arise. Abraham at his right, Isaac at his left, Jacob in front of him, while Moses, the faithful shepherd, will dance at the head of them. The Holy One shall command one of the firmaments, which has been kept in waiting since the six days of creation, to approach. From a certain temple within it, the Holy One shall remove the crown with which he adorned himself when the Israelites crossed the Red Sea: with it will he crown King Messiah. Then he will enter another of the temples and behold there the angels who are called the "mourners of Zion," for they weep without end over the destruction of the holy temple. After thirty days all humankind will witness a blinding light, reaching from the heaven to the earth, and continuing for seven days, during which days the Messiah, surrounded by angels, shall be crowned on earth.

Where shall this be?
On the way to Ephrat
At the crossroads,
Which is Rachel's grave.
To mother Rachel he will bring glad tidings.
And he will comfort her.
And now she will let herself be comforted.
And she will rise up
And kiss him.[32]

GENEALOGY

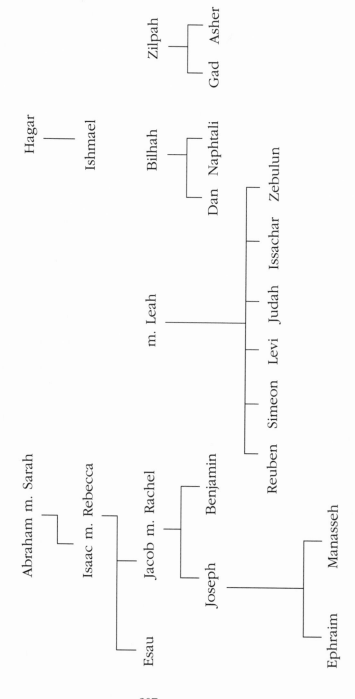

Synopsis

For those unfamiliar with the story, I include here a summary of the events recorded in Genesis (chapters 27 to 50):

Jacob leaves Beersheba for Haran in order to escape the wrath of Esau, whose birthright-blessing he has received through a subterfuge arranged by Rebecca, his mother. He stops to sleep at sundown and sees in a dream a vision of a ladder, set up between heaven and earth, with angels ascending and descending upon it. God appears to him in this dream and promises to watch over Jacob until he returns home. God also promises that Jacob's descendants will inherit the country through which he is traveling. Waking, Jacob renames the place Bethel, that is, house of God, and vows that if God looks after him, "Then God shall be God to me."

Continuing his journey, Jacob comes upon a well covered by a huge stone. Gathered around it are several shepherds and their flocks. When asked, they tell him that they know Jacob's uncle, Laban, and that Laban's daughter Rachel is coming with his sheep. When Rachel appears, Jacob is so deeply affected by the sight of her that he singlehandedly removes the huge stone from the well. He waters the flocks, then, kissing Rachel, he bursts into tears. Rachel runs to tell her father, Laban, that his sister's son has arrived, and Laban welcomes him into his household.

Asked by Laban to work for him, Jacob agrees to serve seven years in return for Rachel's hand. Laban agrees but, at the end of the term, tricks Jacob into marriage with Leah and then extorts Jacob's assent to another seven-year term in return for marriage to Rachel one week after the first wedding.

Over the next seven years, Leah bears Jacob six sons and a daughter. Bilhah and Zilpah, the handmaids of Rachel and Leah, each bear two sons to Jacob. Finally, Rachel, barren for seven years, gives birth to Joseph. Jacob asks Laban for permission to return home, but Laban, anxious not to lose so good a worker, persuades Jacob to stay on and continue working for him. Jacob does so and begins, by careful management of his affairs, to acquire wealth.

After six more years, Jacob realizes that Laban and his sons bear him ill will for his great wealth. God tells Jacob to return home, and Jacob, having obtained his wives' assent, sets off in secret. When Laban discovers that Jacob has gone, he sets off in hot pursuit; God, however, warns him in a dream not to do anything to Jacob. Laban overtakes Jacob, and the two argue but part on peaceful terms.

Returning home, Jacob sends messengers ahead in order to smooth the coming encounter with Esau, from whose murderous wrath he had fled more than twenty years previously. The messengers return with the news that Esau is approaching with a force of four hundred men. Jacob prays for divine assistance and prepares to face his brother. Sending messengers ahead with gifts, he divides his camp into two, so that one-half at least will be spared. When all the arrangements have been made and Jacob is alone, an angel appears in the likeness of a man and wrestles with him. The angel, unable to prevail, dislocates Jacob's thigh and asks to be let go. Jacob demands a blessing as the price of release, and the angel changes his name from Jacob to Israel in commemoration of his successful struggle.

The meeting with Esau is peaceful, and the two part company on good terms.

The next chapter records the rape of Dinah, Jacob's daughter, by Shechem, a local princeling, and the murderous vengeance practiced on his entire clan by Simeon and Levi, two of Dinah's brothers. God appears to Jacob and instructs him to go again to Bethel and build an altar there. Jacob does so, and God confirms the change of names performed by the angel with whom Jacob had struggled. God reiterates the earlier assurance that Jacob's children will inherit the land promised to him as to his fathers, Abraham and Isaac. Jacob continues his journey, and it is here, on the road from Bethel to Ephrat, that Rachel dies when giving birth to her second son, Benjamin. Jacob buries her by the roadside and pitches camp a little further on. During this brief stop, Reuben, Jacob's oldest son, loses his right to the birthright by committing adultery with Bilhah, his father's concubine. Jacob returns to Isaac, his father, in Hebron; when Isaac dies, Jacob and Esau bury him.

Joseph next appears center stage, seventeen years old and his father's favorite son. His brothers hate him for his favored place in their father's estimation and hate him more when he tells them of dreams that suggest that he will be elevated above his family. Their response is to sell him into slavery, thus setting in motion the very sequence of events that will bring him to viceroyship of Egypt and total power over his brothers.

The brothers allow Jacob to believe that Joseph has been killed by a wild animal, and he goes into deep mourning. Meanwhile, Joseph is beginning to prosper. Purchased in Egypt by Potiphar, an officer in the court of the Pharaoh, he rises to stewardship of Potiphar's house. Struck by his beauty, Potiphar's wife attempts to seduce him; when she fails, she accuses him of trying to rape her, and Joseph is immediately jailed.

In jail he soon becomes the favorite of the prison guard, who entrusts the running of the prison to him. Sometime thereafter, Pharaoh's butler and baker incur their master's wrath and find themselves in jail. There they are troubled by similar dreams, which Joseph interprets for them, telling the butler that he will be returned to his old post and the baker that he will be hanged. Joseph then pleads with the butler to return the kindness by helping him get out of jail.

Events come to pass precisely as Joseph predicts, but the butler, returned to Pharaoh's favor, forgets Joseph's plea, and Joseph languishes in jail for a full two years. The butler remembers the Hebrew interpreter of dreams only when Pharaoh is troubled by dreams that his magicians cannot interpret. Pharaoh, hearing of Joseph, summons him and charges him to interpret his dreams. Joseph explains that Egypt will experience seven years of fine harvest followed by seven years of crippling famine and advises Pharaoh to appoint a skillful administrator to supervise stockpiling of food against the advent of famine. Pharaoh, suitably impressed by Joseph's interpretation, appoints him on the spot as his right-hand man, and Joseph becomes governor of all Egypt at the age of thirty. He stores enormous amounts of grain over the next seven years, during which time he has two sons, Manasseh and Ephraim, by an Egyptian woman.

When famine strikes the area, Jacob sends his sons down to Egypt to buy food. Benjamin he keeps at home, especially solicitous of the welfare of Rachel's younger and, he thinks, only surviving son. The brothers come before Joseph to beg for food; he recognizes them but does not reveal himself. Instead he accuses them of being spies and jails Simeon, telling them that, if they hope to see Simeon again, they must prove themselves to be who they say are by returning home and bringing Benjamin down to Egypt with them. Jacob refuses to let Benjamin go, and the subject is dropped until the famine presses so hard that Jacob tells his sons to return to Egypt. Judah points out that they cannot return without Benjamin. Jacob at last assents, and the brothers set off.

When Joseph sees Benjamin, he instructs the overseer of his domestic affairs to take the brothers to his house. The overseer does so and, quieting their fears at this strange treatment, brings Simeon out to them. Joseph joins them, saving a special greeting for Benjamin. Then, overcome with emotion, he retires to weep in private. He feasts his brothers, who are astonished to find themselves seated in order of age. They are given food and set off for home, but before they leave, Joseph has his steward plant his silver goblet in Benjamin's sack. He then sends the steward after the departed brothers to accuse them of the theft. Challenged, the brothers confidently volunteer the death of whoever is found to have the goblet in his possession. It is discovered in Benjamin's sack, and the brothers return to Egypt in despair. Joseph announces that he will keep Benjamin as a slave and informs the brothers that they may return to their father.

Judah steps forward and in a moving plea states that Jacob will not survive the blow if the brothers return without Benjamin. Joseph is so stirred by Judah's request to be enslaved in Benjamin's stead that he reveals himself to his brothers. Stunned, they cannot respond. He assures them that their actions were all part of a larger divine plan and urges them to return with all speed to Jacob. He instructs them to inform his father that he is still alive and to bring him down to Egypt.

Jacob is struck dumb by the news, but rallies and declares his intention to see his son before he dies. He comes down to Egypt with all his goods and is met by Joseph. Pharaoh grants Jacob an audience, and Jacob blesses him, after which Jacob settles with his family in a fertile section of the land.

The famine continues, and, in the process of paying Joseph for the food he distributes, the entire population of Egypt mortgage themselves and their land to Pharaoh.

After seventeen years in Egypt, Jacob feels death drawing near and calls for Joseph. He makes Joseph swear that he will bury him back in Canaan. Shortly thereafter Joseph hears that his father has fallen ill, and he brings his two sons, Manasseh and Ephraim, to him. Jacob claims the two grandsons as his own children and blesses them, taking care to place his right hand, reserved for the older son who will inherit the birthright, on the head of Ephraim, the younger of the two, thus continuing the tradition, unbroken since Abraham, of the younger son's inheriting the birthright.

Jacob then calls his sons together and reveals to them what their futures will be. He adjures them to bury him in the cave of Machpelah in Canaan, where Abraham and Sarah, Isaac and Rebecca, and Leah are buried. Jacob dies, and Joseph travels to Canaan with all his family and an Egyptian entourage to bury his father.

The story closes where it began. Just as Jacob expected Esau to take revenge for the stolen birthright when once Isaac, their father, had died, so here Joseph's brothers fear for their safety after Jacob's death. Joseph assures them of his goodwill. Later, at his death, his last act is to make his brothers swear that, should they return to Canaan, they will take his bones up from Egypt for burial. When the children of Israel are liberated from Egyptian slavery several hundred years later, it is Moses, Joseph's spiritual successor, who performs this service for him.

Abbreviations and Bibliography

EncJud	*Encyclopaedia Judaica.* Edited by C. Roth. 16 vols. Jerusalem, 1972.
Esth. R.	*Esther Rabbah.* Translated by M. Simon. London, 1939.
Exod. R.	*Exodus Rabbah.* Translated by S. Lehrman. London, 1939.
Gen. R.	*Genesis Rabbah.* Edited by R. Theodor-Albeck. Jerusalem, 1965. Translated by H. Freedman. 2 vols. London, 1939.
HUCA	*Hebrew Union College Annual*
JE	Jewish Encyclopedia
Lam. R.	*Lamentations Rabbah.* Translated by J. Rabbinowitz. London, 1939.
Lev. R.	*Leviticus Rabbah.* Translated by Israelstam-Slotki. London, 1939.
MhG	*Midrash Hagadol.* Edited by Margoliut-Fish. 5 vols. Jerusalem, 1947–1972.
Num. R.	*Numbers Rabbah.* Translated by J. Slotki. 2 vols. London, 1939.
PdRK	*Pesikta deRav Kahana.* Edited by B. Mandelbaum. 2 vols. New York, 1962.
PR	*Pesikta Rabbati.* Translated by W. Braude. 2 vols. New Haven, 1968.
RaLBaG	Rabbi Levi ben Gershom (1288–1340).
RaN	Rabbi Nissim Gerondi (d. 1380). In *TB.*

Tan	*Tanhuma.* Reprint Tel Aviv, n.d.
TanB	*Tanhuma.* Edited by Buber. 2 vols. Jerusalem, 1963.
TB	*Talmud Babylonia.* 10 vols. Vilna, 1865.
TJ	*Talmud Jerusalem.* 7 vols. Vilna, 1921.
TSH	*Torah Shlemah.* Encyclopedia of Biblical Interpretation. New York and Jerusalem, 1949–.
Zohar	Edited by R. Margoliut. 3 vols. Jerusalem, 1956.
Zohar	Translated by M. Simon and H. Sperling. 5 vols. London, 1934.

$\mathcal{N}otes$

PREFACE

1. L. Kass, "A Woman for All Seasons," *Commentary* 1 (September 1991): 30.

2. A. Heschel, *God in Search of Man* (Philadelphia, 1956), 242.

3. *Otzar Hatefilot,* ed. A. Gordon (Vilna, 1925), 65.

4. R. Carroll, *Jeremiah* (Philadelphia, 1986), 598.

5. W. Herberg, *Judaism and Modern Man* (Philadelphia, 1951), 246.

6. J. Heinemann, "The Nature of the Aggadah," in *Midrash and Literature*, ed. G. Hartman (New Haven, 1986), 48–49. Commenting on the uniqueness of the midrash, Joseph Dan writes: "The Hebrew midrash is alien to western literary, exegetical, and homiletical tradition because of the vast differences between the Jewish and Christian scriptures. Christian preachers had to rely, when interpreting scriptures and revealing their hidden meaning, mainly on the ideonic side, the implications of the content of the verse. Jewish preachers could use a total text, hermeneutically discussing not only the meaning of terms and words, but also their sound, the shape of the letters, the vocalization points and their shapes and sounds, the *te'amim* (the musical signs added to the Hebrew words), the *tagin* (the small decorative additions to the letters), the frequency with which words and letters appear in a verse or a chapter, the absence of one of the letters from a biblical portion, the variety and number of divine names included

in the text, the numerical value of letters, words, and whole verses, the possible changes of letters (*atbash, temurah*), the new words formed from the initial or final letters of a biblical section (*notarikon*), and the countless ways other than ideonic content and meaning by which the scriptures transmit a semiotic message. It should be emphasized that these methods are in themselves not mystical, and any message, even the mundane or humorous, can be and was reached in these ways. This kind of midrashic treatment is completely neutral on possible meaning and was used in the Middle Ages and modern times . . . by every Jewish preacher and exegete, each according to his own preferences and tastes. Pietists, philosophers, traditionalists, and mystics shared the same midrashic tradition.

"The possibility of using the totality of the text is created by the nature of the original Hebrew language of the Jewish scriptures. This is in marked contrast to the fact that Christians in the Middle Ages and modern times have usually had to use a translated text. Some of the Christian scriptures were written originally in Greek, but in most Christian Bibles, all of the Old Testament and most of the New are translations. In reading the Vulgata, most Christian preachers in the western church had a text which in many cases had undergone two translations. Such a text cannot preserve the sanctity of the shape of letters; at best, it can convey the ideonic meaning of the original. . . . These two differences—the ability to use the total semiotic message of the text, and the use of an obscure, and therefore polysemous, Hebrew original—create a most significant gap between Jewish and Christian exegetes and preachers. . . . Protestants . . . who rely on the literal meaning of the twice or thrice translated text (Protestantism to a great extent began with the third translation to European languages) . . . are thus removed as far as one can imagine from the atmosphere of the Jewish ancient and medieval midrash" (J. Dan, "Midrash and the Dawn of Kabbalah," in *Midrash and Literature,* pp. 128, 129).

CHAPTER 1. THE COVENANT

1. *Gen. R.* 14:6.
2. *Mishnah Abot* 1:2.
3. *Gen. R.* 42:8.
4. Rashi ad loc.

5. L. Kass, "A Woman for All Seasons," *Commentary* 1 (September 1991): 31. Leon Kass goes on to suggest that although Scripture does not reveal the reason for the failure of transmission in the family of Noah, it does provide an intriguing clue—"the absence of a proper wife and mother, or, better, the absence of proper regard for the wife and mother of Noah's sons. We know the name of Noah and his three sons, Shem, Japheth, and Ham, but we do not know the name of Noah's wife, and she does not figure in the story with the sons. This neglect of the importance of the wife seems to be the uninstructed way of the human race—and this crucial defect is perhaps the first object of God's instruction for the patriarchs, and, through them, of us. "God, in fact, had subtly tried to instruct Noah, but Noah—whether from simplemindedness or instinctive male chauvinism—missed the point: when the earth dried after the Flood, God told Noah to leave the ark, *'thou and thy wife, and thy sons, and thy sons' wives with thee'* (8:16); but Noah, changing the instructions, went out, and after him, first his sons, and only then his wife and then his sons' wives with him (8:18). Could Noah's demotion of his wife be related to his inability properly to transmit?"

6. *TB Sanhedrin* 70a.

7. *Gen. R.* 60:16.

8. *Gen. R.* 58:2.

9. *TB Baba Batra* 92b. The Bible first introduces Egypt to the reader as a land whose people, upon seeing the attractive wife of a traveler, may put him to death and take her (12:12-15).

10. See *Sifrey* Deut. piska 31, ed. Finkelstein (New York, 1969), 49–50.

11. J. Bailey, "Josephus' Portrayal of the Matriarch," in L. Feldman and G. Hata, eds., *Josephus and Christianity* (Detroit, 1987), 157, 165.

CHAPTER 2. THE JOURNEY

1. A. Heschel, *The Insecurity of Freedom* (New York, 1966), 158.

CHAPTER 3. AT THE WELL

1. J. Romains, *Men of Good Will*, vol. 2, Eros in Paris, no. 7.

2. Whittier, *Mogg Megone*, vol. 2.

3. *TB Kidushin* 11a.

4. The parallels between Rachel and Rebecca are notable. Both are objects of family matchmaking, both are lovely shepherdesses, and both are met after long travel at a well (perhaps the same well) in the key encounter that determines their betrothal. But note this difference: after Jacob kissed her, Rachel *ran and told her father* (29:12); when Rebecca was approached on a similar occasion by Eliezer on Isaac's behalf, she *ran and told her mother's house* (24:18). For a young woman to go first to her mother at such a time seems more natural. Why, then, did Rachel choose her father? Rashi explains that Rachel's mother was no longer alive at the time. Nahmanides proposes that, whereas Rebecca went to her mother to show her the gifts that Eliezer had brought her, Rachel approached her father because it was proper for the head of the house to welcome the arrival of a relative.

5. As different as is Eliezer's meeting with Rebecca from Jacob's with Rachel, one feature is common to both—the well. Was it simply happenstance that Scripture introduces at the well two women who would henceforth guarantee through their character and their children the continuation of the covenant? The well of the matriarchs may allude to the powers of purity, renewal, and sanctity that, in Jewish belief, water possessed for women.

6. *Midrash Sekhel Tov,* section vayetze.

7. *Tan,* section vayetze.

8. Zohar 1.153a.

9. L. Feldman, "Josephus' Portrait of Jacob" (unpublished manuscript), p. 9.

10. It is suggested that the public reading of the Five Books of Moses during the synagogue service on the Sabbath afforded an occasion to demonstrate this. The weekly portion of the Torah is divided into seven sections. On the Sabbath when the Jacob-Rachel story is read, the second section concludes with the sentence *Rachel was beautiful of form and fair to look upon* (29:17). Its immediate continuation, *[And] Jacob loved Rachel* (v. 18), is made to commence the third section of the reading. Dividing Rachel's beauty, the conclusion of sec. 2, from Jacob's love for her, the beginning of sec. 3, suggests that physical appearance was not a factor, or not the central factor, in the joining of the two, for they were destined for one another from the beginning. One manuscript, which has no problem with the proximity of

the two statements—Rachel's beauty and Jacob's love for her—claims that Jacob saw by the holy spirit that Esther and Mordecai would issue from Rachel and bring deliverance to the people Israel. Esther's resemblance to Rachel is ingeniously drawn by the author from several bits of evidence: (1) the similar Hebrew wording of the phrase, "The king loved Esther" (Esth 2:17)—also famed for her beauty—to the phrase *[And] Jacob loved Rachel;* (2) the *gematria* or numerical equivalents of the Hebrew letters of the phrase, *beautiful of form,* to "Mordecai the Jew and Esther the queen," and of the letters of the phrase, *Rachel, your daughter,* to "Esther"; as well as (3) the number seven representing the years Jacob worked for Rachel and the seven maidens who served Esther and the fact that "Esther was taken to King Ahasuerus . . . in the seventh year of his reign" (Esth 2:16) (cf. *TSH,* s.v. "Gen." 29 n. 56).

11. *Yalkut Shimoni,* eds. Y. Lehrer and Y. Shiloni (Jerusalem, 1973) 2:824. *Maggid Devarav Le-Ya'akov,* ed. R. Schatz-Uffenheimer (Jerusalem, 1976), pp. 29–30, no. 15. Cf. Dov Ber of Mezritch, *Or Ha-Emet* (Zhitomir, Ukraine, 1900), p. 78. Dov Ber continues: "Similarly, we must understand the passage from Canticles 3:13, 'King Solomon made him a palanquin . . . backed of gold . . . decked with love by the maidens of Jerusalem. O maidens of Zion go forth and gaze upon King Solomon.' 'Maidens' represent bodily beauty, while [the Hebrew word] 'Zion' means 'sign' or 'symbol.' Thus the juncture of these words in the phrase, *maidens of Zion,* suggests that bodily comeliness is but a 'sign' of the heavenly source of all beauty, a spark of which the maidens possess. [Indeed] one is permitted to embrace earthly beauty only if this leads one to espouse heavenly beauty [King Solomon, who here represents the Lord]."

12. *Pirkey deRabbi Eliezer* (Warsaw, 1852) 36.

13. *Gen. R.* 63:9.

14. R. Alter, *The Art of the Biblical Narrative* (New York, 1981), 55.

15. The one exception in Proverbs concerns a harlot (7:13).

16. *Gen. R.* 70:12.

17. Ibid.

18. *Ibn Ezra* Gen. 27:27 and Cant. 1:2; *Shulhan Arukh,* section even ha'ezer 21.

19. *Calvin Opera,* 23.400. Ibn Ezra, RaLBaG, and Abarbanel ad

loc. attempt to solve the problem by reading the verb in the past perfect. Thus, *Jacob kissed Rachel . . . for Jacob had told Rachel that he was her father's relative* (29:12).

20. Zohar 146a–147a. The translation is a composite and makes use of several versions, Soncino (London, 1934), D. Goldstein (New York, 1989), and A. Green, "Creating a Feminist Theology of Judaism," *On Being a Jewish Feminist*, ed. S. Heschel (Philadelphia, 1983), 257–58. Note that kissing is followed by weeping among the circle of R. Shimon as in the Jacob and Rachel encounter.

21. *Exod. R.* 2:2-3. He is called "the faithful shepherd."

22. *Gen. R.* 70.

23. C. Chalier, *Les Matriarches* (Paris, 1986), 154, quoting E. Levinas, *Difficile liberté*, 53–54.

24. *TB Berakhot* 3b.

25. *TB Gittin* 52a; cf. *TB Shabbat* 118b.

26. *Gen. R.* 60:12.

27. "In the Biblical account (29:12) Rachel does not speak a word. In Josephus (1:286) it is Rachel who speaks, who weeps, and who embraces Jacob. . . . In Josephus' version Rachel acts with childish delight highly reminiscent of the reaction of Nausicaa (Homer, *Odyssey*, Book 6), when the stranger tells her whence he has come and when she offers to supply him with his wants. Just as Odysseus, after first considering whether he should throw his arms around Nausicaa's knees, decides that she might take offense at such immodest behavior, so Josephus (1.287) omits the Biblical statement (Gen. 29:11) that Jacob kissed Rachel almost immediately upon meeting her." Feldman, "Josephus' Portrait of Jacob," p. 10.

28. *Lekah Tov,* section vayetze 10.11.

29. Chalier, *Les Matriarches,* 155.

CHAPTER 4. LABAN

1. H. Heine, *Rabbi of Bachrach* (New York, 1947), 20.

2. J. Campbell, *Lives of the Lord Chancellors,* 1:13.

3. I. Maclarne, *The Days of Auld Langsyne,* 7:2.

4. Composite. For sources, JE, "Akiba," 1:309, and *EncJud* "Rachel," 13.1490. "In the future, at Judgment, Rabbi Akiba is going to impose guilt [for failing to study] on the poor [who use

their poverty as an excuse not to study]. For if they say to them, 'Why did you not study the Torah,' and they reply, 'Because we were poor,' they will say to them, 'But was not R. Akiba poorer?' If they say, 'Because of our children [whom we had to work to support],' they will say to them, 'Did not R. Akiba have sons and daughters?' So they will say to them, 'Because Rachel, his wife, had the merit [of making it possible for him to study], and we have no equivalent helpmates; our wives do not have equivalent merit at their disposal'" (J. Neusner, *The Fathers According to Rabbi Nathan* [Atlanta, 1986], 6:5:5, 6).

R. Akiba's love for Rachel appears reflected in his answer to the question, "Who is wealthy? . . . He whose wife is beautiful in deeds" (*TB Shabbat* 25b).

See Louis Finkelstein's flawed but still useful *Akiba* (Philadelphia, 1936), and, more recently, Adin Steinsaltz's attempt to portray Rachel as a talmudic prototype for modern women, in his *Strife of the Spirit* (Northvale, N.J., 1989), 150–65.

5. The talmudic tale of R. Akiba concludes with the report that "Rabbi Akiba's daughter acted similarly [to her mother] with Ben Azai [i.e., encouraging him to study], and this is the meaning of the [Aramaic] saying, '*rehilah batar rehilah*,' 'one lamb follows another, as the mother acts so the daughter'" (*TB Ketuvot* 63a). The wordplay is upon the name of R. Akiba's wife, Rachel; the letters form the Aramaic noun *rehila* from Heb. *rahel*, meaning "lamb."

6. The parallel between the two stories has not yet been noted.

7. C. Depew, "Woman," chap. 4 in *Orations* (New York, 1910), 3.

8. *Gen. R.* 70:17.

9. Ibid.

10. Yehezkel Kaufman argues this case convincingly in *The Religion of Israel* (Chicago, 1960), part 1.

11. *TB Megillah* 13b.

12. *Lam. R.* petikhta (introduction), 24.

13. *TB Megillah* 13b.

There were those who, believing self-discipline the foundation of all moral life, looked at this tale more from the point of view of training in moral restraint than in deception. "The old mystics had a wiser sense of what the world was worth. They ordained a severe apprenticeship to law, and even ceremonial, for the gaining of freedom and mastery over these. Seven years of service for Rachel were to be rewarded at last with Leah. Seven other years of faithfulness with her were to win them at last the true bride of their souls. Active Life was with them the only path to the Contemplative" (J. R. Lowell, "Thoreau," in *Literary Essays* [New York, 1890], 219).

CHAPTER 5. LEAH

1. A. H. Clough, *The Bothis of Tober-Na-Vuolich* chap. 9.

2. M. Nahmanides, *Gur Arye; Tikuney Zohar* 40. According to Menahem Nahum of Tchernobyl, an eighteenth–nineteenth century Hasidic leader, Jacob's trip from the holy land to Haran and Laban was for the purpose of removing the evil that inhered in that place in order to prepare for the future revelation of the Torah. For this reason, he had to marry both Leah and Rachel, for there are two Torahs, one written and one oral (Menahem Nahum of Tchernobyl, *The Light of the Eyes* [Maor Eynayim], trans. A. Green [New York, 1982], 206, 210. Cf. Yaakov Yosef of Polnoy, *Ben Porat Yosef* [Lemberg (Lvov), Ukraine, 1845], section vayetze 49c-d).

3. S. Singer, *Judaism* (1988), 252.

4. I. Manger, *Khumesh Lider* (New York, 1935; trans. K. Hellerstein; 1994), 61–62.

5. C. Chalier, *Les Matriarches* (Paris, 1986), 156.

6. For a discussion of the role of procreation as the sole sexual function of woman, see D. Feldman, *Birth Control in Jewish Law* (New York, 1968), chaps. 2 and 3.

7. I. Arama, *Akedat Yitzhak,* shaar 60 to Gen. 30:1-2.

8. Some of the names of the other children, although not all clearly understood at this stage of biblical research, refer to past events (Gen 29–30). Rachel, for example, in naming her handmaid Bilhah's child, says: *God has vindicated me (danani) . . . and given me a son. Therefore she called his name Dan.* In similar vein, she could have called her own son "Asaf" after *God has gathered up (asaf) my reproach* (30:23). Instead she chooses to call him Joseph—*May he add another son for me.* Several of the names Leah gives are followed by expressions of hope for Jacob's love (as pointed out in this chapter, for example, Reuben and

Zebulun), but the names themselves seem not to allow such an inference (see Moshe Hayim Ephraim, *Degel Mahaneh Ephraim* [Zhitomir, Ukraine, 1874], 30, section vayeytze).

9. M. Teitelbaum, *Yismah Moshe* (Berlin, 1928), section vayetze 75b–76a.

10. *TB Baba Batra* 123a. *Gen. R.* 71:2; 70:19. See Zohar 2.316.

11. *TSH*, s.v. "Gen." 30:21. Why is it written *Afterwards, she bore a daughter* and not, as in all of Leah's other births, *She conceived and bore . . .*? Because she did not conceive a daughter but a son. This is the force of *afterwards*, i.e., *after* she conceived a son, *she bore a daughter.* See *Torah Temimah*, B. Epstein (Tel Aviv, 1956), 2.140, Gen 30:21.

12. *Mikhtav me-Eliyahu* (New York, 1985). Cf. Zohar 2.316; *Zohar Hadash* Ruth, 106; Zohar 1.168b; 158b; 223a.

An example of Leah's superiority to Rachel in Hasidic literature, influenced by the Zohar no doubt, can be found in *Maor Vashemesh* by the nineteenth-century Polish leader Kalman Kalomonos of Krakow. Taking Rachel and Leah as spiritual states, he explains Jacob's rejection of Leah and his preference for Rachel as stemming from his willingness to settle for a lower level of spirituality. "For he feared to ascend to such a lofty stage [as Leah] and would not have done so had not Laban deceived him. So he complained to Laban, *Why have you done this to me? Did I not serve you for Rachel? Why have you raised me* (29:25) to a rung to which I feared to ascend [by giving me Leah]?" (reading *romamtani*—"Why have you raised me?"—for *rimitani*—"Why have you deceived me?") (*Maor Vashemesh* [(Breslau?), 1842], 242b).

13. *Gen. R.* 29:31.

14. Teitelbaum, *Yismah Moshe.* Cf. *Kedushat Levi,* R. Levi Yitzhak (Jerusalem, 1958), 53.

15. *Esth. R.* 6:12. The midrash adds that "all the greatest of her [Rachel's] descendants forced themselves to be silent" and cites Esther, Benjamin, and Saul as examples.

16. *Kedushat Levi,* 24b.

17. *Gen. R.* 71.

18. *Gen. R.* 73:4; 71.

19. Zohar 1.225b; 168b; 2.29b.

20. On the other hand, *Jubilees* gives a different picture of Jacob's relation to Leah: "And Leah his wife died in the fourth

year of the second week of the forty-fifth jubilee, and he buried her in the double cave near Rebecca his mother, to the left of Sarah, his father's mother. And all her sons and his sons came to mourn over Leah his wife with him, and to comfort him regarding her. . . . For he loved her exceedingly after Rachel her sister died; for she was perfect and upright in all her ways and honored Jacob, and all the days that she lived with him he did not hear from her mouth a harsh word, for she was gentle and peaceable and upright and honorable. And he remembered all her deeds which she had done during her life, and he lamented her exceedingly; for he loved her with all his heart and with all his soul" (36:21-24).

21. Composite: *Rashi* Gen. 34:1; *Tan,* section vayishlah 7; *TJ Sanhedrin* 2:6; *Gen. R.* 80:1. Cf. *TSH* Gen. 34 n. 2.

In another opinion, Leah's apparently brazen approach to Jacob—*And Leah went out to meet him, and said, "You are to come in unto me. . . ." And he lay with her that night* (30:16)—is taken as the proof case for the opinion cited in the name of R. Yohanan that "One who is summoned to his marital duty by his wife will beget children such as were not to be found even in the generation of Moses." For from this coupling of Jacob and Leah was born Issachar, the ancestor of scholars, as it is written, "And the children of Issachar were men who had understanding of the times" (1 Chr 12:33). The Talmud proceeds at once to qualify R. Yohanan's view that it is virtuous for a wife to summon a husband to his marital duty by adding that she may act thus only if her behavior is delicate and not explicit, as, in fact, he argues, was Leah's, who merely invited Jacob into her tent without mentioning intercourse. For, it is suggested, she did not use the expression *Come in unto me,* in its common scriptural sense, i.e., to have intercourse, but only as an invitation to "come in to my tent" (*TB Nedarim* 20b; RaN ad loc.; *TB Eruvin* 100b. A survey of the sources is found in *TSH* Gen. 30:16 n. 57).

The Zohar, as well, defends and spiritualizes the action of Leah. "*And Leah went out to meet him, and said: You must come in unto me* (30:16), etc. On the surface this language appears to be immodest, but in truth it is a proof of Leah's modesty. For she said nothing in the presence of her sister, but *went out* to meet Jacob, and there told him in a hushed tone that, though he properly was Rachel's, she had obtained permission from Rachel.

She spoke to him outside and not in the house, that he not become upset before Rachel. Should Jacob once enter Rachel's tent, Leah felt it would not be right for her to ask him to leave it, and so she intercepted him outside. Thus, before he could enter Rachel's tent, Leah brought him into her own tent by the door which faced the road, so that she should not say anything intimate in the presence of Rachel. Leah went to all this trouble because the Holy Spirit stirred within her, and she knew that all those holy tribes would issue from her; and so she hastened the hour of union in her loving devotion to God . . ." (Zohar 2.157a; [Soncino, ed., trans., H. Sperling and M. Simon, 5 vols. (London, 1931) 2.103]).

22. R. Zak, *Kerem Yisrael* (Lublin, Poland, 1930).

23. Zohar 1.175a.

24. Cyril of Alexandria 4.213–24. Cf. E. Giannarelli, "Rachele e il pianto della madre nella tradizione cristiana antica," *Annali di storia dell'esegise* 3 (1986): 215–26; L. Zatelli, "Lea e Rachele," in *Atti del seminario "Giacobbe, o l'avventure del figlio ruinore,"* Biblia (Florence, 1990), 51–74. Zatelli also refers to Ruperus Tuitiensis, *De Sancta Trinitate et operibus euis I–IX*, ed. R. Haocke, Corpus christianorum continuatio mediaevalis, no. 21 (Turnhout, Belgium, 1971), p. 464. See also Justin, *Dialogue* 134: *The Anti-Nicene Fathers,* trans. G. Reith, 1.267.

25. Dante Alighieri, *The Divine Comedy,* Purgatorio 27.100–108, trans. D. Sayers (New York, 1962), 284–86. "In mystical writings, particularly those of Richard of St. Victor (d. 1173), whom Dante places in the Heaven of the Sun (*Para.* X. 131), the two wives of Jacob are frequently interpreted as allegories respectively of the Active and Contemplative Life; and this is the function they fulfil in Dante's third dream.

"The Active Life is the Christian life lived in the world; it is abundantly fruitful in good works, but those who pursue it cannot see very far into the things of the spirit because, like Martha (another type of the Active Life) they are 'cumbered with much serving.' The Contemplative Life is that which is wholly devoted to prayer and the practice of the Presence of God; it is less prolific in good works than the Active Life, but the fruit it bears is the most precious of all (Leah bore Jacob ten [*sic*] sons; but the two sons eventually born of Rachel were Joseph and Benjamin, the best-beloved). The Active Life is in no way to be condemned;

it is indeed necessary to the existence of the Contemplative Life (Leah must be wedded before Rachel), for if there were no Marthas to do the work of the world, Mary could not be nourished, nor find leisure for contemplation. Nevertheless, Mary's is the 'better part,' and the Active Life exists, in a manner, for the sake of the Contemplative. The complete Christian life is a blend of action and contemplation, the former leading to the latter, and being subdued to it as the means to the end."

26. H. Hibbard, *Michelangelo* (New York, 1978), 174. Whereas the Zohar sees Leah representing the "hidden world" and Rachel the "public world," Dante, and Michelangelo following him portray the opposite, Leah symbolizing the "active life" and Rachel the "contemplative life."

27. C. Depew, "Woman," chap. 4 in *Orations* (New York, 1910), 3.

28. R. Browning, *The Ring and the Book*, ed. C. Porter and H. A. Clarke (10 vols.; New York, 1899), 5:1.235.

29. *TB Baba Batra* 123a.

30. See above pp. 8–9.

31. Sir James George Frazer's view, in *The Golden Bough*, that Israel evolved from animism through polytheism and henotheism to monotheism has long been rejected by most scholars, who see a kind of eruption of religion at the beginning. The "central elements of Biblical faith . . . are so unique and *sui generis* that they cannot have developed by any natural evolutionary process from the pagan world in which they appeared" (G. Wright, *The Old Testament against Its Environment* [London, 1953], 7). As with the divine so with the family mode: the movement is not from polygamy to monogamy but the reverse.

32. Monogamy is characteristic of the biblical wisdom literature, as evidenced by the "woman of valor" described in Proverbs 31. "In the Talmudic period, no instance of plural marriage among the more than two thousand Sages is recorded" (D. Feldman, *Birth-Control in Jewish Law* [New York, 1968], 37).

33. The "great mutiny" against Moses, when he took the children of Israel through the wilderness toward the Promised Land, was lead by Korah from the tribe of Levi and Dathan and Abiram from the tribe of Reuben. Dathan and Abiram, who vilified Moses—"Is it not enough that you brought us from a land flow-

ing with milk and honey to have us die in the wilderness, that you would also make yourself a lord over us?" (Num 16:13)— were listed by the sages among the five most wicked persons of antiquity and are blamed for endangering Moses' life by betraying the secret of his slaying an Egyptian; for trying to convince the Israelites at the Red Sea to return to Egypt; for violating the Sabbath and for disobeying the rules regarding the miraculous manna—which list comprises the major crimes of the period (L. Ginzberg, *Legends of the Jews* [7 vols.; Philadelphia, 1968], 3:297, 48; 6:360). Levi and Reuben, from whom Korah, Dathan, and Abiram were descended, were, with Simeon, Leah's eldest sons. Zimri, whose public coupling with a Midianite woman in the "great seduction" at Baal Peor was ended by Pinhas's spear, came from the tribe of Simeon (Num 25:6-9), and Nadab and Abihu, who perpetrated the "great blasphemy," were from the tribe of Levi. In the trip through the wilderness the leadership position of Reuben, the firstborn, had already been taken by Judah. (See J. Milgrom, *Numbers* [Philadelphia, 1990], 340–41.) On the other hand, Joseph (Ephraim and Manasseh) and Benjamin are among the tribes placed on Mount Gerizim to bless the children of Israel as they crossed the Jordan into the Promised Land (Deut 27: 11-12).

34. C. Chalier, *Les Matriarches*, 158.

35. C. Weissler, "The Traditional Piety of Ashkenazic Women," in A. Green, ed., *Jewish Spirituality* (2 vols.; New York, 1987), 2:266 n. 59. The *tekhineh* literature comprises the Yiddish folk prayers written for, and often by, Jewish women in eastern and central Europe from the late sixteenth to the nineteenth centuries.

36. Ginzberg, *Legends of the Jews,* 3:24 n. 141.

37. *Gen. R.* 73.

38. The mystics held various views as to the role of Rachel, associated sometimes with joy, as in the Hasidic tale recounted above, and more often with sorrow.

For a description of the midnight *Tikkun,* see G. Scholem, *On the Kabbalah and Its Symbolism* (New York, 1965), 149–50. "According to this Kabbalah, Rachel and Leah are two aspects of the Shekhinah, the one exiled from God and lamenting, the other in her perpetually repeated reunion with her Lord [this second representation, symbolized as the 'rite of Leah,' is variously known as the 'rite of Jacob and Leah,' because it refers to the fruitfulness of their unions]. Consequently the *Tikkun Rachel,* or 'rite of Rachel,' was the true rite of lamentation. In observing it, men 'participate in the suffering of the Shekhinah' and bewail not their own afflictions, but the one affliction that really counts in the world, namely the exile of the Shekhinah.

"The mystic, then should rise and dress at midnight; he should go to the door and stand near the doorpost, remove his shoes and veil his head. Weeping, he should then take ashes from the hearth and lay them on his forehead, on the spot where in the morning the tefilin, the phylacteries, are applied. Then he should bow his head and rub his eyes in the dust on the ground, just as the Shekhinah herself, the 'Beautiful One without eyes,' lies in the dust. . . .

"After the great messianic outbursts of 1665–6 this rite [of Rachel] became a subject of dispute between the Sabbatians and their adversaries. The Sabbatians declared, though with varying degrees of radicalism, that the rite for Rachel had become obsolete now that the Shekhinah was on her way home from exile. To mourn for her now was like mourning on the Sabbath day. Accordingly they performed only the second part of the ritual, the rite for Leah, expressive of messianic hopes. . . . Orthodox Kabbalists continued to insist on careful observance of the ritual of lamentation."

See the first part of *Shaarey Zion* by Nathan Hannover (Prague, 1662), for the classic text of the rite.

39. *Kedushat Levi,* R. Levi Yitzhak (Jerusalem, 1958), 53.

Another Hasidic master, R. Shlomo of Radomsk, also portrays only selfless love between the sisters in a passage quoted here at length to give the full flavor of the free Hasidic style of interpretation. *"And the Lord saw that Leah was unloved and he opened her womb, but Rachel was barren* (29:31). Several questions are raised by this verse: Why the juxtaposition of Leah's fertility and Rachel's barrenness? And why is the expression *He opened her womb* used only for Leah [in the verse above] and for Rachel (in 30:22), but not for the other matriarchs Sarah and Rebecca, of whom it is written of the one: *The Lord took note of Sarah. . . . Sarah conceived and bore a son* (21:1); and of the other: *The Lord responded to (Isaac's) plea and his wife Rebecca conceived* (25:21)?

"We shall first refer to our explanation of Psalm 36:1: 'For this let every Hasid pray at the time when you can be found: that the [divine, beneficent] outpouring not reach him' (Ps. 31:6). The verse lays out the proper course for one who would follow the ways of Hasidism, namely, not to pray for one's own needs but for the needs of the other. . . . So the spelling of the word 'Hasid' is similar to that of *hesed* or compassion, HSD, in the center of which is the letter yud [*Yehudi*, 'Jew.' The Hasid, then is] one who seeks the welfare of his people (Esther 10:3). . . . If the other is not benefited, only oneself, there is no *hesed* or compassion. . . . It is the other who should receive heaven's outpourings. As it is said of Rabbi Hanina, that his virtue sustained the world but was himself sustained with a mere carob fruit. For he did not benefit from the outpouring of heaven.

"And this is the matter of Rachel and Leah. For it is written, *He opened her womb*, and the Hebrew for 'womb' is *rehem* which is related to *rahmanut* or 'compassion.' . . . Therefore, we are told, *And the Lord saw that Leah was changed.* [Reading *shinui*, 'changed,' instead of *sanuah*, 'unloved.'] For Leah sought heaven's mercies not for what she herself required but for her sister. This explains the proximity of Leah's fecundity and Rachel's barrenness in the same sentence [the first question raised above]. And the words, *And the Lord opened her rehem*, means that the Lord opened her capacity for compassion for the other. . . . This is alluded to in the verse, 'He sets the childless woman among her household as a happy mother of children' (Ps. 113:9). Now Rachel is usually associated with 'the childless woman' and Leah with 'the happy mother.' But, according to our interpretation, when the Lord gives the 'childless woman'—Rachel—a 'household,' then 'the mother of children'—Leah—'is happy.'

"So the sisters Rachel and Leah sought the welfare each of the other. For of Rachel too it is written, that *The Lord opened her rehem* or womb [and this answers the second question about the verse]" (Shlomo of Radomsk, *Tiferet Shlomo* [Tel Aviv, 1962], 58).

CHAPTER 6. BARREN

1. S. Blumberg, "Akara," *Shema* 17/323 (12 December 1986), 1.

2. Cf. P. Brown, "The Notion of Virginity in the Early Church," in *Christian Spirituality*, ed. B. McGinn (2 vols.; New York, 1986), 1.427–44.

3. Aphraat, *Demonstration,* 18.1, cited in Brown, "The Notion of Virginity in the Early Church," 1:427.

4. B. Friedan, *The Feminine Mystique* (New York, 1982), 37, 77; K. Millett, *Sexual Politics* (New York, 1978), 79, 87; G. Greer, *The Female Eunuch* (New York, 1972), 343, 364. Cf. N. Davidson, *The Failure of Feminism* (Buffalo, 1988); and M. Levin, *Feminism and Freedom* (New York, 1987).

5. M. Gallagher, *Enemies of Eros.* The comments on this book are partly drawn from D. Feder, "Feminism Contributes to Woes," *The Boston Herald,* 27 November 1990.

6. C. Chalier, *Les Matriarches* (Paris, 1986), 179.

7. *Gen. R.* 71:6.

8. Zohar, ed. R. Margoliut (3 vols.; Jerusalem), 1.48a, 61a.

9. *Gen. R.* 71:2. Isaiah (56:4, 5) states that "As for the eunuchs who keep my sabbaths . . . and hold fast to my covenant—I will give them a name better than sons or daughters."

10. Lending an urgent contemporary note, Leon Kass concludes his splendid study of Rebecca by asking how it is possible "to transmit the way of life directed and sanctified by the God of Abraham, Rebekah, and Jacob, amidst the natural dangers and cultural temptations that stand in the way? Today, the fatal attractions for Jewish fathers (and not for Jewish fathers only) are more prevalent and tempting than [Isaac's] venison: money, power, and status; board rooms, country clubs, and ESPN; the Ivy League, the Chicago [Bulls], and the bottom line; and, alas, for a growing number, alcohol, promiscuity, and even cocaine. These fatal attractions, thanks to our newly found equality, are also open, without discrimination to women. What will become of the children of Israel (and, again, of children generally) if women, too, live only for the here and now, if they opt only or mainly for personal self-fulfillment? Whatever might be the case for America or for the world, the way of Jewish people, now and forever, depends absolutely on the right ordering of the household, devoted wholeheartedly to the noble and sacred task of rearing and perpetuation. For this task—and there is, for Jews, none higher—women, we learn from Bible, have special access and special gifts, especially if they hearken to the call . . ." (L. Kass, "A Woman for All Seasons," *Commentary* 1 [September 1991]:35).

11. Chalier, *Les Matriarches,* 179–80.

12. *Gen. R.* 63.

13. A free translation. For a full discussion of the sources of the text, see D. Goldschmidt, ed., *Mahzor Layamim Hanorayim, High Holy Days Prayerbook* (2 vols.; Jerusalem, 1970), 1, 69–70.

14. K. Hellerstein, "Kadya Molodowsky's 'Froyen-Lider,'" *Association for Jewish Studies Review* 13, nos. 1 and 2 (1988):66. I have made slight changes in Hellerstein's fine translation.

CHAPTER 7. DEATH

1. *Gen. R.* 84:5.

2. The Hebrew for *replied* is singular. See *Targum Jonathan* and *RaLBaG* to 31:14.

3. G. von Rad (Philadelphia, 1961), 305. Cf. Lev 15:19-f. For a mystical view of the theft, see *Kedushat Levi,* (Jerusalem, 1958), 57b.

4. C. Chalier, *Les Matriarches* (Paris, 1986), 202–3.

5. *Tan,* section vayishlah 6.

6. Esth 3:2; 2:5; *Midrash Aggadat Esther* 3. When Jacob met Esau, Benjamin had not yet been born!

7. *Sifrey* Deut. 33:12; Gen 49:10; 33:7.

For the Zohar, ed. R. Margoliut (3 vols.; Jerusalem, 1956), 1.71, the problem of Jacob's servility to Esau does not present itself, since, according to this source, it was not before his brother that Jacob displayed obeisance but before the Shechinah (the divine Presence), who had arrived to protect him.

8. *Yalkut Makhiri* Psalm 61; *TJ Taanit* 2:6.

9. *You have striven* (Heb. *saritah*) *with God* (Heb. *El*) *and man and prevailed* (32:29). See Hos 8:4. It is also associated with *Yeshurun,* "to be upright" (Deut 32:15; 33:15; Isa 44:2), suggesting "he who is upright with God," a contrast to *yaakov* or "crafty one" (27:36). N. Sarna, *Genesis* (Philadelphia, 1989), 404–5; von Rad (Philadelphia, 1961), 317.

"All Israel were to be called by his name. At that moment the Holy One, blessed be he, sanctified Israel unto his name, as it is said, 'Israel, in whom I shall be glorified' (Isa 49:3)" (*Tan,* section kedoshim 2).

Benno Jacob points out that just as Jacob becomes "Israel" only after he repents his earlier behavior, symbolized by his struggle with the angel when the new name is given, so the sons of Jacob are called the children of Israel only after they have repented their earlier behavior. Before the Joseph story begins, Jacob is called Israel three times in contrast to *the sons of Jacob* (35:21-22). "Gen. 35:21f indicated that initially only the patriarch Jacob had achieved the name Israel. The sons must earn it, especially after they have sinned against their father and Joseph. When they have been purified by trials and reunited as brothers with Joseph, they bring their father to Egypt (Gen. 46:5 and Ex. 1:1) as *the children of Israel"* (B. Jacob, *Exodus* [New York, 1992], 5–6).

10. *Lev. R.* 30:10.

11. Strangely, the only left-handed persons mentioned in the Bible come from the tribe of Benjamin!

The name could also mean "son of the south" (cf. Ps 89:13), for he alone was born in the Promised Land, to the south of Haran, and his tribal territory was in the southern part of the land. Yemen, for example, was a land of the far south. Another possibility is to take *yamin* for "days": thus *ben-yamin,* "son of my days," or old age, as in Gen 44:20, where he is called *son of his old age* (Sarna, *Genesis,* 1989), 243; (*EncJud,* s.v. "Gen." 2.522.

12. *PdRK* 1:310.

CHAPTER 8. JOSEPH

1. Zohar, ed. R. Margoliut (3 vols.; Jerusalem, 1956) 1.176b; *TB Baba Batra* 12b; *Tan,* section vayeshev.

2. *Gen. R.* 84:5. See the remarks of Abraham Steinberg in his edition, *Midrash Rabbah Hamevuar* (Jerusalem, 1988), 4:7.

3. *TSH,* s.v. "Gen." 37 n. 137.

4. *Midrash Mishley,* ed. B. Visotzky (New York, 1990), 31:14.

5. J. W. von Goethe, *Truth and Fiction.*

6. "*Potiphar, a eunuch of Pharaoh, bought Joseph from the Ishmaelites* (39:1) [reading the Hebrew *seris* as 'castrato' instead of 'courtier']. He bought him for the purpose of sodomy, but the Lord emasculated him [Potiphar]" (*Gen. R.* 86:3; *TB Sotah* 13b). Therefore was "he called Potifera (vs. 41), because he uncovered himself [*po'er*] before idols" (*Gen. R.* 86:3). The reference is to Baal Peor and the association of sexual immorality with idolatry (see Num 25:1-9).

7. *Gen. R.* 43:6.

8. *Tan,* section vayigash 5. Cf. *TSH,* s.v. "Gen." 44:18 n. 66.

9. *Gen. R.* 42.

10. *Vifey toar vifey mareh.*

11. Zohar 1.216b.

12. *Gen. R.* 98:18. Cf. *Pirkey Rabbi Eliezer* (Warsaw, 1852), 39.

13. *TB Berakhot* 20a. *Aley ayin. Ayin,* which means "fountain"— "by the fountain"—also has the meaning of "eye" and receives numerous interpretations. Thus *aley ayin* is read *oleh ayin,* "He ascended from lusting after other women" (*Song Rabbah* 4:12). Or *ileym ayin,* "who blinded his eye to Potiphar's wife, or upon any other Egyptian women during his reign as ruler" (*Num. R.* 14:6).

The sages, in discussing Joseph's mastery of the eye—linked by the warning of Scripture against forbidden desire: "You shall not lust after what your eyes behold" (Num 15:39)—cite the case of R. Matya. Once Satan observed him sitting and learning in the house of study, his face shining like an angel, for he had never in his life gazed upon a woman. Wondering that there could be a person who had never sinned, Satan gained heaven's permission to put him to the test and thereupon changed himself into a seductress so ravishing, the very angels were enthralled. R. Matya, turning every which way to avoid looking at her, but, regardless of his efforts, knowing that the evil eye of desire would in the end gain control, blinded himself with red-hot nails. Taken aback, Satan repaired to heaven once again, whereupon Raphael, the angel of healing, was dispatched. R. Matya, however, refused all remedies until he was assured that "henceforth temptation will not prevail against you" (*TanB,* section hukkat 66a).

14. *TB Berakhot* 20a. Cf. *TSH,* s.v. "Gen." 49:22 n. 299.

15. *TB Berakhot* 20a; cf. 55b.

16. *TB Berakhot* 20a. The comeliness of these two, Joseph and R. Johanan, is joined in describing the just before the doors of paradise. "The least fair of the just is as beautiful as Joseph or Rabbi Yohanan" (*TB Baba Metzia* 48c).

17. *PR* 12. "This was the intent of Jacob's praise, *aley ayin,* 'above the eye,' that is, he hid his mother from that evil man's eye."

18. *Tan,* section vayeshev 5.

19. *MhG* ad loc.

20. Zohar 1.194b; 2.23a. Cf. 1.59b, 158a, 189b, 246b. Later

commentators relate the words of the last blessing Jacob bestowed upon Joseph (49:22-26) to Joseph's encounter with Potiphar's wife. Cf. *TSH*, s.v. "Gen." 49:22-26.

21. *Gen. R.* 86. For a more critical view of Joseph see *TB Sota* 13b.

22. *Yalkut Temani; TSH,* s.v. "Gen." 46:29 n. 176; *TanB,* ad loc.; *Hayashar.* According to Nahmanides' reading of the verse, it was "Jacob who fell upon Joseph's neck." The Talmud asserts that Joseph was punished for not sufficiently defending the honor of his father *(TB Sotah* 13b).

23. This is based on the words *Joseph went up to Goshen to meet* [*likrat,* suggesting *kriat shema*] *his father* (46:29). See *Siftey Hakhamim* (Warsaw, 1882), 46:29, for some of the problems this explanation raises—e.g., if it was time for the recital of the Shema, why did Joseph fall on his father's neck at all, and why did Joseph not say the Shema as well?

24. "Jacob foresaw that Joseph was unlisted among the [holy], whose bodies would not be devoured by worms in their graves. For seven are [so holy as to be] free of worms: Abraham, Isaac, Jacob, Moses, Aaron, Miriam, and Benjamin (some add David)" *(TSH,* s.v. "Gen." 46:29 no. 177; *TB Baba Batra* 17a).

25. The proof-text quoted there is "The bow was quite naked" (Hab 3:9). *Masekhet Kalah* 3; *TSH,* s.v. "Gen." 46:29 n. 177 and 49:24 n. 318.

R. Yohanan of the Talmud, famed for his handsome features, was understandably more knowledgeable of the traps of passion and, consequently, harder on Joseph. Indeed, he finds him sufficiently involved with Potiphar's wife as to be denied a place among the patriarchs. "What caused you to be rejected from the company of the mighty ones [*eytanim,* 'patriarchs']? Because of the passion you had for your mistress, as it says, *His bow remained firm [be'eytan kashto]*" (*Gen. R.* 98:20). *MhG* ad loc., on the other hand, has the reverse reading: "Why was Joseph worthy of being counted among the patriarchs? Because of the firmness he displayed with his mistress" (cf. *TB Sotah* 36b; *TSH,* s.v. "Gen." 49:24 n. 319). Further, R. Yohanan sides with Shmuel, who takes the word *work* in the verse *On a certain day he went into the house to do his work* (39:11) to mean "immoral work" and not his "normal chores," as Rav understands it. "It teaches," says R. Yohanan, "that both of them [Joseph and his mistress] had immoral intent and lay down naked in bed" (*TB Sotah* 36b; *Yalkut Makhiri Mishley* 29:3, p. 81b).

26. *Tan,* section vayeshev 9. Cf. *TB Sotah* 36b; *TSH,* s.v. section "vayeshev" 99, 100.

Another version reads: "When he was about to have intercourse with her, the image of his father appeared to him, and his ardor grew weak, as it is written, *The vigor of his bow relaxed* (49:24). She said, 'My darling, why have you weakened?' He replied, 'I have seen my father.' 'Where is he?' she asked. 'For *there is no one in the house'"* (39:11) (*Midrash Avkir,* cited by *Yalkut Shimoni* and *MhG* ad loc.; cf. *TSH,* s.v. "Gen." 39:11 n. 100).

Vateyshev b'eytan kashto (49:24) is translated in the passages quoted in the text and notes as, alternately, *The vigor of the bow relaxed,* or *The bow remained firm.* See R. Yohanan's view in n. 25 above.

27. *Gen. R.* 87:6.

28. *Gen. R.* 98:20 (24); *TJ Horayot* 2:5; *Midrash Avkir,* cited by *Yalkut Shimoni* 1.145 and *Yalkut Reuveni* vayeshev; *Derekh Eretz.* Cf. Zohar 3.202b.

29. *Matnat Kehunah* to *Gen. R.* 98:20; *Gen. R.,* 98:20; *Luria* to *Pirkey deRabbi Eliezer,* 39 n. 21.

30. *Gen. R.* 98:20 (24); *TJ Horayot* 2:5; *Derekh Eretz.*

31. A. Enzil, *Korban he-Ani* (Lemberg [Lvov], Ukraine, 1882), 13b.

32. *Midrash Tehillim* 110a.

33. *Gen. R.* 84:10.

34. G. Ashkenazi, *Tiferet HaGershuni* (Frankfurt am Main, 1699), section vayeytze. This passage, which supports the argument of Rachel's centrality, was not seen until this work had been completed.

35. *Lev. R.* 32:5; *Num. R.* 3:6. See *Gen. R.* 84:5.

36. Zohar 1.222a.

37. Zohar 1.229a.

38. *TSH,* Gen 46:20, vol. 7, p. 1685, no. 109 and note.

39. *Num. R* 20:23.

"Why was Benjamin given the title zaddik [along with Joseph], for, although he never committed a sexual transgression, neither was he tempted in the manner of Joseph? So why was he called Zaddik? . . . Because he abstained from conjugal relations all the while that his father mourned for the loss of Joseph. For he said, 'Joseph guards the sign of the holy covenant, as our father did. Since he is lost, I must take the place of my brother'" (Zohar 2.153b–154a). (Text unclear.)

40. *Gen. R.* 97:6.

41. Mishnah Abot 4:1.

42. *Lev. R.* 32:5. Although various other reasons are given in rabbinic literature for Israel's being worthy of being redeemed from Egypt, sexual morality is the central one. A passage from nineteenth-century Hasidic literature brings together several of the elements of the Joseph story drawn upon here without, however, relating him to Rachel. *"Joseph could no longer control himself . . . and said to his brothers: 'Draw near to me.' And when they drew near, he said, 'I am Joseph your brother whom you sold into Egypt. Now do not be distressed that you sold me hither. It was to save life that God sent me before you . . . to ensure your survival on earth, and to save your lives in an extraordinary deliverance'* (45:1, 4-5, 7).

"Rashi observes that Joseph told his brothers *Draw near to me,* in order to reveal that he was circumcised. But was it really necessary to confirm his identity in this fashion, when his confession of being sold into Egypt—known only to the brothers and to himself—would have sufficed? Further, why were the self-evident locations, *into Egypt* and *hither,* added to the words *whom you sold?* And finally, why does Scripture say *God sent me before you to ensure your survival,* when Joseph, in fact, preserved not merely his own family but the entire world by saving Egypt from famine?

"I shall explain. God surrounds us with his holiness, but, dull of eye, we fail to perceive his beneficent intent. . . . Thus the mystical books tell us that the purpose of our exile in Egypt, the land of sexual licentiousness par excellence, was that the holy sparks which fell and had been swallowed up there, might be raised to their holy higher source . . . until no spark would remain in that place of depravity. . . . And it was because the Israelites in Egypt achieved this, that they were ultimately redeemed.

"Furthermore, this *tikkun* or means of putting right could not have been accomplished in any land other than Egypt, which Scripture calls *the land of nakedness* (42:12), and the sages depict as the land 'overflowing with filth.' Only there was a *teshuvat hamishkal* [a correction commensurate with the evil] possible by instituting a code of conduct to counter the temptation to sexual sin and thereby delivering the holy sparks. Thus the sages tell us that 'Israel was delivered from Egypt because they did not change their "tongue,"' which word refers to sexuality as well as to language, and implies the *tikkun* of the holy covenant of the flesh (*brit kodesh*). To repair the sign of the holy covenant, then, they had to be exiled to Egypt. And this is the meaning of *teshuvat hamishkal* in this case: to raise up the holy sparks which fell in that precise place which was most soaked in filth.

"However, that was no simple matter. And it would have been impossible for the people Israel to achieve had not Joseph the zaddik been sold into Egypt, the land of nakedness, overflowing with filth, and the primal source of uncleanliness. It was there that God tested him with Potiphar's wife and it was there that he resisted, not defiling the sign of the holy covenant, a feat of which none of his brothers was capable. In fact, Joseph, who was proclaimed 'zaddik' because he guarded the sign of the covenant when assaulted with temptation, began to mend the blemish which Adam's sin had wrought. The people Israel in Egypt followed his example in disciplining themselves in sexual matters and completed the *tikkun* of guarding the covenant by raising up all the sparks, until Egypt became as a pond without fish. Had Joseph not initiated this work, however, the children of Israel would not have had the strength to complete the task and deserved to go up out of the land. Thus was the redemption from Egypt made possible through Joseph who commenced the effort that the Israelites completed.

"[That this was the role of Joseph is born out in the midrash that attributes the splitting of the Red Sea before the fleeing Israelites to the merit of Joseph] by explaining the words of the psalmist, 'The sea saw it and fled' (114:2) to mean, that 'The sea saw the casket of Joseph sinking into the water, and hearkened to the Lord's words: "Let the waters flee from him who fled from sin," as it is written, *and he fled* [from Potiphar's wife]' (39:13) (*Midrash Tehillim* 114:9).

"Now we can understand the verses in question.

"*And Joseph said to his brothers, 'Draw near to me.'* Rashi's explanation, that he revealed his circumcision to them, must be taken in the spiritual sense, namely, that he told them he had not defiled the sign of the holy covenant in the land known as *the land of nakedness*. He did so in order that their children might follow in his footsteps to keep from sexual sin . . . by virtue of which merit they would be redeemed from Egypt, so that [in the end of days] the complete redemption would come. And he further said to them *Be not distressed that you sold me hither . . . into Egypt*, for in Egypt alone was this *tikkun* credible. Thus it was that the sale of Joseph made the redemption possible. It was destined to be, for so he told them, *God has sent me before you to ensure your survival* from the exile. Amen" (*Maor VaShemesh*, 49).

In another Hasidic work we are told that Joseph redeemed the quality of love from its perversion in Egypt, which was the work of the *yetzer hara* or evil impulse "who rode astride the snake when he went to seduce Eve. . . . Joseph set right that which the snake had damaged" (Menahem Nahum of Tchernobyl, *Maor Eynayim,* trans. A. Green [Ramsey, N.J., 1982], 267–68).

43. *TB Yoma* 35b.

CHAPTER 9. JOSEPH AND JACOB

1. Note the words of Jacob that Judah quotes, *You know that my wife bore me two sons . . .* (44:27). Speaking to the ten children of Leah and the handmaids, Jacob refers to Rachel as his "wife," as if he had no other; and to Joseph and Benjamin as his "two sons," as if he had no others.

2. *Yashar* section vayeshev, 82b–84a.

3. *Gen. R.* 94:3.

4. *TSH,* s.v. "Gen." 45:26 n. 70.

Serah, the daughter of Asher, became a legendary figure in Jewish folklore. She was one of the seventy souls Jacob brought into Egypt and the only one of the seventy to have survived the captivity. Not only did she perform the delicate task of informing Jacob that Joseph was still alive, but she knew the secret of Joseph's burial place, which Joseph revealed to his brother Asher who in turn told Serah. For Joseph had sworn his people not to leave Egypt without taking his bones with them. Failing to locate the grave—for even Joseph's sons had forgotten the place—Moses turned to Serah, who disclosed the secret. She who had told of Joseph's survival in Egypt now assured the redemption by revealing Joseph's grave and ensuring his burial in the Holy Land.

Somewhat as Rachel, Serah became a folk hero to Jewish women. Esther Boylan remembers her grandmother singing this song of Serah bas Asher: "Serah bas Asher hut geshpilt/Oif a fiddle/Far Yaakov Avinu/A gants sheyn lidel./Zee hut durt gezungen/Zee hut durt geshreeun:/'Yosef HaZaddik iz a kenig in Mitzrayim.'"

"Serah bas Asher/Would play on her fiddle/A song of great beauty/For our father Jacob./She sang and proclaimed:/'Joseph is king in Egypt.'"

E. Boylan, "Serah bas Asher: A Jewish Woman for All Ages," *Jewish Action* (Summer 1990): 77–78. See also L. Ginzberg, *Legends of the Jews* (7 vols.; Philadelphia, 1968), 7:424, index.

5. *PR* 3; *Tana Debe Eliyyahu*, ed. W. Braude (Philadelphia, 1981), 75. Cf. *TB Sanhedrin* 22b.

6. G. von Rad, *Genesis* (Philadelphia, 1961), 410.

7. *TSH,* s.v. "Gen." 48:5 n. 22.

8. *Lev. R.* 2:3.

9. *PR* 37.

10. *Gen. R.* 98:25; *Targum Jonathan* and *Targum Jerusalem* to Gen. 49:25.

11. *Abarbanel* Gen. 49:22.

12. *TB Pesahim* 56. Liturgically, "Hear O Israel . . ." (*Shema*) is followed by "Blessed be his glorious kingdom . . ." (*Barukh Shem . . .*).

CHAPTER 10. EPHRAIM

1. A. Heschel, *The Prophets* (New York, 1962), 226, 5.

2. Rachel grieves "because they are gone" (Jer 31:25). The Hebrew *eynenu* is singular, suggesting "For they are gone, every one of them."

3. Zohar 2.29b.

4. *TB Baba Batra* BB 123; *Gen. R.* 70:16.

5. It has been suggested that Jeremiah's use of the word *sakhar,* "reward," harkens back to the tale of Rachel and the mandrake plant, the similarity of whose roots to a baby may have led to a belief that it encouraged fertility. Rachel, observing that Reuben, the son of Leah, has come upon some, offers Leah a night with Jacob in exchange for the plant. Leah thereupon approaches Jacob with the words, *You are to sleep with me, for I*

have hired you (sakhor sakhartikha) with my son's mandrakes (Gen 30:16). From this meeting came another son, whom Leah named accordingly. *God has given me my reward (sekhori). . . . So she named him Issachar* (v. 17). "The reward and hire in this story is a son, and the reward which God announces to Rachel in Jeremiah's vision is the restoration of her exiled children" (T. Frymer-Kensky, *In the Wake of the Goddesses* [New York, 1992], 268 n. 26).

6. Among other comments on this passage from Jeremiah, Theodore H. Gaster, following Sir James George Frazer, suggests that the "Image of the mother weeping for her dead children may be an echo of the folk belief that women who die in childbirth haunt the earth in search of their babies" (T. H. Gaster, *Myth, Legend and Custom in the Old Testament* [New York, 1969], 605). Even more bizarre, however, is the remark of Robert Carroll, in his most recent and comprehensive commentary to Jeremiah in which he attempts to replace the image of Rachel weeping for her children as follows: since Rachel as the wife of Jacob "is hardly ever mentioned outside the stories of Jacob," and since the Hebrew word *rahel* means "lamb," "a bleating ewe-lamb" can be substituted for weeping Rachel. Which gives us "a mother sheep lamenting on the highlands [*ramah*, 'height'] for the loss of her lambs" (R. Carroll, *Jeremiah* (Philadelphia, 1986), 598).

7. A. Camus, *The Fall* (New York, 1957), 112.

8. Dante Alighieri, *The Divine Comedy* (New York, 1954), Inferno 2.15.

9. H. Melville, *Moby Dick*, ed. C. Feidelson Jr. (Indianapolis, 1964), 671.

10. See L. Finkelstein, *New Light from the Prophets* (London, 1969).

11. *Lam. R.* 24; *TSH,* s.v. "Gen." 29:25 n. 74.

12. Cf. Jer 31.7, 21; *MhG* Gen. 48.16.

13. *Gen. R.* 71:2; *MhG* Gen. 48.16. This midrash, which came to my attention after I had completed this study, summarizes its thesis. Here the entire passage is given and interpreted. It follows the statement that Rachel was the head (*ikarah*) of her household, a play on the Hebrew *akarah* in *Rachel was akarah,* "barren" (29:31). A euphemism for *akarah,* "barren," is *akeret habayit* (Ps 113:9), which takes on the later meaning of "mistress of the house" (Cf. D. Marcus, "The Barren Woman of Psalm 113:9,"

Journal of the Ancient Near Eastern Society (of Columbia University) 11 [1979]: 81–84).

14. Cf. Amos 6:16; Obad 1:18; and *TB Sanhedrin* 19b.

15. Passages refered to in this paragraph are Deut 33:6; Judg 5:15-17; Gen 35:22; 49:3-4; 1 Chr 5:1; Numbers 16; Deuteronomy 33; Judg 3; Deut 33:7; Gen 49:8-12. Cf. N. Sarna, *Genesis* (Philadelphia, 1989), 402.

16. J. Milgrom, *Numbers* (Philadelphia, 1990), excursus 3, pp. 340–41.

17. *Targum Jonathan* ad loc. *Targum Jonathan* uses the word *rivah,* usually denoting a "young woman." *Targum Jerusalem,* however, understands it as *yeled* or "boy." Dr. Eric Freudenstein kindly supplied this reference. Cf. Num 1:32-37.

18. *Gen. R.* 97; *MhG* Gen. 43:20; *Tan* 20; *TB Sukkah* 52a.

19. The play on words adds to the literary power of this section. For example, "return" (*shuv*) has a double meaning here: geographical and spiritual. In v. 17 it is twice used to mean the return of the exiles to their land, whereas in v. 18 it signifies the return to God and is in the causative, "enable me to return" (*hashiveni*). This double entendre persists thoughout the chapter with still further amplifications.

20. Thus, at the Rosh Hashanah service the verse *Is not Ephraim a precious child to me? . . . (Haben yakir li Ephraim?)* receives special musical emphasis.

21. *PR* 36 and 37. Cf. piska 31:10.

PR piska 37:1 deserves fuller citation. "'Rejoicing I will rejoice in the Lord, my soul shall be joyful in my God; for he hath clothed me with garments of salvation, he hath covered me with the robe of victory, as a bridegroom putteth on a priestly diadem, and as a bride adorneth herself with her jewels' (Isa 61:10).

"This verse is to be considered in the light of what Jeremiah was inspired by the Holy Spirit to say. 'For I will turn their mourning into joy, and will comfort them and will make them rejoice from their sorrow' (Jer 31:13). What did Jeremiah have in mind in this verse? He had in mind the days of the Messiah. . . . In the month of Nisan the patriarchs will arise and say to the Messiah: Ephraim, our true Messiah . . . for the sake of Israel thou didst become a laughingstock and a derision among the nations; and didst sit in darkness . . . and thy skin cleaved to thy bones, and thy body was as dry as a piece of wood . . . and thy strength

Notes

was dried up like a potsherd—all these afflictions on account of the iniquities of our children. . . .

"Then the Holy One will lift the Messiah up to the heaven of heavens, and will cloak him in something of the splendor of his own glory as protection against the nations, particularly against the wicked Persians. He will be told: Ephraim, our true Messiah . . . the nations would long since have destroyed thee had not God's mercies been exceedingly mighty in thy behalf, as is said 'Ephraim is a precious child to me. . . . I will have boundless compassion for him, saith the Lord. . .' (Jer 31:20).

"'As a bridegroom putteth on a priestly diadem' (Isa 61:10). This text teaches that the Holy One will put upon Ephraim, our true Messiah, a garment whose splendor will stream forth from world's end to world's end. Blesssed is the hour in which he was created! Blessed the womb whence he came! Blessed the generation whose eyes behold him! Blessed the eye which waited for him whose lips open with blessing and peace. . . . Blessed are the forebears of the man who merited the goodness of the world, the Messiah, hidden for the eternity [to come]."

See the entire piska 37, as well as 36 and 31. The return of the exiles from Babylonia, the redemption from the rule of Rome, and the battle of Gog and Magog are all here associated with the Messiah Ephraim. Cf. above, Chap. 9 nn. 8 and 9, and below, Chap. 11 n. 32. Because this seems to be the only time in rabbinic literature that the Messiah is referred to as Ephraim and is there described as bearing the sins of the people, some Jewish scholars have questioned its authenticity (see N. Krochmal, *Moreh Nevukhey Hazeman,* ed. S. Rawidowicz, 255; Azariah dei Rossi, Maor Eynayim, ed. Cassel [Vilna, Poland, 1866], 250; and B. Bamberger, "A Messianic Document of the Seventh Century," *HUCA* 15 [1940]:429).

22. Verses 15-22 seem to form a single poem of contrasts and fulfillment. Its striking linguistic character is fully evident in Hebrew, where words with similar sounds but different meanings are used throughout. Thus, *tamrurim,* which earlier connoted the "bitter tears" Rachel shed when the people went off into exile (v. 14), now signifies the "signposts" that will guide the people on their return along the very same road. Or the word *shuv,* which is used both geographically ("Return"—*shuvi*—"to those cities of yours") and spiritually ("How long will you waver, O wandering

daughter"—*shovevah*). Of special note is the fact that the verb *shuv* has now taken on the feminine form, which, although not evident in English, is clearly feminine in Hebrew—*shuvi* ("return"), *shovevah* ("wandering daughter"), and *teshovev* ("enfolds") are all in the feminine. Further, "Return (*shuvi*) . . . O wandering daughter" (*shovevah*), is the female counterpart of "Return O faithless sons" (*shuvu banim shovevim*) (3:29). Cf. Frymer-Kensky, *In the Wake of the Goddesses*, 268 n. 30.

23. The contrast between the old and the new is suggested by a wordplay in the final verse of the poem. On the one hand, the woman is addressed as a "faithless one" (*hasobeba*, v. 22a); on the other hand, she will "encompass" or "enfold" (*tesobeb*) a man. The latter verb seems to have been chosen because of its assonance with the adjective describing God's daughter (*hasobeba/tesobeb*). The poetic juxtaposition of the two words draws a sharper contrast between Israel's faithlessness, which led to divine judgment (exile from the land), and God's faithfulness to the people despite their infidelity.

24. B. Anderson, "The Lord Has Created Something New," in *Essays in Jeremiah Studies* (Indiana, 1984) 376–80. See also P. Trible, "God, Nature of, in the OT," G. A. Buttrick, ed., *Interpreter's Dictionary of the Bible*, suppl. vol.:368–69; and Frymer-Kensky, *In the Wake of the Goddesses*, 268 n. 30.

25. The contrasting allusions to Rachel mark these verses, while Ephraim is designated as *my firstborn*. Jacob, who is Israel, the husband of Rachel, is prominent in the chapters surrounding 31 in a loving-forgiving-rejoicing sense. "Fear not my servant, Jacob . . . for I shall save you from afar, and your seed from the land of their captivity. And Jacob shall again be quiet and none shall make them afraid. For I am with you, to save you" (Jer 30:10-11).

A portion of this passage—*The Lord will ransom Jacob from a foe too strong for him*—was made part of the Jewish evening worship service, preceding the prayer for peace, the blessing that results from divine guidance and concern.

CHAPTER 11. *KEVER* RACHEL

1. *Rashi* Gen. 48:7.
2. *Rashi* Gen. 48:7; *Ramban* Gen. 48:7; *TSH*, s.v. "Gen." 48:7.
3. *PR* 3; *Ramban; TB Moed Katan* 27a.

4. *PR* 3; *Ramban; TB Moed Katan* 27a.

5. *Ramban* Gen. 35:16.

6. *TSH,* s.v. "Gen." 48:7; *Sforno* 48:7.

7. *Gen. R.* 82:10; *PR* 3:4; *Rashi* Gen. 48:7; *TSH,* s.v. "Gen." 48:7.

8. R. Hayward, *The Targum of Jeremiah* (Edinburgh, 1987), 131. There are "sufficient grounds for discerning the origins of Targum Jeremiah in the land of Israel during, or slightly before, the first century A.D." (p. 38). Cf *Gen. R.* (the earliest of the midrashim) 61:2; I. Zatelli, "Rachel's Lament in the Targum and Other Ancient Jewish Interpretations," *Rivista biblica* 39 (1991):477–90. On Rachel's intercession for her children, see L. Ginzberg, *The Legends of the Jews* (7 vols.; Philadelphia, 1968), 1:361, 415; 2:135; 5:299 n. 202.

9. *PR* 26:7. See the entire piska.

10. Zohar 3.187a; 2.29b.

11. Zohar 3.187a.

12. *Tanna deBe Eliyyahu,* ed. W. Braude (Philadelphia, 1981) (30) 28, pp. 365–66; A. Lifshitz, *Yesod Likra* (*Limud* K*ever* R*ahel* I*menu*) (Jerusalem, [1967?]), 147.

13. The Talmud cites this verse as the source for the custom of erecting a tombstone at the grave (*matzevah,* "pillar," "tombstone").

14. The location of Ephrat is problematic. According to 35:19 and 48:17, it is Bethlehem. David is called "the son of a certain Ephratite of Bethlehem in Judah" (1 Sam 17:12; see also Ruth 1:2 and Mic 5:1). But why bury Rachel in the territory of Judah, a son of Leah, and not within the borders of the tribes of Joseph or Benjamin, as 1 Sam 10:2 suggests. Kimhi and *Targum Jonathan* attempt to resolve the problem by taking the Hebrew *ramah* (Jer 31:14) to mean "on a height." See also *Tosefta Sotah* 11:11; *Gen. R.* 82:10; N. Sarna, *Genesis* (Philadelphia, 1989), 404–5; A. Demsky, "Queburt Rachel," *Encyclopedia Mikrait* (in Hebrew) (9 vols.; Jerusalem, 1988), 8:360–63.

15. See Joseph Son of Isaac Orleans, *Bekhor Shor* and *Sefer HaYashar.*

16. *Lekah Tov* Gen. 35:20; I. Eisenstein, "Gelilat Eretz Yisrael," in *Otzar Masaot* (New York, 1927), 182; Petahya of Regensburg, *HaSibuv.* See selections in E. N. Adler, *Jewish Travelers* (Philadelphia, 1930).

17. *Yesod Likra,* 219.

18. *Yesod Likra,* 39.

19. Furthermore, it tells us that when the twelve spies were sent to view the land before it was conquered, Caleb, whose enthusiasm for the land was not shared by the majority, traveled to Hebron to the graves of the patriarchs and prostrated himself upon them, imploring: "O my forefathers, deliver me from the party of the spies" (*TB Taanit* 16a; *TB Sotah* 34b).

20. Zohar 3.69b–70a.

21. *Shulhan Arukh* orah hayim 293. Cf. responsum of *MaHa-RaM Shick,* and M. Krassen, "Visiting Graves," *Kabbalah* (Fall 1988), 3:1.

22. *Yesod Likra,* 39.

23. *Yesod Likra,* 35. Two further prayers are of particular interest. Rabbi Nahman of Bratslav (1772–1810), the great-grandson of the founder of Hasidism, the Baal Shem Tov, and one of the luminaries of the Hasidic movement, has left us a superb volume of prayers, one of which is often said at the grave of Rachel. The land of Israel, which he visited in 1798, was central to Nahman's thinking. This prayer differs from others cited in that it reflects his belief in the role of the Hasidic masters (zaddikim) and reveals his unusual personality. The zaddikim whose loss he laments are the disciples of the Baal Shem, whom he mentions by name. "Master of the world, we have been compelled to compose eulogies for our great loss . . . of the holy saints . . . who have gone to their eternal rest and left us in sorrow. . . . You, O Lord, know that it is not within our power to eulogize saints such as these. . . . I stumble in my words to you, O merciful one. . . . Weep for us, this orphaned generation. . . . But what is passed is passed. Now teach me how to cry out and lament . . . in such a way that I might appropriate some of their holiness, through the residue of which they have left through their holy books. For the complete soul ascends on high but also descends below to awaken all souls, even those who dwell in the nethermost reaches of hell, lest we give way to even the least despair.

"Master of the world, take pity on the tears and the wailings of our mother Rachel, who is the Shechinah and who moaned over our great anguish. For Rachel wept for her children who were dismissed from their father's table and exiled from their land, 'weeping sorely at night, her tears upon her cheeks, and among all her friends none to comfort her' (Lam 1.2). For her 'friends' are the zaddikim . . . who are no longer. We are left as a solitary pole on the mountaintop and as a lonely banner in the valley. We are orphaned, with none to console us, O master of the world. Who will take pity upon us and who will inquire after us? It was for the sake of those who worked wonders and saved souls without number that you lit up our way. . . . For the zaddikim of the generations since the time when the hidden light—that wondrous man of God, our teacher Baal Shem Tov, who illuminated the world and raised up many holy and wondrous zaddikim and Hasidim . . . have been taken from us over the years. . . . So take pity upon us, O merciful one. . . . Strengthen me in your ways, that I might merit to rise up and recite the midnight vigil (*Tikkun Hatzot*) and to sorrow over the destruction of the temple. . . .

"Master of the world, O master of the world, what has happened has happened, for the holy temple has been destroyed and the zaddikim have departed from us, but it is for this that I weep, that my sins have, in some measure, delayed the rebuilding of the temple, and who knows, perhaps, in a former incarnation, my sins contributed to the destruction of the temple itself. Woe for my sins . . . woe for the sins I committed in each of my incarnations. Woe that so ugly a one as I has caused the destruction of the holy temple and delayed its rebuilding and the redemption of the people Israel, that they might return to their land. . . . Woe that through my sins I burned the holy temple and I exiled the children of Israel among the nations and I continue to prolong the exile through my evil and ugly passions" (*Yesod Likra,* 253–57).

The following prayer is, strictly speaking, not one of those listed in the manuals to be used at the grave of Rachel, though it does mention the grave. Taken from the *tekhineh* literature, the Yiddish prayers written for, and often by, Jewish women, it was to be recited on the Sabbath before the new month and refers to all four of the matriarchs, following the name of the author, "Mistress Sarah Rebecca Rachel Leah," daughter of the Rabbi Yokel Segal Horowitz of Glogau and wife of Rabbi Shabbetai of Krasny. Once again, as with the pleas in the midrash to Lamentations and in comparison with the prayers said at the grave of the other matriarchs in Hebron, Rachel's role far exceeds the others.

"Therefore, we spread out our hands before God, and pray that you do bring us back to Jerusalem, and renew our days as of old. For we have no strength, we can no longer endure the hard, bitter exile, for we are feeble as lambs. . . . Therefore, we pray you, lord of the world, take revenge on those who cause us suffering, for the sake of the merit of the patriarchs and matriarchs. O God, just as you answered our forebears, so may you answer us this month.

"By the merit of our mother Sarah—for whose sake you have commanded, 'Touch not my anointed ones' [Ps 105:15], as if to say: 'You nations! Dare not lay a hand upon my righteous ones!'—may no nation have the power to harm any of Sarah's children today.

"By the merit of our mother Rebecca, who caused our father to receive the blessings from father Isaac [Gen 27], may these blessings soon be fulfilled for Israel her children!

"By the merit of our faithful mother Rachel, for whose virtue you promised that we, the children of Israel, would have an end to our exile. For when the children of Israel were taken into captivity, they were led by a way not far from the grave in which our mother Rachel lay. They pleaded with their captors to permit them to go to Rachel's tomb. And when the Israelites came to the sepulcher of our mother Rachel and bewailed, 'Mother, mother, how can you bear to see us being led into exile before your very eyes?' Rachel ascended before God crying bitterly, 'Lord of the world, surely your mercy is greater than the mercy of flesh and blood. I had compassion on my sister Leah when my father switched us and gave her to my husband Jacob in my place. I told her the secret signs which my husband and I had decided upon, so that my husband would think that I was the one [beside him]. No matter the agony it caused me; it was because of my compassion for my sister that I gave her the signs. Thus, even more so [than I], is it fitting for you, O Lord, most compassionate and gracious, to show mercy.' And God answered her: 'You are right, Rachel. I shall redeem your children from the exile.' So may it soon come to pass, for the sake of her merit.

"And for the sake of the merit of our mother Leah, who wept day and night that she not fall to the lot of the wicked Esau, until her eyes became dim, may you enlighten our eyes to see a way out of this dark exile." (Trans. C. Weissler [somewhat altered],

"Images of the Matriarchs in Yiddish Supplicatory Prayer," *Bulletin of the Center for the Study of World Religions*, 14, 1 [1988].)

24. *Mekilta de-Rav Ishmael*, ed. and trans. J. Z. Lauterbach (Philadelphia, 1976), piska 1.60–61.

25. *Targum Jonathan* translates "And your [i.e. Rachel's] work shall be rewarded" (Jer 31:16) as "There is reward for the deeds of your righteous ancestors." See Smolar-Aberbach, *Studies in Targum Jonathan* (New York, 1983), 220 n. 576. Cf. Marmorstein, *The Old Rabbinic Doctrine of Merit;* R. Hayward, *The Targum of Jeremiah* (Edinburgh, 1987); Zatelli, "Rachel's Lament in the Targum."

26. I. Gurzinski, *She'erit Yisrael* (Brooklyn, 1957), 220.

27. *Tanna deBe Eliyahu,* chap. 18, p. 256.

28. E. Shiller, *Kever Rachel* (in Hebrew) (Jerusalem, 1977), 32–35.

29. S. Sered, "Rachel's Tomb and the Milk Grotto of the Virgin Mary," *Journal of Feminist Studies* (Fall 1986): 7–21.

30. Sered, "Rachel's Tomb," 14.

31. A red string as protection against the evil eye seems to have been exempted from the prohibition against superstition. See *Tosefta Shabbat* 7.8 and *TB Shabbat* 67.

32. Zohar 2.7a–9a.

Indexes

INDEX OF BIBLICAL REFERENCES

251

INDEX OF NAMES AND TOPICS

Indexes

Indexes